JOURNALISM FOR THE PUBLIC GOOD

BIGHORN

Journalism for the Public Good

The Michener Awards at Fifty

KIM S. KIERANS

Bighorn Books
An imprint of University of Calgary Press
2500 University Drive NW
Calgary, Alberta
Canada T2N 1N4
press.ucalgary.ca

LIBRARY AND ARCHIVES CANADA CATALOGUING IN PUBLICATION

Title: Journalism for the public good : the Michener Awards at fifty / Kim S. Kierans.
Other titles: Michener Awards at fifty
Names: Kierans, Kim S., author.
Description: Includes bibliographical references and index.
Identifiers: Canadiana (print) 20240355741 | Canadiana (ebook) 2024035575X | ISBN
    9781773855356 (softcover) | ISBN 9781773855349 (hardcover) | ISBN 9781773855387
    (EPUB) | ISBN 9781773855370 (PDF) | ISBN 9781773855363 (Open Access PDF)
Subjects: LCSH: Journalism—Awards—Canada. | LCSH: Journalism—Canada. | LCSH:
    Journalists—Canada.
Classification: LCC PN4914.A87 K54 2024 | DDC 071/.1079—dc23

The University of Calgary Press acknowledges the support of the Government of Alberta through the Alberta Media Fund for our publications. We acknowledge the financial support of the Government of Canada. We acknowledge the financial support of the Canada Council for the Arts for our publishing program.

Printed and bound in Canada by Imprimerie Gauvin
✪ This book is printed on Enviro natural paper

Copyediting by Brian Scrivener
Cover art: Олег Фадеев, Golden feather logo icon illustration design template, generated using AI tools, downloaded 2024, Adobe Stock, File #603425379, https://stock.adobe.com/ca/images/golden-feather-logo-icon-illustration-design-template/603425379?prev_url=detail
Cover design, page design, and typesetting by Melina Cusano

*For the media outlets that invest in in-depth news and
to the teams of reporters, editors and photo/videographers
who produce journalism that makes a difference.*

TABLE OF CONTENTS

Acknowledgements

This book honours the in-depth journalism of Canadian reporters, editors, producers, broadcasters and publishers who, over decades, have stood up to bullies, uncovered secrecy, fraud and wrongdoings, and given voice to marginalized communities. Their stories had an impact. They mobilized voters to defeat corrupt officials and brought down governments, they explained and exposed systemic injustices, and they shamed politicians to change laws and policies and forced transparency. *Journalism for the Public Good: The Michener Awards at Fifty* pays tribute to their ongoing mission to speak truth to power and in the process strengthen our democratic institutions. Their journalism is the heart and soul of the work of the Michener Awards Foundation and this book.

As a Michener judge, I had the honour to read, watch and listen to twelve years of the best in investigative journalism from across the country. I am grateful to the Michener Awards Foundation and my fellow judges — you know who you are — for your combined wisdom and shared purpose. A special thank you to former board member Tim Kotcheff for giving me unfettered access to the Michener archives, which he single-handedly built and maintained until he left the board in 2014.

I would be remiss if I didn't thank Bill Lahey, president of the University of King's College, and my colleagues in the School of Journalism, Writing and Publishing. King's was my intellectual home, first in the Foundation Year Program as a student, and years later, as a journalism professor. King's was the springboard that launched this project.

Journalism for the Public Good was conceived, researched and written at Massey College at the University of Toronto. Thank you to the late Hugh Segal, principal of Massey College, and Amela Marin, registrar, for opening the iron gates to welcome me as a visiting scholar in 2018, to Tom Kierans and Mary Janigan for their support, to principal Nathalie Des Rosiers for inviting me back in 2021 as a Senior Fellow and resident, and to the Junior Fellows at

Massey College. These phenomenal graduate students encourage and inspire me daily with their intellect, humour, compassion and dedication to making the world a better place.

In researching this book, thanks go to Sophie Tellier at Library and Archives Canada, Liseanne Cadieux and Mélanie Frias from Rideau Hall Library, and Allan Thompson, Emily Hotton and Cindy Kardash-Lalonde at Carleton University's School of Journalism and Communication.

I am ever grateful to the collective of people who kindly waded through the manuscript at various stages. Their sage advice and editing helped to shape my ideas into this book: developmental editor Karen Dewart McEwan, Elizabeth Hanton, Henry Roper, Sally Reardon, Margo Goodhand, James Baxter, Chris Waddell, Pierre-Paul Noreau, George Cooper, Alexander Sallas, and Jamie Deacon.

I also want to thank the many people not mentioned in these acknowledgements who contributed to this book over the years. All omissions and errors are mine alone.

To the wonderful team at the University of Calgary Press, director Brian Scrivener, editorial coordinator Helen Hajnoczky, designer Melina Cusano, and marketing specialist Alison Cobra. You got me to home base.

A special thank you goes to my partner, Ian Porter, who believed in what I was doing even when I had my doubts. Thank you for your ears and eyes and encouragement, and for keeping the home fire burning while I've been away researching, writing and editing.

The Michener Award.

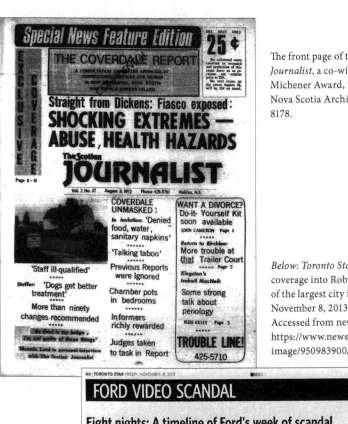

The front page of the *Scotian Journalist*, a co-winner of the 1972 Michener Award, August 3, 1972. Nova Scotia Archives, microfilm 8178.

Below: *Toronto Star*'s ongoing coverage into Rob Ford, mayor of the largest city in Canada, November 8, 2013. Accessed from newspapers.com, https://www.newspapers.com/image/950983900/

Fluoride pollution killing Cornwall cattle: Human health in danger, pathologist says

By SYLVIA WRIGHT
Staff writer

Above: Front page of the *Whig-Standard*, June 12, 1979, winner of the 1971 Michener Award for its in-depth reporting about fluoride poisoning on Cornwall Island, an Indigenous community. Accessed from newspapers.com, https://www.newspapers.com/image/730543211/?terms=

Sunday Star 25 years old
NEWS, A7

THE SUNDAY STAR

October 20, 2002

thestar.com

Police target black drivers

Above: Race and Crime. A *Toronto Star* investigation into Race and Crime led by investigative reporter Jim Rankin won the 2002 Michener Award. The ongoing series revealed the Toronto police department treated blacks differently than whites in the world's most ethnically diverse city. The ongoing reporting has led to the end of carding and other discriminatory practices. Image courtesy of Jim Rankin, *Toronto Star*.

Right: *Daily News* (Halifax) wins the 1997 Michener Award for its series covering the mistreatment of children at Nova Scotia reform schools over several decades. Accessed from Halifax Regional Library, Central Library microfilm.

Daily News wins national award

Abuse series takes Michener Award for 'public service in journalism'

His Excellency Roland Michener giving the first Michener Award to Clive Baxter of *The Financial Post* and Alan Elrich of CBC-TV for the 1970 series "The Charter Revolution."

Foreword

The Honourable David Johnston, 28th Governor General of Canada and Chair of the Rideau Hall Foundation

Robert Schuman, a founder of the European Union, once observed that the successful creation of the union comes about through people and institutions together — people of courage and wisdom focussed on the public good and specific organizational institutions that are part of a broader network of connected institutions which, if good fortune prevails, ensure a fully functioning democracy and a healthy, constantly reinvigorated society.

This book embraces both observations. First, it is about the people who created and supported the Michener Award for public service journalism, as well as those whose courageous truth-telling is at the heart of the award. Second, it is about the institutions — the Award itself as an institution reinforcing freedom of the press and informed communities that, in turn, strengthen the broader range of institutions that underpin a healthy democracy.

The Michener Award was established by one of my predecessors in the Office of the Governor General of Canada, The Right Honourable Roland Michener, who served in this role between 1967 and 1974. Over its first half-century, between 1970 and 2020, fifty-seven Michener Awards and 221 honourable mentions and citations of merit have been presented at Rideau Hall. While they have each told very different stories and focused on a wide variety of themes, the common thread that knits them all together is, of course, courage. The courage it takes to shine a light on something that those in power would rather remain in the dark. The courage to question decisions, chase facts and give voice to the voiceless, all with the goal of effecting change, whether to policies or, more intimately, to individual lives. The great George Orwell famously said "Journalism is printing something that someone does not want printed. Everything else is public relations." I have no doubt that Roland Michener would have agreed with that statement wholeheartedly. In essence, that is the spirit of the Michener Award, and those are the stories that are told with such care and vibrancy within the pages of this book.

It is worth noting early in your journey through the history of the Michener Award that they are not given to individual journalists. This Award is about more than bylines. Instead, it recognizes the news organization as a whole, the institution above the individual. Unique among journalistic awards, the Michener Award celebrates teamwork. In this way it also recognizes how resource-heavy these types of investigations are for newsrooms: how many people, how many hours and how much money needs to be invested in the name of uncovering truth and bringing about immediate and lasting change. The Michener Award is also special in its determined recognition of small newsrooms and the sacrifices they make to tell the stories that are important to their communities and that will have real impact on the lives of their readers.

Ensuring these Awards continue to be relevant in a dramatically shifting media landscape has required its own form of leadership and, frankly, the same kind of dogged determination its recipients demonstrate through their journalism. Through a volunteer board of directors and independent judging committees made up of experienced journalists, the Michener Award Foundation has worked to preserve the integrity of Roland Michener's vision and legacy. So, we see in this book a thoughtful exploration of five decades of journalistic evolution and the leaders who created and then stewarded the Michener Awards in celebrating, promoting and solidifying the importance of public service journalism as a key element to a fully functioning democracy. The Michener Award story also serves to illustrate that institutions, and the individuals who care for them, *can* make a difference.

This begins with Roland Michener and is followed by so many others, including this book's author Kim Kierans, who continue to shepherd the Michener Awards. It is a journey that has had its share of challenges, near misses and threatened extinction. So, gear yourself up to be inspired and delighted by the stories illuminated in the pages that follow. Yes, they are the stories that make up the history of the Michener Award, but just as importantly they also document our country's flawed past — lies, corruption and injustice — and the valiant members of Canada's fifth estate who wielded pen and paper to hold those in power to account.

Now, before *you* begin *your* journey through the history of the Michener Awards, let's imagine its next fifty years. I, for one, am excited for the future of this award. It has persisted time and time again, despite facing all manner of challenges. It now finds itself supported more widely through its partnership with the Rideau Hall Foundation, to help ensure its broad reach and impact and sustainability into the future.

While the future of the Michener looks bright, it's easy to become complacent, and in complacency lies disaster, not just for an important institution, but for our democracy as whole. According to Edelman's Trust Barometer, Canada's trust in media has eroded from 2022 to 2023, and now stands at 50 per cent overall — with only 21 per cent trust in social media. Edelman's central theme for 2023 is polarization, with the Battle for Truth highlighted as one of four main contributing factors. What's more, media organizations and newsrooms across the country continue to face dark and difficult days: declining ad revenues, rising costs of operations and disappearing web views as a result of Meta's response to Canada's Online News Act.

As I write this introduction, we mourn the loss of yet another local newspaper and Michener Award finalist from 2021. *Kamloops This Week* published its last paper on October 25, 2023, after thirty-five years in business, leaving its community without a local paper. As Margo Goodhand, current President of the Michener Award Foundation, so eloquently said about the paper's demise, "Kamloops is losing more than twenty-six local jobs. It's losing a newsroom with integrity, something that has become increasingly rare in the media landscape. And that's sad news for people who still believe journalism is a fundamental pillar of democracy."

While the weight of preserving journalism as a means of serving the public good and safeguarding our democracy cannot rest solely on the shoulders of one relatively small organization, the Michener Awards clearly have a role to play in turning the tide on Canadians' trust in the media. This will be done by continuing to recognize and celebrate the kind of journalism that is both powerful and transformative, that requires taking risks which often result in few rewards. The kind of journalism that epitomizes the selflessness of its supporters. So, as you flip the pages of this very fine book, join me in saying cheers to the journalists who continue to shine light into dark corners. Cheers to the newsrooms and media organizations who champion and make space for their work. And, of course, cheers to the Michener Award, for its enduring commitment to lifting up dynamic, independent and important journalism, and in so doing, reminding the rest of us of the peril we would find ourselves in without it.

The Honourable David Johnston
28th Governor General of Canada and Chair of the Rideau Hall Foundation
October 31, 2023

Introduction

The Michener Award for public service journalism honours independent, fearless journalism. Journalism that informs, challenges power imbalances, exposes corruption and empowers those on the margins. Journalism that changes policy and practices to improve the lives of citizens.

These are groundbreaking stories that have impact and bring about results. For example, fair compensation for victims of thalidomide after a *Globe and Mail* series. Twenty million dollars to upgrade logging roads after the *Prince George Citizen* documented a staggering number of road deaths in northern British Columbia. A new mayor and council for Toronto after the *Toronto Star* unmasked the illegal and reckless behaviour of Mayor Rob Ford. Regular testing of Taser stun guns after an in-depth independent analysis by CBC/Radio-Canada and The Canadian Press exposed potentially fatal problems.

These stories come from politics, environment, health and social policy, public affairs and international issues. These stories were honoured with a Michener Award because they achieved impact in the public interest and helped to improve the lives of Canadians.

The Michener Award emerged from a long-held understanding of the role of journalism as a pillar of democracy. Lindsay Crysler, who was the senior editor at the *Ottawa Citizen* in 1970 when the award was founded and would later become the executive editor of the *Montreal Gazette* and founder of the journalism program at Concordia University, said "My idealistic view of journalism in that early era was that it was a public service and we were looking out for the public. This award is exactly for that. This one was specifically for something you improved in the community or showed the community how to improve. And I thought that was terrific and something we should really all be doing."[1]

Back in 1970, while other journalism organizations gave industry awards for categories such as spot news, sports, feature writing and business, no award specifically recognized the public service aspect of journalism. The Michener, as it's called, has become Canada's most coveted journalism award, like the Pulitzer Prize for Public Service in the United States.

"It's the one," said David Walmsley, editor-in-chief of the *Globe and Mail*, sweeping his arm to the right where the framed citation hangs proudly behind his desk. "It's the Michener that goes on this wall: nothing else. The reason for that is that it's because of its unimpeachable excellence and it stands the test of time."[2]

The Michener Award is the only award in Canada with a singular focus on journalism in the public service. It honours the collective effort of a media organization to produce measurable change through its journalism produced in a calendar year. It stands out because it is open to all media — French and English news organizations, daily and community newspapers, periodicals, online publications, and radio and television stations from every corner of Canada.[3] To level the playing field for smaller media organizations, an independent panel of judges considers the resources of each applicant. It is not the quality of writing or layout or visuals that make a Michener; it is the impact of the journalism and the degree of arm's-length public benefit the journalism has generated.

For longtime journalist, author and educator John Fraser, the Michener Award is unique because of its focus on stories that address wrongs in society; they can spark changes in public policy and processes. He explains it this way: "They lead to civic responsibility and civic citizenship. So, you can point to the idealistic, but in fact, what the Micheners sort of underpin is the practical world of journalism that can affect change in society. Rather than seismic changes, it's just regular honest reporting of stuff that's slightly out of kilter. I think of the Micheners as something that helps us be a decent and better society."[4]

No one was more passionate about the Michener Awards than the late John Honderich, a longtime Michener director, editor and publisher of the *Toronto Star* and chair of Torstar, the parent corporation. From his corner office in One Yonge Street in the heart of downtown Toronto, Honderich ran the largest daily circulation newspaper in the greater Toronto area with fierce pride. "An exultant force"[5] in the industry, he lived and breathed the *Toronto Star*; it was his passion to the exclusion of everything else.

It was no secret that Honderich liked to win. When the *Star* didn't, the chief judge could expect a phone call about two weeks after the awards ceremony. Honderich, with his big booming voice, would let loose, unsuccessfully probing for some insider information. But once he had blown off steam, he'd concede that the judges had made the right choice and added quickly that the *Star* would be back next year. The attraction of the Michener, Honderich said, is that it has the respect and distinction that do not exist with other journalism awards. "The public service aspect of it, that you hear you've done particular articles to that end, that they have had impact. . . . So it's at the highest level and that's how it's viewed," and not just by the *Toronto Star*.[6]

The following pages highlight fifty years of award-winning journalism through the lens of a volunteer organization that has maintained its focus on journalism that benefits the public. From the media silos of the 1970s to the contemporary world of digital and multi-platform media, the Michener Awards Foundation has kept step and, like the industry, adapted to drastic changes.

Advocates, like Governor General Roland Michener (1967-1974), Bill MacPherson of the Federation of Press Clubs and Paul Deacon of the Michener Awards Foundation, believed in the purpose of the award and fought to keep it relevant. Media organizations funded in-depth journalism, even in tough economic times. Reporters and editors, who through their passion for and commitment to journalism, gave voice to the marginalized, shamed and challenged the powerful, and brought about legislative and policy changes to make our country a better place. Fifty years of award-winning journalism are woven into each chapter of this book.

The Michener Award is a signal to the public that the work of media organizations matters. In 2024, this kind of support is more critical than ever. Fact-based journalism is under attack from a flood of misinformation and disinformation peddled as news on social media and the deep web. Professional journalists face threats and harassment fuelled by those who label journalists as the enemy and dismiss their stories as "alternative news."[7] Various opinion polls rank journalists fairly low on the trust scale, down with lawyers and bankers.[8]

The journalism recognized by the Michener Awards stands in stark contrast to that dark view of the media. At the 2021 virtual awards ceremony, APTN reporter Cullen Crozier captured the essence of the award when he described Michener stories as those that are "challenging status quo, holding truth to power, forcing conversations and hopefully effecting meaningful and lasting change."[9] He and fellow reporter Kenneth Jackson received the

2020 Michener Award for the Aboriginal Peoples Television Network's investigation into the failings of child protection agencies following the suicide of three sisters in seven months.

The Michener Award, and the values it represents, remain highly relevant today. In many countries around the world such freedom is at risk. Media outlets face closures and suppression from authorities, big businesses and hostile governments. Viceregal patronage from the highest office in Canada gives lustre to the Michener Award. More importantly, as Kenneth Jackson of APTN said, the award highlights the value the state puts on the essential role of independent journalism as a "guardian of the public interest" in our democratic society.[10]

As former Governor General David Johnston explains, "Professional journalism is key to how democracy, the economy and healthy communities function. And so, you use a Governor General's award like the Michener Awards to celebrate the best of the profession and use it as a kind of light to encourage all Canadians to cherish that profession and to attain even higher standards."[11]

For fifty-plus years the public service values of the Michener Award have propelled publishers, editors, senior producers and reporters at news organizations to "aspire to higher ground."[12] As Edward Greenspon, former editor-in-chief of the *Globe and Mail,* sees it, the "Michener values" naturally align with the mission of news organizations in fulfilling their democratic function.[13] For media outlets, a Michener nomination is coveted proof that their work is contributing to the health of their geographic or virtual community.

For reporters, editors and producers, the Michener is the holy grail of journalism, but it is more than just the prestige. It is evidence that journalism has an important role to play in helping to improve society. "It demonstrates to those who care what journalism means to the country," said George Hutchinson, a reporter at the *London Free Press* in the 1970s.[14]

Data journalist David McKie has won his fair share of journalism awards, but, above all, he treasures the one Michener Award he earned in 2009 for a CBC/Radio Canada and Canadian Press investigation into the use of Tasers by the RCMP. "Because of what it stands for," he said with a big smile. "Your work has led to measurable change. You've actually saved lives in many instances. Your work has resulted in the implementation of important public policy that has made lives better."[15]

As Michener chief judge Margo Goodhand said at the opening of the virtual ceremony for the 2020 awards, "Micheners change lives and laws and speak for those who cannot speak for themselves."[16] The stories from the six finalists that year gave a platform to the silenced voices of public health officials, abused hockey players, trafficked children, seniors in long-term care, employees of Rideau Hall and children lost in the child protection maze.

Since its creation in 1970, various journalism organizations (now the Michener Awards Foundation) have administered the award — handling communications, advertising, fundraising and organizing the annual awards ceremony at Rideau Hall hosted by the governor general.

The volunteer directors of the Michener Awards Foundation have always taken great care to ensure the judging panel — made up of a chief judge and four or five other members — is arm's-length and impartial. The judges bring diverse journalism experience; they're often retired editors, reporters, publishers or journalism educators with no current ties or obligations to media outlets. Their independence from meddling from outside influences, including the Michener board, the industry and Rideau Hall, has given the award its elite status. It also gives the judges the freedom to break from the pack, as they did in 2013 when the *Toronto Star* won for its exposé of Toronto Mayor Rob Ford, even though the same submission did not receive a single nomination from the prestigious National Newspaper Awards.

Since 1971, ten governors general — five with journalism backgrounds — have hosted the Michener Award ceremony.[17] They have opened their residence at Rideau Hall to honour hard-hitting, investigative public service journalism. Journalism that exposes, angers, shames and, in the process, brings about meaningful change in the lives of Canadians. No institution is off limits — not even Rideau Hall and the Office of the Governor General.

If the founders and Roland Michener had been online for the virtual ceremony honouring journalism from 2020, there might have been a moment of discomfort when the president of the Michener Foundation, Pierre-Paul Noreau, read the citation for CBC News — "Inside Rideau Hall." The coverage exposed Rideau Hall as a "house of horrors" with "a toxic work environment, evidence of questionable spending and a flawed government vetting process."[18] The CBC stories led to an investigation and the resignation of Governor General Julie Payette and her top bureaucrat. But then the founders probably would have taken a deep breath and nodded. They would have understood that the award was set up to encourage independent journalism in the service of the public. "It's about forcing conversations and getting answers the public can't," said CBC's Jamie Strashin, a 2019 award finalist.[19]

Between 1970 and 2020, fifty-seven Michener Awards and 221 honourable mentions and citations of merit have been presented at Rideau Hall. The healthy number of entries year upon year, even in a pandemic, is a repudiation of claims that independent journalism is dead and that it has no value in our wired and social world. The award is an affirmation that citizens benefit from accurate, reliable, fact-based information.

Journalism for the Public Good: The Michener Awards at Fifty

This project started during a sabbatical at Massey College at the University of Toronto in 2018-19, where I was a visiting scholar. For almost fifteen years, I had a unique behind-the-scenes view of the Michener Awards Foundation. I served as an awards judge, chief judge, vice president, president and secretary to the board between 2007 and 2022. This project was undertaken independently of the Foundation and is self-funded. I had unfettered access to the internal electronic minutes and documents from the Michener Awards Foundation, including its historic documents — four bankers' boxes, stored at Carleton University's School of Journalism and Communications, crammed with meeting minutes, correspondence, emails, annual reports and other gems that go back to 1967.

My research also took me to Library and Archives Canada and the Rideau Hall archives. I am profoundly grateful to former Michener director Tim Kotcheff for access to his archival website, a repository of Michener history. *Journalism for the Public Good: The Michener Award at Fifty* also includes excerpts from interviews, conversations and email exchanges with more than fifty people, including five retired governors general, former presidents of the Michener Award Foundation going back to 1990, board members, judges, members of the Michener family, along with publishers, editors and journalists. Combined, these resources document the story of how an inspired idea to honour media organizations for journalism in the public interest developed into Canada's premier journalism award.

This story begins in the late 1960s and early 1970s — a time of tremendous growth, prosperity and optimism in Canada. Chapter One explores the pivotal role of Roland Michener in the creation of the award during a time of change in the journalism industry. In its very creation, the Michener Award responded to industry needs and a movement among journalists. The

Micheners honoured media outlets that produced investigative stories with measurable impact and sent a strong message to the industry that journalism in the public interest was the highest form of journalism.

In the early 1970s, investigative journalism was starting to take hold and challenge the boundaries of reporting. Chapter Two examines how the Michener Award administrators worked with little support to position the Michener Award as Canada's Pulitzer Prize for Public Service within the industry.

Chapter Three links the creation of the Michener Awards Foundation/*La Fondation des Prix Michener* in 1983 to the growing reputational success of the awards in the 1980s and a commitment by media companies to invest in public service journalism. Chapter Four focuses on expanding the mission of the new foundation. In addition to honouring investigative journalism, the directors built a culture of journalism in the public interest through the creation of special awards, education opportunities and outreach.

As we see in Chapter Five, by the end of the 1980s, the award earned the respect of the industry for the integrity and independence of its judging and the ongoing patronage of the governor general. It was at this moment that an overture from the Canadian Journalism Foundation in 1989 forced the Michener board to choose its path — a financially stable partnership or independence.

Chapter Six looks at the 1990s, a decade of leadership changes with the loss of its key founders — Roland Michener, Bill MacPherson and Paul Deacon. A series of new leaders addressed the perpetual challenge of attracting entries from French-language and small media outlets outside the golden triangle of Ottawa-Toronto-Montreal. The organization struggled through a fresh round of financial difficulties that emerged from the changing journalism landscape.

A new century brought the rise of the Internet and social media and panic among established media outlets. Chapter Seven documents a vicious newspaper war and the frenzy of consolidation, closures and mergers in the early 2000s that left media organizations heavy with debt and light on journalists. Despite institutional constraints, journalists found ways to pursue public interest stories through collaboration and other methods. A Michener nomination was more than validation of a job well done; it was a way to leverage resources for the next story.

The collapse of the media business model hit regional and smaller broadcasters and newspapers hard. By the 2010s, big media organizations dominated the roster of Michener finalists. Chapter Eight looks at some of the investigative stories that resonated nationally — racial profiling, cancer care and systemic intuitional problems in Canada's armed forces and policing.

Chapter Nine details how in 2017-18 the Michener Foundation faced and resolved internal governance issues and its ongoing relationship with the Office of the Governor General.

Journalism for the Public Good: The Michener Awards at Fifty concludes with the story of an unexpected opportunity from former governor general David Johnston. In 2019, in an interview for this book, he suggested the Michener Awards Foundation partner with the Rideau Hall Foundation (RHF), an organization formed to "amplify the impact of the Office of the Governor General as a central institution of Canadian democracy."[20] Its focus on democracy fits with the Michener mandate of journalism in public service.

The 2020 union has given the Micheners access to professional resources it lacked as a volunteer organization — communication, marketing and fundraising. This is a renaissance for the Michener Awards Foundation as it takes stock, reimagines and expands to provide impetus for public interest journalism for the next fifty years.

These are difficult times for journalism in Canada. Social media is a marketplace for mis- and disinformation that undermines and threatens fact-based journalism. Media organizations, faced with declining advertising and readership and rising costs, are laying off journalists by the hundreds and shuttering outlets to save their business. To stanch further closures of legacy media and provide help for startups, the federal government introduced tax measures in 2019. This move, along with the Online News Act, Bill C-18, raises questions about government meddling and the independence of media. While news organization sort out their business model, journalists continue to produce stories that uncover wrongs, catalyze policy changes and in the process win the Michener Award, the highest honour in Canadian journalism.

The Birth of the Michener Award

When Governor General Roland Michener's press secretary sliced open the envelope in September 1969, Guy Robillard likely recognized the signature. The letter was from C.W.E. MacPherson, president-elect of a new national journalism organization, The Federation of Press Clubs of Canada/*La Fédération des Cercles des Journalistes*. Robillard knew him as Bill MacPherson, the avuncular long-time managing editor of the *Ottawa Citizen*. His letter contained an intriguing proposition. Would His Excellency endorse a new national award for meritorious public service in journalism?

The time was right for a new award that focussed on journalism in the public interest. The 1950s and 1960s brought significant changes and prosperity for many. By the end of the 1960s, Canadians enjoyed subsidized health care and could look forward to government-funded pensions in their old age. The introduction of no-fault divorce and the legalization of the birth control pill led to more women studying in universities and joining the workforce.[1] Rapid changes in technology and industry had ignited "a substantial rise in the Canadian standards of living."[2] The growing middle class had more money to spend on luxury goods like automatic appliances and family cars. Television viewing had moved from crowds huddling in front of store-front windows into living rooms where families watched the six o'clock news sitting comfortably on their sofas eating supper. This was the era of TV trays and Swanson frozen dinners.

The images broadcast on those nightly newscasts were unlike anything Canadians had ever seen. "There were drug scenes and student revolts in universities and colleges, particularly at Simon Fraser University in British Columbia, and Sir George Williams University in Montreal, where the computer centre was destroyed, and the love-in, or live-in, at Rochdale College in Toronto," historian Peter Stursberg observed.[3] Television brought these events, along with the daily carnage of the American war in Vietnam, into our living rooms. Young Canadians crossed the border to take part in anti-war rallies, and Canadians welcomed a northern influx of idealistic draft dodgers into their communities. "The young people were really interested in the Vietnam War and civil rights. They didn't care about reading newspapers like their dad did," said Toronto writer and author David Hayes.[4]

"It was turbulent times. You had assassinations, you had civil rights movements. It was the 60s and everything was in motion. So, how can journalism not be in motion if everything else is," asked Cecil Rosner, author of *Behind the Headlines: A History of Investigative Journalism in Canada*.[5] "It was leading people to think that, hey, why shouldn't I hold some powerful interests to account, or maybe the *status quo* should be challenged, or maybe I shouldn't believe every statement a politician is making. Maybe I should test those. Maybe I should call out a tough question."[6] It was all part of the transformation of journalism that was in step with the times.

Like Canadian society, in the late 1960s, the journalism industry was in motion. In this climate of widespread change, the Michener Award for Meritorious Public Service in Journalism was conceived, developed and launched. It was created to recognize and encourage a new kind of journalism — fierce, hard-hitting journalism that served the public interest and had an impact. It emerged from an uneven and somewhat placid mainstream media in Canada.

Three particular historical developments set the scene for the award's creation. The first was the emergence of a new, more critical culture. The second was a growing concern about the concentration of media ownership in Canada that led to the creation in 1969 of the Special Senate Committee on Mass Media. The third was the appointment of Roland Michener — a lawyer, politician, and diplomat with a reputation as the consummate public servant — as Governor General in 1967. In its very creation, the Michener Award recognized the changing Canadian landscape. It would spur positive changes in journalism, among media organizations and in Canadian society.

Canada's Pulitzer Prize for Public Service

It's not that the quality of journalism went unrecognized before the creation of the Michener. Each year, Canada's journalists competed for individual recognition at a buffet of regional and national industry awards for excellence in news, features, columns and broadcast. The Canadian Women's Press Club Memorial Awards (renamed the Media Club of Canada in 1971) had been judging and honouring the best stories of its members since 1935, while the

National Newspaper Association started its awards ceremony in 1941.[7] In broadcast, the then Radio Television News Directors Association (RTNDA) television and radio awards began in 1962. But in 1969, none of these organ- izations had a category to acknowledge exemplary enterprise investigative journalism — defined by author Cecil Rosner as "stories that hold a powerful interest to account, and also use a rigorous methodology for doing so."[8] It was time to set the bar higher. Bill MacPherson, with his easy smile, even temper and gentle persistence, was the person to turn the idea for a Canadian Pulitzer and create the Michener Award.

Support for the idea grew from a new spirit of independence among Canadians — a confidence buoyed by the adoption of its own Maple Leaf flag in 1965 and Canada's proud welcome to the world for Expo 67. "If the Micheners hadn't come along something else would have had to come along because, in fact, it was part of that spirit of adventure that Canada suddenly found. We were no longer the kind of country that deferred to others. We were a country that could achieve really important things on our own," said Peter Herrndorf, a CBC executive, who in the 1970s led the creation of inves- tigative programs such as *the fifth estate*.[9] The mindset and conditions were right for new ventures.

In the early 1960s, journalists from across the country started to dis- cuss new projects to advance journalism. The concept of an award for public service journalism started to take shape at the founding of the Federation of Press Clubs of Canada in 1968 — a union of eleven independent press clubs in cities from Vancouver to Moncton. The umbrella organization's main job was to provide a national network to connect journalists from all media coast to coast. The group would provide professional and administrative help through supports such as a national directory of reporters and editors. But that wasn't enough. Organizers wanted a project that would knit the new group together and give the Federation a national profile. At its first national conference in Kitchener, Ontario, members settled on a single national journalism award; one that would stand above other industry awards given to journalists by their peers.

Delegates to the Federation of Press Clubs of Canada's inaugural meet- ing selected Bill MacPherson as the incoming president who set his sights on viceregal support. In a letter to the governor general's press secretary, MacPherson made his pitch. This journalism award would stand out from other journalism awards because it would honour the collective effort of a media organization, not individual journalists working in a specific medium as the other awards did. As MacPherson wrote in his letter, "The Toronto Men's Press Club has, through its National Newspaper Awards program, a long-established record of recognizing individual efforts in journalism. There is, however, no national award to recognize such an effort by a Canadian publication or broadcasting station."[10]

With the support from the Federation of Press Clubs, MacPherson set out a vision for Canada's version of the Pulitzer Prize to honour "disinterested and meritorious public service" journalism.[11] In 1969, the U.S. Pulitzer Prize was in its fifty-second year. Like the Pulitzer, Canada's new journalism award would be truly national and embrace all media — broadcast, print and magazine journalism, big and small. "Just as the Canadian Broadcasting Corporation, for example, would be eligible to enter for some great national achievement, so should a small weekly newspaper that stretches its resources to the limit to achieve perhaps a modest but important community improvement," MacPherson explained to Robillard in a follow-up letter.[12] There was "a kind of flowering, a sudden awakening of Canada, that almost everything was possible in this country," recalled Herrndorf. Aggressive news coverage of the American war in Vietnam and the civil rights protests south of the border were inspiring a new generation of journalists in Canada to be bolder and bigger. From Herrndorf's perch at the CBC, the Michener was the perfect way to recognize that trend, and it came at a perfect time for Canada.

This idealism found its expression in a developing critical culture and optimism that investigative journalism had the power not only to point out injustices and wrongdoing but also to improve our institutions and communities. Canadian journalists were awake to the challenges. The unfolding events of the late 1960s and early 1970s were exciting times for many reporters and editors working in Canadian newsrooms. They read exposés such as Seymour Hersh's coverage of the My Lai massacre in Vietnam. The New Journalism of Truman Capote, after the publication of *In Cold Blood* in 1966, attracted younger journalists. They were intrigued by the gonzo storytelling of counter-culture hero Hunter S. Thompson. "I think that had a ripple effect across journalism in that it increased the number of people going to journalism schools. It changed the ambition that newsrooms had to look into serious things," said John Miller, who started at the *Toronto Star* as a junior copy editor and was rising through the ranks when the burglary at the Democratic

National headquarters in the Watergate building in Washington, D.C., happened in 1972.[13]

When *All the President's Men* was published in 1974, "suddenly journalism, a romantic calling to begin with, became downright sexy, an outlet for all those baby-boomers wondering what to do with an English or History or Philosophy degree," wrote David Hayes.[14] Students lined up to get into journalism programs at Ryerson Polytechnical Institute, Carleton University and the University of Western Ontario. Hayes saw it as "an expression of the times . . . growing out of the values of 'critical culture'."[15]

Compared to our colleagues south of the border, however, reporters working for the mainstream media in Canada had been slow to embrace investigative journalism and its watchdog role of exposing wrongs and corruption in institutions.[16] This emerging critical culture had a hard time finding a home in Canadian mainstream newsrooms of the late 1960s and early 70s — but a crack opened at the CBC in 1964 with the debut of *This Hour Has Seven Days*, a spicy television current affairs program. Co-producers Patrick Watson and Doug Leiterman wanted "to tell the truth about social inequities."[17] The two pitched a "program for a mass audience to be produced like a variety show, with live music, satire and a singing cover girl."[18] The producers and CBC management were at odds even before the first show aired on October 4, 1964. Watson and Leiterman flouted a CBC executive order that forbade broadcasting dissenting views of the Queen's visit, and the program mocked royalists.

This Hour Has Seven Days broadcast fifty shows over two seasons. Ratings soared as the "rebellious freedom fighters" defied CBC rules at every turn, using a hidden camera to do a story that resulted in a man being released from a psychiatric hospital. They grilled politicians "contravening CBC's demand for good manners."[19] In the end, CBC President Alphonse Ouimet had enough. Despite an audience of 3.2 million and a vocal national lobby called "To Save *Seven Days* and the Integrity of the CBC," Ouimet ignored appeals from Prime Minster Lester Pearson and cancelled the program.

This new journalism could not be suppressed. It found expression through alternative newspapers and magazines that became the editorial outlet for "disaffected conventional journalists" in the late 1960s and early 70s.[20] Young journalists such as Mark Starowicz at the *Last Post*, Donald Cameron (later known as Silver Donald) at the *Mysterious East,* Brenda Large and Nick Fillmore at the *4th Estate* and Cy Gonick at *Canadian Dimension* were uncovering social, political and business wrongdoings, holding powerful interests to account and discussing new ideas in the public interest. Cameron described the role of the alternative press as "a corrective for a press that had fallen away from what we considered its duties to be."[21]

The introduction of an award that focused on public service journalism in Canada was overdue, not only because of the growing number of critical voices among journalists but also because of a newly released report of the Special Senate Committee on Mass Media. Senator Keith Davey, a former Liberal organizer and campaign strategist known as The Rainmaker, initiated the study "to investigate the mass media in Canada, particularly with respect to their influence and concentration of ownership."[22] The Davey report, released in 1970, painted a dismal picture of Canada's media with its low-quality journalism and trend to consolidation as a way to make more money. At public hearings held over fourteen months, his committee heard from a parade of 125 witnesses. Committee members also found their desks piled high with submissions from 500 individuals and groups. Everyone had an opinion on what was wrong with the media, how to fix the industry and how to improve the quality of journalism.

The committee's final report, *Mass Media: The Uncertain Mirror*, predicted further media concentration. It recommended government intervention to protect the public interest against "the greed or goodwill of an extremely privileged group of businessmen."[23] The Davey report didn't stop there; it dripped eloquently with contempt for the work of many of Canada's print and broadcast media organizations:

> Some newspapers dig. Some newspapers are a constant embarrassment to the powerful. Some manage to be entertaining, provocative and fair at the same time. There are a few such newspapers in Canada. The *Vancouver Sun*. The three Toronto dailies. *Le Devoir*. The *Montreal Star*. The *Windsor Star*. *La Presse*. The *Edmonton Journal*. A handful of others. There should be more. There are also newspapers which, despite occasional lapses into excellence, manage to achieve a consistent level of mediocrity. The *Montreal Gazette*, and the dailies in Ottawa, Winnipeg and Calgary fit into this category. There is a third kind of newspaper in Canada — the kind that prints news releases intact, that seldom extends its journalistic enterprise beyond the coverage of

the local trout festival, that hasn't annoyed anyone important in years. Their city rooms are refuges for the frustrated and dis-illusioned, and their editorial pages are a daily testimony to the notion that Chamber-of-Commerce boosterism is an adequate substitute for community service. It is our sad impression that a great many, if not most Canadian newspapers, fall into this clas-sification. Among them are some of the most profitable newspa-pers in the country.[24]

The point was that greedy media organizations were opting for profits and fail-ing to honour their public service watchdog role. Broadcasters didn't escape condemnation for doing the bare minimum of reporting as required by law. The Davey report criticized the networks for filling prime time with imported programs. But even worse, the news had become "for the most part a sideline for broadcasters," with little original reporting; newscasts were re-writes of newspaper stories and the police blotter.[25] Private radio and television stations had not embraced Canada's new 1968 *Broadcasting Act* that required them to use the public airwaves "to safeguard, enrich and strengthen the culture, political, social and economic fabric of Canada."[26] Like their print counter-parts, broadcasters had turned a blind eye to what Davey considered their primary purpose: to provide in-depth, accurate information so that citizens could make informed decisions as members of society. Davey, like Michener, set the bar high because both held firm to a view that journalism played an essential role as a pillar of democracy.

The Davey report shamed media owners about the quality of journal-ism, especially in smaller newsrooms across Canada. The committee didn't hold back: "Every reporter soon learns that there are only a few newspapers where excellence is encouraged. If they are lucky or clever or restless, they will gravitate to those newspapers. If not, they will stay where they are, growing cynical about their work, learning to live with a kind of sour professional de-spair. Often you can see it in their faces. Most Canadian city rooms are bone-yards of broken dreams."[27] The report had a bleak, prophetic tone of Charles Dickens's novella, *A Christmas Carol*. Davey, the ghost of media present and future, wrote that if nothing was done to put the brakes on media concentra-tion, then ownership's interests will collide "with the public interest."[28]

The Special Senate Committee on Mass Media recommended a Press Ownership Review Board with the power to prevent "*all* transactions that increase the concentration of ownership in the mass media [that] are undesirable and contrary to the public interest."[29] The Liberal government of Pierre Elliott Trudeau faced a wall of resistance from independent and unregulated publishers. It had no appetite for a protracted tussle with the media, so the report with its recommendations gathered dust. The concession from media organizations was the creation of local and regional press councils. The first was in Windsor, Ontario, in 1971, followed by provincial councils in Ontario and Alberta in 1972, and in Québec in 1973 — with limited participation from publishers.[30]

While press councils adjudicated complaints and held participating media outlets accountable for their quality of journalism, they did nothing to stanch the primary concern of the Davey report — media consolidation and concentration. As CBC journalist Cecil Rosner explained — apart from the public broadcaster, CBC/Radio Canada — most media organizations are for-profit businesses, many with business interests outside journalism. "It can get sticky and tricky because the owners of a lot of large media corporations travel in the same circles as the powerful, the very people good investigative journalists are trying to hold to account."[31] Without some form of regulation, like a Press Ownership Review Board, Davey predicted the waves of media buying, selling, mergers and closures would accelerate and intensify the conundrum watchdog journalists and editors faced in pursuing stories in the public interest.

In 1970, in the aftermath of the Davey report, publishers and private broadcasters made it clear that they did not want any federal intervention. While frontline reporters and backroom editors wanted more resources for investigative reporting, most were not interested in shaming their bosses. The executive of the Federation of Press Clubs of Canada/*La Fédération des Cercles des Journalistes* had come up with a strategy to entice the media bosses. A new prestigious award that rewarded "meritorious and disinterested" journalism would surely co-opt media executives who managed budgets and made editorial decisions to put more money into investigative journalism. The award could be one industry response to the Davey report's criticism of Canada's lacklustre journalism.

The Special Senate Committee shared the view that publishers and broadcasters had to up their game and invest in serious journalism that served the public interest. Much of that burden, the Davey report observed, fell to the staid and somewhat dysfunctional public broadcaster, the Canadian

Broadcasting Corporation, in particular CBC television, "which has all too often been the empty-headed service."[32] When Peter Herrndorf, a newly minted graduate from Dalhousie University law school, joined the CBC television newsroom in Winnipeg in 1965, he found "the people there were not terribly ambitious, were not terribly aggressive. They had good jobs. . . . And the idea of somebody like myself coming in wanting to be much more proactive, to do aggressive work was thought to be a bit inappropriate."[33] Herrndorf was one of a class of new young bucks who would bring about change and transform news and current affairs at the public broadcaster.

Energetic and enthusiastic young journalists were finding ways into newsrooms and rapidly climbing the executive ladder. At CBC-TV, Herrndorf, inspired by the CBC radio revolution and the success of *As It Happens* (started in 1968), looked to shake up television news and current affairs by creating *the fifth estate* in 1975 and the *Journal* in 1982. Television programs such as *Connections*, a documentary series in 1977 about organized crime, "stunned people" and engaged audiences with "really serious, thoughtful, difficult, investigative reporting for the first time," Herrndorf recalls.[34] Media companies were starting to build a stable of reform minded journalists who found a hungry audience for their hard-hitting stories. The executives found that in addition to the public good, larger audiences were also good for business.

The Michener Awards emerged amid these changes, as journalists and the industry became more focused on public service journalism. At the *Globe and Mail*, long-time editor-in-chief (1963-1983) Richard (Dic) Doyle liked to brag about the members of the *Globe*'s SWAT investigative team — known as "Davey's Hit Squad" or "Davey's Raiders" in homage to Clark Davey, the managing editor — who were busy rooting out injustices in society.[35] On Canada's one hundredth birthday, Doyle wrote a front-page editorial that set out "an agenda for *The Globe* — if not the country to address: Nobody need starve to death, but people do. . . . Who writes with pride of our mental hospitals, our slums, our inability to plug the gaps in social grids conceived to guarantee that no one should live in hopeless destitution? What kind of a country is it that admits to a woeful shortage of housing and at the same time endures a heavy tax upon the materials houses are made of?"[36]

Over at the rival *Toronto Star*, Beland Honderich, the chairman and publisher, pushed a progressive agenda in the paper, based on influential early *Star* editor Joseph E. Atkinson's editorial principles: a strong, united independent Canada, social justice, individual and civil liberties, community and civic engagement, the rights of working people and the necessary role of government.[37] In a speech at the University of Toronto in 1901, Atkinson declared that "the paper which is most human will in the end be found to have the most influence."[38]

His aptly named son, Joseph Story Atkinson, continued that crusading tradition. In a 1957 speech, he reminded employees that "from its inception in 1892 *The Star* has been a champion of social and economic reform, a defender of minority rights, a foe of discrimination, a friend of organized labour and a staunch advocate of Canadian nationhood."[39] The larger media outlets like the *Toronto Star*, *Globe and Mail* and CBC embraced a new award to recognize exceptional journalism. Within smaller news outlets, the culture was rapidly changing as waves of young people fresh out of journalism schools joined the reporting ranks, ambitious to investigate, expose and make a change. An award to recognize public service in journalism would be something to aim for, and one that could garner the support of Governor General Roland Michener.

Michener's Award for Public Service

There was a lot of good fortune and a certain amount of calculation when the president of the Federation of Press Clubs pitched a new journalism award to Rideau Hall in 1969. Bill MacPherson, the long-time managing editor of the *Ottawa Citizen*, was familiar with the political career of Roland Michener. As a young Toronto lawyer, Michener had served as an elected member in provincial and federal Progressive Conservative governments and later as Speaker of the House of Commons in the Diefenbaker government. After the Liberals took power in 1963, Prime Minister Lester Pearson appointed Michener Canada's High Commissioner to India and the first Ambassador to Nepal. Named Governor General of Canada in 1967, Michener had a sterling reputation among all political parties as the ultimate servant of the public.

When MacPherson mailed his letter to Rideau Hall, he knew that as, governor general, Michener's patronage would be vital to establishing the credibility of an award. This request was not out of order. The long history of governors general supporting artistic, cultural, charitable or athletic activities during and at the end of their terms goes back to Lord Stanley of Preston (1888-1890), who established the Stanley Cup. Vincent Massey patronized the arts and established the Governor General's Award for Architecture, while his successor Georges Vanier founded the Vanier Institute of the Family.

When it came to suggesting Michener embrace this new award, MacPherson promised His Excellency that the Federation would assume all administrative responsibilities, set and maintain standards and cover all costs. Like a typical journalist, MacPherson was in a hurry. He wanted His Excellency to respond to the proposal immediately so he could announce it at the Federation's second annual national meeting in a couple of weeks. Michener complied. His agreement "in principle" arrived from Rideau Hall before the October 11, 1969, meeting. As Michener later recalled, Bill MacPherson "soon convinced me of the value of such an idea and collectively we organized the competition, established the trophy and held the first competition."[40] Michener's interest and hands-on involvement were essential to the Award's growth, success and survival, especially in its early years.

The 1969 annual meeting of the Federation of Press Clubs of Canada concluded in a triumphal announcement that the directors of the Federation had unanimously "accepted the responsibility — and the honour — to administer The Roland Michener Award for Meritorious Public Service in Journalism."[41] The news found its way into newspapers coast to coast. "Governor General Roland Michener will present the first award in a ceremony at Government House early next year and his name will be permanently attached to the award," stated the headline in the *Hamilton Spectator* on October 14, 1969. It was a big coup for the Federation, which saw the award's potential to "rank with the most treasured in the field of Canadian journalism."[42] It also established the Federation of Press Clubs as a group that had some clout. The Federation hoped its growing reputation would entice other local press clubs to join the national umbrella group.

Now began Bill MacPherson's long and sometimes thankless work on behalf of the Federation of Press Clubs to establish the award, build its credibility and garner support among media groups nationwide. Over the next two years, MacPherson, with a lot of help from Rideau Hall and Roland Michener, was immersed in behind-the-scenes logistics for the new award. Letters went back and forth between MacPherson and Rideau Hall trying to find a hole in His Excellency's calendar to hold the first award ceremony. In early January 1970, a letter from Michener's assistant secretary to MacPherson suggested the first half of April, November or December of 1970.[43] It was a little premature. It took MacPherson ten months to respond. He was busy forming a judging panel and spreading the news of the new award to press clubs and media outlets with the zeal of a travelling salesman. In October 1970, he finally was able to report that the panel was in place and a call would soon go out by mail to all newsrooms inviting them to submit their stories for "Meritorious Public Service in Journalism" for the calendar year 1970.[44]

The newspaper reports from the Federation's third annual meeting in October 1970 noted that "The item of prime importance will be the finalization of plans for the establishment of the Michener Award."[45] In the new year, MacPherson consulted with His Excellency and Rideau Hall staff about the award's criteria, judging and logistics for a ceremony. Together they drew up a to-do list. Chief among the thirteen points checked off at that meeting was a general agreement "that there would be no difficulty in future presentations by the following governor generals [sic]."[46] This statement implied that Michener and Rideau Hall expected the award to survive and to become part of the range of honours bestowed by future governors general, even those who might have little connection to journalism or even antipathy towards media organizations. It was a promise that would be tested to its limit over the coming decades.

Still to be settled was the name of the award. While it had been announced in 1969 as the 'Roland Michener Award for Meritorious Public Service in Journalism,' Michener's press secretary thought that title was too wordy. As a postscript in the minutes, he scribbled, The Michener Award for Excellence in Journalism/Le Prix Michener pour excellence dans la presse. It took a few more months before Michener and the Federation settled on a trimmed-down version: The Michener Award for Journalism/Le Prix Michener du Journalisme.

The dream of the Federation of Press Clubs was starting to take shape. "The Michener Award . . . establishes our credibility," wrote Barry Mather, a former journalist and the Federation's Secretary-Treasurer.[47] For Peter Herrndorf, who by then was CBC's vice-president for English Services, "It was kind of a Godsend." As he saw it, "a lot of journalists were looking for a big transcending award that could validate, that could in fact say, you did great work. And so, people very early on bought into the Michener Awards."[48]

This award had cachet. So much so that even before the first ceremony, at least one other journalism organization aspired to wrest it from Bill MacPherson. In the spring of 1971, the new award caught the attention of the Canadian Women's Press Club (CWPC). With its 541 members, the CWPC was confident that it was organizationally and financially stronger to represent the press in Canada and run this new award. "The Federation of Press Clubs of Canada has practically no funds, an executive of three and is primarily set up to administer the Michener Awards," CWPC president, Jean Danard, wrote to Senator Keith Davey, former chair of the Senate Special Committee on Mass Media.[49] That was a fair assessment. Behind the scenes, the fledgling Federation of Press Clubs of Canada was struggling. Support from its member press clubs had flagged. Annual dues to cover the costs of the award were slow to come in. It is not clear if the CWPC bid ever reached the ears of Bill MacPherson, but he maintained a firm grip, thus preventing any other journalists' group from swooping in and scooping it up. With a stubborn Scottish streak, MacPherson pushed on with the firm conviction that Roland Michener was critical to the financial stability and success of this nascent award and the Federation.

To outsiders, Daniel Roland Michener might have seemed like an unlikely champion for a crusading journalism award. Roly, as he was called, was athletic — hockey, tennis, jogging — one might have expected him to endorse some athletic prize. Not so, said his daughter Diana Michener-Schatz, a chemist and founder of the Michener Institute. An award focussing on journalism in the public interest was a natural for her father "because he wasn't narrow." She pointed to his rural Alberta upbringing in a politically active Conservative family, his education and his career choices. "It fits with his approach to politics, and I think it fits with his approach to being governor general" — and his support for an award for public service journalism.[50]

Michener devoted his private and professional life to the values of public service — the award's *raison d'être*. After serving briefly in the Royal Canadian Air Force, he went to Oxford University as a Rhodes Scholar in 1921, where he became fast friends with fellow Canadian Lester B. "Mike" Pearson.[51] The two shared a love of politics and sports. They played on the Oxford hockey team, "Roly at centre or left wing and Mike on defence."[52] As Peter Stursberg wrote in his biography of Pearson, "Some might say that's the way they went on to play politics. Despite their divergent politics, Michener said he regarded Pearson as a Liberal conservative and himself "as a liberal Conservative — a small 'l' liberal and a capital 'C' Conservative."[53]

Michener represented a political culture that today would be all but unthinkable. His daughter Diana says her father was not like typical politicians of today with their narrow one-party focus. "He was far more interested in the exchange between people, understanding people. . . . He was definitely interested in the broader spectrum."[54] When Michener died in 1991, a *Toronto Star* editorial described his life as: "King St. law firm, Bay St. directorships,

Rosedale friendships — he approached every task with enthusiasm and every person with civility."[55] But what elevated Michener above others was his service to the public good. For example, when the *Chinese Immigration Act* was repealed in 1947, Michener, a Conservative member of Ontario's provincial legislature, worked to reunite Chinese families. Later, as MP and Speaker of the House of Commons in Ottawa between 1957 and 1962, he won the respect of all parties for — among other rulings — holding to order his party's boss, Prime Minister John Diefenbaker.

When Governor General Georges Vanier died in office on March 5, 1967, Liberal Prime Minister Lester Pearson turned to "Roly," his old Oxford buddy, to take over. Expo 67 was opening in just a few months and Canada was expecting more than sixty official visits as part of the Centennial celebration.[56] Michener, born on April 19, 1900, was only the third Canadian-born individual to fill the position, following Vincent Massey and Georges Vanier. Because of Michener's sterling reputation across the political arena, no one accused Pearson of nepotism. In fact, it was the opposite. The announcement even garnered praise from Walter Stewart, a professed anti-royalist journalist. In the *Star Weekly Magazine*, he wrote, "Roly Michener could make an ideal governor general, but we should make him Canada's first president instead" because Michener brought "flair, dignity and that indefinable something called presence" to the position.[57]

Michener's colleagues from all political and social backgrounds would concur, describing the incoming governor general as civil, congenial, decent and energetic. He possessed perfect qualities for what would be his last public role, the 20th Governor General of Canada. In a moment of self-reflection, Michener said, "You know by temperament I am not a comet and not a rabid partisan and I am more judicial in mind."[58] As governor general, Michener quickly found he needed all his judicial, political and diplomatic skills to navigate the changing landscape of Canada. At the same time as Canadians waved maple leaf flags with nationalist fervour during the Centennial celebrations, in Québec, the growing separatist movement sparked a debate about the Office of the Governor General, the last vestige of colonial rule. Michener clearly saw the viceregal position as a national institution.[59] In that role, he recognized that journalism was essential in informing and encouraging a national conversation about issues and events.

Michener made this very clear in his public support for the higher calling of journalism. Soon after taking office in 1967, in a speech to the Parliamentary

Press Club, he paid tribute to the place of the free press of the Fourth Estate in the life and governance of Canada "for the indispensable service which you render in what I call the Canadian ideal."[60] Later, in a speech to the Canadian Press Association, Michener reminded journalists that when he was practising law in the 1940s at Lang, Michener and Ricketts, as it was called at that time, he worked on the incorporation of Press News Limited, an entity to supply news from Canadian Press to the Canadian Broadcasting Corporation. "I was sometimes called upon to give a snap opinion to your editors as to the risk of libel actions arising from some of the news stories."[61]

Many believe that Roland Michener's impetus for his vice-regal endorsement of the Michener Awards for Public Service Journalism was to honour his daughter Wendy, a celebrated cultural critic, arts journalist, broadcaster and experimental filmmaker, who died suddenly on New Year's Day 1969 from an embolism. She was just a couple of months shy of her thirty-fourth birthday. "It wasn't a story of [Roland] Michener setting out to do a memorial for his daughter and that kind of thing," said her husband, Les Lawrence. "I think of that as part of the background of the story, rather than the initial prompting."[62] As Lawrence remembers it, the Federation of Press Clubs of Canada came to Michener looking for viceregal endorsement. No doubt, Lawrence said, Wendy "must have been in Roly's mind when he accepted to put his name on the award. And I think it might have been in the minds of the press people as well. But I don't think it was a clearcut example of a man setting up something for his daughter." Diana Michener-Schatz agreed, saying her instinct was that her father supported the Michener Award because he was interested in journalism in the public interest and "wanted to see it continued and pursued." The premature death of Wendy may well have been "a catalyst to keep it going" and perhaps "strengthened his activity" in the Michener Awards, she said, especially after his term as governor general ended in 1974.[63]

In the early years of the journalism award, Roland Michener's dedication included pulling out his personal chequebook on occasion to save the fledgling organization from insolvency and pitching in to raise money. Michener said the Michener Award "appealed very strongly to me as a useful means of encouraging excellence in a field of endeavour which was not being given enough attention in Canada. . . . There is no doubt, however, of the importance of the journalist and his counterparts in radio and television as moulders of opinion and essential supporters of a democratic society."[64]

When it came to the logistics of setting up a new journalism award in 1970-71, Roland Michener was hands-on. He wanted "a visible and physical representation of the award — a fitting symbol of journalistic excellence — that a deserving organization could take back to the newsroom."[65] He had agreed to cover the costs of the design and production of the dies and re-make of the trophies during his term.[66] Michener wanted a trophy that would stand out from all the other journalism awards, one that had some heft. He envisioned a large bronze sculpture with his personal Coat of Arms and the name of the award on one side and a symbol and its relation to media on the other side. It would be mounted on a wooden base that would have the winner's name and the year of the award.

Michener asked Bill MacPherson to come up with appropriate images to symbolize journalism. Three weeks later MacPherson reported that his efforts had not been very fruitful. He offered the symbol for Mercury and Hermes — "both at times were portrayed as bearing the caduceus, or herald's wand. Thus, I suppose, both gods as well as the caduceus could portray the dispatch of news." It was that or "the bell-ringing town crier."[67] There would be no town crier on Michener's trophy. Michener turned to Rideau Hall's historian and former chief curator of the National Gallery of Canada in Ottawa. Dr. Robert H. Hubbard recommended Michener hire John Matthews, a twenty-eight-year-old sculptor from Ottawa.

Matthews' vision for the trophy was a rectangular, sturdy plaque in bronze to represent permanency. It would sit on a white marble base sourced from Piggott Construction of Toronto. Together the sculpture would stand nine inches tall. "Initially, the Governor General was surprised the award would be so large, but eventually he realized it would be displayed in different locations, not just on an individual's desk," Matthews explained.[68] One side of the trophy had antique type in a random pattern along with the inscription — The Michener Award for Journalism/*Le Prix Michener du Journalisme*. The reverse side had crossing lines to suggest communication by airwaves and electronics. Michener gave his unreserved approval to the design.[69] Matthews was given a budget of $700 and a tight deadline of October 1, 1971.

That first Michener Award presentation started to take shape. As the administrator for the Federation of Press Clubs, Bill MacPherson had invited newsrooms and press clubs across Canada to submit stories of outstanding public service for the calendar year of 1970. There is no record of how many media outlets submitted entries that first year, where they came from, or the stories they covered. MacPherson had enlisted four volunteers — who were arm's-length and independent of media organizations — to sit on the panel. The judges were a distinguished group that reflected the times: A. Davidson Dunton, former board chair of the Canadian Broadcasting Corporation and president of Carleton University, who served as the chief judge of the panel; George V. Ferguson, editor emeritus of the *Montreal Star*; Yves Gagnon, director of the School of Communications at Laval University; and Sam Ross, a retired Parliamentary radio correspondent living in Vancouver.

The panel was bilingual, represented print and broadcast and included one member from Québec and one from Western Canada. It would be another sixteen years before a woman and more than fifty years before a Racialized or Indigenous person would join the Michener Award judging panel. The judges convened at the National Press Club at 150 Wellington Street across from Parliament Hill in March 1971. Deliberations were held behind closed doors, but no doubt discussions were lively, given the slate of finalists for the 1970 award.

The First Michener

The first Michener Award for Public Service Journalism was not the gala event that media organizations have come to expect. It was a modest and rather perfunctory affair. About fifty people gathered at Rideau Hall at 11:30 on the sunny, nose-chilling Monday morning on November 8, 1971. They stood in a semicircle in the Reception Room. Most were dressed for the office, or wearing, as the invitation from Rideau Hall advised, "leisure suits."[70] The president of the Federation of Press Clubs of Canada, Ken MacGray, opened proceedings by thanking His Excellency for his enthusiastic support and sponsorship. "The Michener Award is an important adornment to Canadian journalism, and you are to be warmly congratulated for such an initiative."[71] His Excellency Roland Michener stepped forward, welcomed "the press" and quickly got to business. "I know that every minute of your time is valuable, and I am therefore all the more grateful that you have found time to join us this morning for the award presentation."[72]

There was none of the suspense of an awards event. The announcement of the inaugural 1970 Michener Award winner had come seven months earlier, on April 13, 1971. The judges had picked two well-heeled media outlets, *The Financial Post* and CBC-TV, for the series, "The Charter Revolution" — a joint investigation into shady practices in the booming charter airline business.

In the early days of air traffic, large groups, who belonged to some club or organization, chartered aircraft to go on special ski adventures, religious pilgrimages or school trips. As Clive Baxter wrote:

> To make sure that these clubs didn't slip into the business of organizing large scale public travel, regulations were drafted that insisted that only clubs or organizations set up for some other purpose could qualify — this is the so-called affinity clause — and that anyone making a trip must have been a member in good standing for six months. What was meant to restrict the growth of charters, has in fact become a bonanza to a growing army of entrepreneurs . . . It becomes, in effect, a government license to charge the general public for — in too many cases — absolutely nothing but the right to qualify for a charter.[73]

Two other media outlets received honourable mentions: the *Windsor Star* for its investigation into the ownership and control of a local television station, and CKLG, an edgy top-40 radio station in Vancouver for its documentary series, "Drugs: A Search for Understanding." The five two-hour episodes probed all facets of drugs and drug culture. In an interview, Miles Murchison, the researcher and writer for the series, recalled how he brought in an outside journalist to grill the morning show host Roy Hennessy about why he played drug-themed songs such as "Lucy in the Sky with Diamonds." Nothing was off limits, Murchison said. "It was the first time I heard a doctor from Montreal say that heroin was easier on the body than alcohol," and according to the doctor, the problem was that heroin led to a life of crime. "We looked at how dope was brought into B.C. from across the border. . . . We explored all of it."[74]

That morning neither the winners nor the finalists had a chance to brag about their journalism and the outcomes. That may not have been such a bad thing, given the content of CKLG's entry and the formality of the event. Governor General Roland Michener was a "traditionalist" and a "stickler for protocol and liked all the ceremony and trappings of the vice-regal office."[75] His wife, Norah Michener, the doyen of good manners, wrote a booklet on etiquette for the wives of Members of Parliament. That could be why the citation from the judging panel for CKLG's "Understanding" series was artfully vague. It read that the radio programs "presented useful material in ways particularly appropriate for young people and to promote understanding between generations."[76] The Michener judges rewarded journalism that investigated current issues in a controversial manner, but the panel, with its extensive experience and expertise, belonged to an older school of journalism where good taste and propriety still mattered. There would be no reference to dope, heroin, LSD or the Beatles, especially at the first awards ceremony with the Governor General of Canada at Rideau Hall.

The judges had no trouble describing in detail the winner of the first Michener Award, "The Charter Revolution," and heaping ample praise on the journalism. *The Financial Post* and CBC-TV combined the respectability of the conservative business press and the audience reach of the public broadcaster. The judges pointed out that the series broke new journalism ground not just because it was an "excellent public exposure of the dangerous developments in the air charter business" or that "the research was excellent and the presentation very striking," but because of the effective combined use of television and the printed media.[77] In those years, it was common for newspaper people such as the *Financial Post*'s Clive Baxter to guest host on a CBC-TV current affairs shows, but not typical for competing media outlets to work together on an investigative story. The cross-exposure of the same story benefitted both media outlets.

Along with Baxter, producer and director Alan Elrich accepted the first Michener Award on behalf of CBC-TV. "The only thing that stands out for me is the stupid grin on my face."[78] That morning when Elrich was getting dressed for the ceremony, he discovered that he had packed one black shoe and one brown shoe. "The shoe store down the street opened early due to my incessant knocking on the door at 9 a.m."[79] When Michener presented the newly minted bronze-and-marble Michener Award trophy, Elrich recalled him saying, "'Be careful it's very heavy.' It was much heavier than it looked."[80] Weighing eight pounds and eight ounces, the trophy could be a metaphor for the important heft of the stories Michener hoped would gain recognition through the award.

Cynthia Baxter beamed as her husband Clive grasped Roland Michener's hand as he accepted the Michener Award trophy on behalf of the *Financial Post*.[81] It was her first "solemn occasion" at Rideau Hall. "I was impressed by all of the pomp . . . and so I loved the whole ceremony, and of course, I was thrilled for Clive. But I remember I saw one dear man and a dear friend with moth holes in his jacket. I remember seeing a spectacular dress, not really a mid-day dress that another woman was wearing," she recalled.[82] The range of attire that morning may well have reflected the newness of the award or the fact that despite all of Bill MacPherson's work, the industry still didn't know much about the Michener Award and occasion. Over the years, the Michener traditions would come to be made and remade.

After the presentation of the trophies and plaques, guests lined up to shake the hands of His Excellency and Mrs. Michener, then briefly mingled over refreshments in the Long Gallery. By 12:15 p.m. the ceremony was over, but not the celebrations. The Federation of Press Clubs of Canada would hold a dinner for the winners and finalists that night. CBC and the *Financial Post* broke new journalistic ground; their joint story foreshadowed collaborative teamwork among media organizations. "So, it was suddenly possible to partner with the *Financial Post*. It suddenly became possible to partner with the National Film Board. It became possible to partner with all kinds of others," recalled Peter Herrndorf. "There were really interesting initiatives that not only relied on the new talent that we had brought to the CBC but in fact relied on the talent that existed at other organizations and with the *Financial Post*. That was a perfect illustration of complementary talent working on a project, each one bringing a lot of expertise to bear."[83]

For the most part, co-productions, especially among competitors, remained the exception in the journalism world until the 2000s. The next collaboration to win a Michener Award would come in 2008. CBC/Radio Canada and The Canadian Press won for their research and reporting into the dangers of police Taser stun guns — thirty-eight years after "The Charter Revolution." The coming years would bring technological developments and new tools to help journalists investigate, expose wrongs and effect change.

It had taken three years for Bill MacPherson to shepherd the concept of a national award for public service journalism through to birth. Roland Michener's patronage gave it a name and won it recognition. As understood by one successor, it fit with Michener's deep belief in public service. Ed Schreyer, who would do much — as we shall see — to enhance the standing of the award during his time in office (1979-1984), believed Michener was motivated to support the award: "He felt that it really had to do with the existence of a free press and journalists of great energy and probity." said Schreyer in an interview. He remembered Michener as a person attuned to societal changes. The creation of the award could be understood as a response to a time of dissatisfaction with authority, criticism of media organizations and the desire for institutional change. The Michener Award was also an incentive for a growing cohort of investigative journalists. More importantly and more specifically, Schreyer said Michener wanted "to continue developing standards of journalism. That's the main reason I think the awards were established."[84]

The Emerging Face of Public Service Journalism

In the first few years of the fledgling Michener Award, entries from media organizations varied wildly in their interpretation of public service journalism. The judges saw the gamut. "We had examples of coverage ranging from crime and violence to storm, slum and near-disaster, from 'investigative' reporting to thinly disguised promotion, and most of it extremely good," the Michener Awards judging panel noted in an early adjudication report.[1] The criteria were clear. Judges were looking for entries that showed evidence of "disinterested journalism" and "impact" for the public good at the local, regional, provincial or national level. So, the announcement of the 1971 Michener winner must have raised a few eyebrows. The CBC-TV retrospective documentary series, "The Tenth Decade," while disinterested, showed scant evidence of impact.

The series told the tumultuous story of the ten years between Canada's ninetieth and one hundredth birthdays — 1957 to 1967. The series used a collage of archival film and tape to look back and reflect on the political, social and cultural changes in Canada through the lens of federal politics. It took viewers behind the scenes of well-known political events of the decade. The judges — all of whom had extensive experience in journalism[2] — opted for CBC-TV's descriptive narrative over two other finalists, both from the Southam newspaper chain. One was a joint investigation by the *London Free Press*, *Ottawa Citizen* and *Windsor Star* into issues surrounding the preservation of the Niagara Escarpment in southern Ontario. The other honourable mention went to the *Ottawa Citizen* for its examination into the Ontario government's Parcost program that put pressure on doctors and pharmacies to prescribe and dispense generic drugs.

In contrast, "The Tenth Decade" re-examined defining political moments and issues of the time, such as the John Diefenbaker Conservative government's refusal to allow nuclear-tipped missiles on Canadian soil. There was the salacious Gerda Munsinger political sex scandal, the defeat of the Tories that led to the ousting of John Diefenbaker as the leader and the failings of the new Liberal government. Building on this was the growing nationalist fervour in Québec — at a time when much of Canada was preparing to welcome the world to Expo 67 in Montreal as part of the country's centennial celebrations.

Given the rapid societal and institutional changes underway in Canadian society, the late 1950s and 1960s were worth documenting and reflecting upon. But was "The Tenth Decade" the kind of storytelling for which the Michener Award had been conceived? Cameron Graham, the executive producer, described it as a feature account of a historical decade. The politics in those ten years, he said, were extremely intricate with a different ethos. "Whatever else it was, Canada was about Canadian politics. We were working in a time when we could go in and ask [politicians] can we cover you guys having this little meeting or can we follow you around and see what you're doing? . . . We would always say, we won't be putting it on the air until after the event you are talking about had occurred. So, they would say, yeah you can come in."[3]

For example, Graham recalled an episode that examined the 1967 Conservative leadership race where John Diefenbaker lost to Nova Scotia's Robert Stanfield. During the convention Graham had three film crews wandering the halls of the CN Chateau Laurier hotel in downtown Ottawa, filming the backroom struggles for power. "I was like a General and I'd say, go here, go there and see what's going on. I would wonder what someone is doing and say, let's send a crew up to their room. So we got all this interesting stuff," Graham recalled. "This was the basis for a lot of the film footage in "The Tenth Decade." . . . A lot of the shenanigans that were going on." It was lively storytelling.

"The Tenth Decade" focused on personalities, issues and ideas with disparate political threads from the decade woven into a compelling narrative. "So, it becomes a pretty interesting film that way. I don't think you could do that now," Graham observed.[4] CBC-TV's Peter Herrndorf acknowledged the wide appeal of the series, but as for impact, "there was very little audience or institutional follow-up. It was just that people had a slightly different take on the history of their own country."[5]

One could say that in giving the Michener to the "The Tenth Decade" the judges recognized the end of an era, not only politically, economically, socially and culturally, but also for journalism. Attitudes and practices were changing quickly. Time was expiring for "insider journalism" when top reporters and columnists regularly cultivated their relationship with powerful politicians to their mutual advantage. Instead, with the rise of investigative journalism in mainstream media, that relationship became more adversarial. The perception of journalists as sympathetic lapdogs of public institutions had changed. Younger journalists saw themselves as watchdogs of public institutions acting on behalf of citizens. Journalists started to go beyond the "who, when, where and what" of stories. They were demanding "how and why" — accountability from those in authority on behalf of the public. At the same time, media organizations started to adopt codes of ethics that stressed independence.

By the 1970s, the ghost of CBC's *This Hour Has Seven Days* was finding expression in mainstream media in Canada. To stay in step with the new decade, the Michener Awards would pivot to reflect the changes and celebrate bold, innovative journalism. But there was work to do. The new award lacked profile and outreach, putting organizers in a tough spot: journalists and media organizations could not submit their work for an award they didn't know existed. Behind the scenes, the two people running the show — Bill MacPherson, as award administrator, and Fraser MacDougall, who became head of the judging panel in year three — worked singlehandedly throughout the decade to build the award's reputation for excellence, pay the bills and raise the profile among media outlets to ensure the award took its rightful place in the industry. Their efforts to boost the award were bolstered by the governor general's annual ceremony at Rideau Hall.

Watchdogs in the Public Interest

If the Roland Michener Award, as it was called then, was about rewarding media outlets for stories with impact for the public good, then the two winners in 1972 set the bar high. The *Scotian Journalist*, a muckraking Nova Scotian bi-weekly newspaper, and Toronto's *Globe and Mail* tied. "*Ex aequo*," wrote Judge Bill Boss. "The results might be interpreted as meaning that the panel had difficulty in reaching its decision. This was not the case. . . . The panel had little difficulty in reaching the consensus that equal excellences this year had been demonstrated by two of them so markedly that a distinction could not be drawn."[6] Boss went on to write that, when the judges considered resources, both organizations demonstrated excellence.

The winning story from "Davey's Raiders" at the *Globe and Mail* exposed the self-interest and blatant conflicts of interest among municipal and provincial politicians in performing their public duties. In one case, two Toronto aldermen voted to change the zoning in areas they held an interest.[7] At the provincial level, it was no better. Ontario's Attorney General resigned after the *Globe* revealed he had bought land northeast of Toronto while the Cabinet was planning to promote growth in the area. Another story involved the Department of Municipal Affairs approving a subdivision of land in which a minister had a financial interest.[8] The public shaming was enough to nudge the new Conservative government of William Davis to pass legislation requiring all political parties in Ontario to disclose financial contributions; it also introduced conflict of interest regulations that were considered the most progressive in the country. In 1974, the Trudeau Liberals followed with the *Election Expenses Act* that provided the first regulations to limit funding for federal candidates and parties and their campaign spending.

Globe and Mail legislative reporter Jonathan Manthorpe had written extensively about financing inequities in political parties and was part of the team recognized for the 1972 series. On the day of the ceremony, the *Globe* team had lunch at the Chateau Laurier in Ottawa with Prime Minister Pierre Trudeau and several other federal ministers. "I remember Trudeau looking as though he'd rather be somewhere else. He seemed to be fairly bored by the whole process,"[9] Manthorpe recalled with a grin and twinkle in his eye. "It was a pleasant lunch but no sparkling conversation." Then they were off to Rideau Hall for a brief stand-up ceremony. Roland Michener presented the award to *Globe* editor Richard ("Dic") Doyle "a very cheerful man, especially in situations like that," Manthorpe said in a soft accent that reflected his upbringing in England's Suffolk County. He chuckled as he recalled that Doyle "almost hopped, skipped and jumped" as he went to collect the trophy. "I never saw it again. It disappeared into his office. . . . The reporters who actually had done the work, we had no mementos of the thing at all."[10]

Manthorpe used his research, much of it targeting Bill Kelly, the "chief bag person for the provincial Tories," to write a book on the history of the Ontario Conservative Party, *The Power and the Tories*.[11] The bottom line for Manthorpe is that the *Globe* series and his subsequent book had lived up to the Michener values and had an immediate and significant impact on how political parties collect money. "I think it did a fair bit to lessen patronage and corruption. It was worthwhile." This was a clear message to politicians and others that the days of "The Tenth Decade" were over; the media would be watching and holding those in positions of authority accountable. The Michener judges described the *Globe and Mail* series as "a classic case of a 'biggie' taking on the mighty by persistently digging for facts" and praised the *Globe* for upholding "the best traditions of journalism as a bastion of democracy" and helping to improve the quality of democracy through journalism.[12]

If the *Globe* was the established biggie, then the *Scotian Journalist*, the other 1972 Michener Award winner, was the polar opposite. It was an example for smaller media outlets that they, like the upstart alternative from Halifax, could produce stories that changed the lives of people. In this case, it was women living in a regional minimum-security prison on a farm in Riverview, now a suburb of Moncton, New Brunswick.

The newspaper's owner and editor Frank Fillmore, a dyed-in-the-wool leftie, and reporter Debbie Sprague devoted an entire ten-page edition of the *Scotian Journalist* to the deplorable conditions at the Coverdale Interprovincial Home for Women.[13] The so-called home was founded in the 1920s by the Anglican, Baptist, Methodist and Presbyterian churches with the stated intention to rehabilitate up to a hundred women at a time serving "terms of two years or more and had committed crimes of prostitution, vagrancy, theft, forgery and other offences."[14]

When the three-storey building opened in 1926, it boasted dorms, a chapel, classrooms, a room for hair-dressing instruction and a gymnasium. The administration claimed a high success rate of rehabilitation and pointed to the low number of repeat offenders.[15] A much different picture emerged in 1972 from a confidential official 400-page report by Glenn R. Thompson, an expert in prison management and the treatment of offenders. Thompson found that the institution was more of a work camp than a place of rehabilitation. The women did chores on the farm and in the kitchen, laundry and dining room six days a week; many spent their time serving the needs of the staff. Thompson found the teachers and staff ill-qualified.

He also identified a litany of health and safety issues. For example, staff shortages resulted in the women being locked in their rooms with a chamber pot from 5:30 p.m. to seven o'clock the next morning. Those in detention for breaking rules, some as minor as spilling water, were denied basics such as regular meals, water and sanitary pads.[16] The complaints came from both residents and staff. A staffer told the paper that "dogs are better used than residents."[17]

Fillmore, citing the public interest, reprinted the recommendations and stories from on-the-ground reporting. They had the intended effect. A week later, the women were moved and the institution closed. That was the kind of impact for the public good that the Micheners wanted to encourage among media outlets.

The *Scotian Journalist* belonged to a new breed of alternative newspapers that dug into issues not often seen on the front pages of the established daily newspapers of record — stories such as racial and gender inequities, environmental wrongdoings and injustices in the policing, justice and correctional systems. For example, reporters at the competing *Mail Star* and Halifax *Chronicle Herald* often found themselves playing catch-up with investigative scoops in the then-independent weekly *Dartmouth Free Press* and other alternative papers. Competition was fierce and often personal and helped to raise the quality of journalism.

Frank Fillmore and his son Nick started with a newsletter — *People and Community News* — and then, in 1969, the weekly, *The 4th Estate*. Each of these startups came with a pledge to tell it like it is: "Sometimes, you won't like that, for if we have one over-riding purpose and dedication it is to shake the community and force it to face that which is so difficult to face — Truth."[18] The father-son partnership dissolved after two years with Fillmore Sr. taking his brand of social activism journalism to start the *Scotian Journalist* in 1971. Paul Willies was a fifteen-year-old high school student who became a cub reporter for the bi-weekly. "Frank was such a maverick, he just wanted to do things his way," recalled Willies. "He [Frank] was always taking on the establishment and doing everything on a wing and prayer."[19] For audiences in small cities like Halifax, stories like Coverdale were eye-opening, and they built audiences.

The announcement that the *Scotian Journalist* had won the Roland Michener Award and would be going to Rideau Hall on May 9, 1973, produced absolute fury in the publisher of the rival *Dartmouth Free Press*. Bruce Cochran was quick to tell *Globe and Mail* correspondent Lyndon Watkins that the *Free Press* had done the Coverdale story six weeks earlier. "Everybody in the plant is irate about it," he told Watkins. "All he [Frank Fillmore] was doing was publishing a report which it [the Free Press] had leaked and whose contents were already well known."[20] Cochran claimed that the paper would have submitted its material for a Michener Award "because it had measurable and good effects," but it had not received an entry form.

Fillmore acknowledged that the *Free Press* had reported on Coverdale and went on to say the *Scotian Journalist* had published far more detail, including an exclusive interview with the matron of the jail. "They [the *Dartmouth Free Press*] were cleaned out and they know it," Fillmore told the *Globe*'s Watkins. "Nothing was done about the home until we came out with the report. Four or five days after, the place was closed."

The *Dartmouth Free Press* felt differently. Within days, managing editor Gerard McNeil fired off a letter of protest to the governor general's secretary. McNeil wrote that he was "flabbergasted by the award" to the *Scotian Journalist*. "It is inconceivable to me, as a reporter and editor of some experience, that a newspaper could get a national award for a story that was at least five weeks old."[21] McNeil had professional standing. He'd been a respected reporter in the Ottawa bureau of the Canadian Press before returning to Nova Scotia as editor of the weekly. He submitted a dossier of stories the *Free Press* had done and credited *Mysterious East* in Fredericton for being first to the story and prompting the government investigation by Glenn Thompson.

This was the first challenge to a decision of the Michener panel. "Whoever the judges were, they must have made the award to the *Scotian Journalist* without checking the context," wrote McNeil. "Some remedy seems to be in order, if only to uphold the standard of the Michener Award itself." He appealed to the Office of the Governor General to undertake an impartial study of the press clippings "in the interests of the award if nothing else."[22] There is no record of Rideau Hall's reply to McNeil. Protocol would dictate that this matter would be sent to the Federation of Press Clubs of Canada.

Award administrator Bill MacPherson lobbed this hot potato over to the judging panel for review.[23] Chief Judge Fraser MacDougall consulted other members who didn't have much time for the "shrieks of anguish"[24] from the *Free Press*. McNeil's indignant protest went nowhere. MacDougall responded that the panel worked with the material it received. He added that if the *Dartmouth Free Press* felt its story was worthy, it should have submitted its collection of stories. MacDougall did not address the issue that the *Free Press* claimed it had not received an entry form. It may have been a coincidence, but the following year the *Dartmouth Free Press* received an honourable mention at the Michener Awards ceremony. The terse citation praised the *Free Press* for "its courage in the face of a hoodlum invasion that threatened the lives of its staff and the security of its plant."[25]

If nothing else, this incident brought to light the Michener's growing pains. The Michener Award wasn't high on the agenda of the journalists who belonged to the Federation of Press Clubs. The annual mailouts and word-of-mouth encouragement simply weren't good enough to reach all the newsrooms. This lack of public profile and outreach meant that media outlets overlooked or disregarded the Michener Award when submitting their high-quality work for national and regional newspaper or broadcast industry awards. In those early years, the Michener lacked the institutional heft to raise its profile, but what it stood for — excellence in journalism in the public interest — was gathering momentum.

Digging deeper

Media organizations started to see the value of going beyond the daily news cycle and giving journalists the freedom to dig deeper. This new generation of journalists didn't regard those in authority as allies, and they were pushing for greater access to information and challenging the boundaries of reporting. What was professional and ethical behaviour when, for example, it came to undercover reporting and using new technologies to get a story? The Michener judges inadvertently entered the debate when they gave the 1973 Michener Award to CTV News for a story that spoke directly to using new technology to challenge authority.

The announcement that CTV's program *Inquiry* would get the 1973 Michener Award for its program "Hear No Evil, See No Evil, Speak No Evil" was greeted with some skepticism in rival newsrooms. Reporter Tim Ralfe and his producer Jack McGaw had decided to expose the lax standards of Canada's anti-eavesdropping laws that allowed secret recordings of some third-party conversations which invaded personal privacy.[26] Ralfe — a reporter with a reputation for "fight and courage"— was gung-ho for the assignment.[27]

There are various accounts of what happened on the morning of Wednesday, October 17, 1973. Apparently, Ralfe walked into the main block of the Parliament building carrying a roll of duct tape and a store-bought $185 listening device. About an hour before a New Democratic Party caucus meeting, Ralfe secretly slipped into the room and taped a "matchbox-size radio transmitter"[28] under the boardroom table.

It was high drama. CTV parked its unmarked van outside Centre Block on Parliament Hill. Ralfe, McGaw and an audio engineer sat inside, waiting to record the NDP caucus meeting, "the most secret type of gathering in

Parliament," NDP Leader David Lewis declared that afternoon in the House of Commons.[29] An RCMP officer approached the van just at the moment when the transmission stopped. The CTV crew thought they had been busted, but all the officer did was write a parking ticket and stick it under the windshield wiper. As the officer moved on, the bug started transmitting again and the crew let out a collective sigh of relief.

What they didn't know was that inside the boardroom, NDP caucus leader Ed Broadbent had brushed up against something under the table and he pulled up the tiny transmitter. "This looks like a bugging device," Broadbent told caucus members. He then put the transmitter on the table and the caucus carried on with the confidential meeting as the tape recorder in the van captured the conversation.[30]

Meanwhile, CTV's McGaw and Ralfe had already decided to admit to the illegal taping. As soon as the caucus meeting ended, they handed over the tape recording and assured NDP leader David Lewis that the audio engineer had been the only one to hear what had been said at the meeting and he was sworn to secrecy.[31] Lewis was furious with CTV's underhanded actions. The aftermath of the phone bugging and subsequent break-in of the Democratic National Committee headquarters in Washington, DC, was fresh in people's minds and still unfolding on the front pages of the newspapers.

When Lewis took his seat in the House of Commons that afternoon, he stood on a question of privilege to announce that CTV had bugged the NDP caucus meeting. "Whether or not it is illegal under the present Criminal Code . . . is irrelevant. Certainly, it is totally illegal as far as the rules of Parliament are concerned." Lewis went on to call the actions of CTV "morally and socially wrong in every respect" and described the bugging as "indecent and anti-social." MPs were in an uproar and gave unanimous support for a motion of censure against CTV that ordered Ralfe to return all the tapes immediately.[32]

This "was typical of McGaw's style of activist, advocacy journalism in which events are devised and filmed to make an editorial statement," wrote Tim Kotcheff, a former CTV executive.[33] In news reporting, this only happens as a last resort, when all other avenues to get the information have been exhausted. In his *Globe and Mail* column, Geoffrey Stevens called the CTV stunt a "distressing, disgusting episode," especially since the show's producers knew that the wiretap laws were at the committee stage and would become law soon.[34]

In *Behind the Headlines: A History of Investigative Journalism in Canada*, Cecil Rosner wrote that the CTV program raised the question of whether the news magazine *Inquiry* was nothing but "a form of cheap 'gotcha' journalism" to attract viewers and ratings.[35] It was a time when the two established Canadian networks, CBC and CTV, found themselves competing with new players: Citytv in Toronto and a third national network, Global Television, had entered the field. With all of them vying for audiences and advertisers, journalists were pushing boundaries.

None of the criticism or controversy over the CTV win was evident as media gathered on May 16, 1974, in the foyer of Rideau Hall for a late afternoon award ceremony. At the stand-up reception Governor General Jules Léger, a former associate editor at *Le Droit*, university professor and diplomat, held out his hand to CTV producer Jack McGaw. "I hope you haven't got an electronic bug on you," Léger joked. McGaw replied, "No sir, not today."[36] The citation of the Michener judges praised CTV, noting that the program "took a series of facts, which were being reported by all media at the time, and, using imagination and courage, probed beyond the surface." They described the episode of *Inquiry* as "an outstanding example of in-depth reporting by a medium still discovering its ability to dig with impact, instead of being content to skim superficially."[37] The Michener jury was likely attracted to the enterprise journalism of the story because CTV was using the latest technology to push conventional boundaries, and the program had achieved concrete impact.

Despite his initial fury, even NDP leader David Lewis was of two minds about the show. In an interview with Ralfe, Lewis condemned CTV's actions, and at the same time, he applauded the editorial objective of the documentary. A few months later Parliament passed Bill C-175, the *Protection of Privacy Act* that made it illegal to use secret wiretaps or any electronic listening devices.[38] CTV's wiretapping story showed that journalists were prepared to push those in power to the point of risking access to power and insider information.

As Rosner writes, "Hidden cameras, concealed microphones and night lens equipment were frequently the only means of accomplishing the task" of exposing the darker sides of society.[39] For example, CBC-TV's two-part documentary "Connections" received an honourable mention at the 1977 Michener Awards ceremony for its shocking undercover video of the world of organized crime in Canada. Two and a half years in the making, and at a cost of more than $300,000, "Connections" was a far different kind of journalistic storytelling from "The Tenth Decade" five years earlier. Audiences went behind the scenes with CBC and listened as crime figures described in graphic terms how a network of crime from the United States had spread into Montreal, Toronto and Vancouver. Ratings for the broadcasts over the two nights went through the roof. Peter Herrndorf, then head of planning at CBC, recalled how viewers were "stunned" by the revelations. So were politicians, who called for a royal commission and for the provinces to band together to fight organized crime. "In those six, seven months after that came out, there was a lot of change in the way banks, credit organizations and all kinds of other organizations that dealt with the public because they'd learned some lessons from the organized crime documentary," said Herrndorf. "So, both government and the private sector changed their practices and policies. That was part of what we had hoped to do."[40] Most journalists get into the business to achieve results like that in their reporting and the latest technology started to open new possibilities.

As Rosner points out in *Behind the Headlines,* journalists of the 1970s looked beyond wrongdoings and injustices. They drilled down to examine how the policies and practices of institutions — like banks, businesses, churches, government courts and police services — affected the lives of citizens.[41] One such Michener Award-winning example was the *Vancouver Sun*'s reporting in 1976 into the illegal activities of the Royal Canadian Mounted Police Security Service, SS (replaced by the Canadian Security and Intelligence Service, CSIS, in 1986).

The *Vancouver Sun*'s Ottawa reporter John Sawatsky relied on sources in the RCMP to tell the story of misdeeds and a cover-up that extended into the senior management levels at RCMP headquarters in Ottawa. His investigation started after a member of the RCMP SS admitted during a trial that he was working for the Mafia in his off hours and had planted a bomb at the home of a Montreal supermarket executive. Constable Robert Samson also testified that in his day job with security service, he had been ordered to do much worse. Just four months after the Watergate break-in, Sampson said he was part of a joint police force team called "Operation Bricole" that illegally broke into the *Agence de Presse Libre du Québec* (APLQ) and took documents.[42]

Swasey's front page story unmasked a web of deception at the highest levels:

Sources indicate that the RCMP knew the truth about the raid soon after it took place and, knowing the raid was illegal, turned a blind eye to it. The RCMP took no action to see that the matter was prosecuted as it does routinely on other break-ins. Instead, the RCMP acted to hide the material in filing cabinets under the responsibility of John Starnes, who as director-general of the security service was the country's top spy chaser.[43]

The Michener citation praised Sawatsky's "tenacity and skill" and said the story shook "the very foundations of Canada's legal system — respect for law and order of those sworn to uphold them on behalf of Canadians."[44]

As Sawatsky told Rosner, it was the first public evidence of a Watergate in Canada where RCMP management had been implicated in methodical illegal activity." As Rosner wrote: "Faith in the RCMP was so strong that it seemed preposterous to think that the organization could be deliberately involved in flagrant law breaking."[45]

Sawatsky's story was so hot that no other media outlets tried to match or advance the story. Even the New Democratic Party refused to raise it in the House of Commons the day the story broke. But subsequent inquiries by the Québec government and Ottawa revealed more RCMP wrongdoing, including arson, break-in and theft.

Over the years, the Michener Award would validate media outlets that exposed structural failings of institutions and, in doing so, helped to change public policies and attitudes, tighten operational procedures and improve the lives of marginalized and voiceless people.[46] Journalists would embrace and adapt the latest technology, like cameras and data, to get to the truth.

Award in Jeopardy: Federation of Press Clubs falters

In the decades since those early awards, media organizations have come to applaud the Michener for its impact on the quality of journalism and society. In the early 1970s, though, it was an uphill climb. Outside of the Ottawa-Toronto axis, the award was an *arriviste* in the competitive field of journalism awards. Publishers and broadcasters still gravitated to established, high-profile national journalism awards such as the National Newspaper Awards, Canadian Women's Press Club Memorial Awards and RTNDA broadcast awards.[47] Even regional awards appeared to have more sway. At the Federation's annual meeting in Montreal in 1973, Bob Weber of the London Press Club spoke of the media's keen interest in the Western Ontario newspaper awards, "But there is not all that interest in the Michener Awards."[48] If the purpose of this award was to recognize and celebrate the best of journalism in the country, then it had to become better known in the industry. Acting on behalf of the Federation, Bill MacPherson and Fraser MacDougall embarked on a long and arduous road to increase the profile and reputation of the fledgling Michener Award in Québec and the regions.

When it came to the Michener, this industry *ennui* was reflected in the very organization responsible for the award — the Federation of Press Clubs. While delegates at the 1973 annual meeting of the Federation discussed adding more categories of awards and had suggestions for new sponsors — private industry, insurance companies, government and media companies — no one actually volunteered to do the leg work. Bill MacPherson, the chair of the Michener Award, read the room correctly when he advised caution. "We shouldn't be beating the bushes for awards, but we should be ready to act if somebody comes to the Federation and suggests an award."[49] He was not keen to add more awards to the roster. Neither were the members of the judging panel.

By May 1976, the judges, some of whom had now clocked four years of judging, wrote to express their "misgivings" about the Federation's support for the award and concerns that the Michener Award is either "not effectively promoted or it is not being taken seriously by media management in the various media."[50] Their letter complained that the Federation had not put enough effort into attracting Francophone, regional and small media — a problem that still haunts the Michener Awards. The judges noted the award was short on "both the number and calibre of meritorious public service it was expected to display." They pointed to the number of entries for 1975: zero for weeklies, news agencies, radio or television networks, and magazines, and only one French-language entry from a TV station.

The judges claimed they knew of stories "of a calibre comparable to the better entries submitted this year" that were published and broadcast but not entered for a Michener Award. They urged member press clubs to designate "monitors" to identify possible Michener entries and suggested the Federation crowdsource to "enlist the co-operation of readers."[51] That message was repeated at the annual meeting in the fall when Bill MacPherson urged local clubs to "talk up" the awards. [52] The growth and success of the award depended on it. However, other issues dominated the meeting. Delegates seemed more interested in grumbling about the Federation's poor communications and lack of administrative support for member press clubs in cities across the country than in finding ways to promote the award.

There is no record of how many media outlets submitted stories for 1975, but the paucity of entries may have been why the list of finalists was short. The news release announced a tie for the Michener: the *Montreal Gazette* and the *London Free Press*. No runners-up, and no honourable mentions. Remarkably though, each of the two entries that shared the Michener Award that year was an outstanding example of the kind of unrelenting inquiry and initiative that the awards were intended to inspire. Both finalists addressed issues ripe for urgent attention back then and provided the impetus for actions that are still unfolding some fifty years later.

The *London Free Press*, a mid-sized daily, tied for the 1975 Michener for its five-part series about mercury poisoning in Indigenous lands of Grassy Narrows in northwestern Ontario. The *Free Press* revealed extensive mercury poisoning and health issues in the communities of Asubpeeschoseewagong (First Nation) and Wabaseemoong Independent Nations of One Man Lake, Swan Lake and Whitedog.

Reporter George Hutchinson's investigation began as a follow-up story on the "Mercury Crisis of 1970" in the Sarnia area, south of Lake Huron. Five years earlier, Del Bell of the *London Free Press* had detailed the findings of Norvald Fimreite, a young graduate student at the University of Western Ontario, who found evidence of toxic mercury discharges from the Dow Chemical Chlor-Alkali plant in Sarnia. Since 1949 the effluent had seeped into the St. Clair River, Detroit River, Lake Ontario and Lake Erie and had contaminated fish.[53] The revelations ended a $1.2 million fishery for forty families in Lake St. Clair in southwestern Ontario.[54] As Hutchinson was to discover, Sarnia was just the tip of an industrial environmental disaster in Ontario. Some 1700 kilometres northwest of Sarnia, another environmental disaster had been ignored — mercury contamination of the land and waters of Grassy Narrows.

Hutchinson, the Queen's Park provincial reporter, was on assignment following Ontario Liberal leader Robert Nixon. During a stop at a fishing lodge up north he landed a couple of pickerel and "had them quick frozen," he said with a laugh.[55] Tests conducted at a University of Toronto lab found Hutchinson's catch had "four to five times the acceptable level [of mercury] for human consumption."[56] Effluent from Dryden Chemicals and Reid Paper

Limited, a pulp and paper operation, had polluted the English-Wabigoon River system on Indigenous lands.

The Ontario government immediately banned guiding and commercial fishing, but the ban did not extend to eating the fish, the main food source for the Anishinaabe Nation. With the mercury in the food chain, people eating the toxic fish were slowly being poisoned.

As Hutchinson's Michener Award-winning series showed, the devastation from the loss of guiding and fishing was more than economic and social. There was a serious health crisis — one that government officials were denying. Similar to Minamata, a small city on the southern tip of Japan where the release of toxic chemicals from an industrial plant had accumulated in fish, which were then eaten by residents, the first signs of mercury poisoning in northwestern Ontario appeared in the local cat population.

> Now there is only one [cat]. "They all died," explains Chief Andy Keewatin. The most recent was in March. The cat was seen convulsing, performing a 'dance' of death, racing in circles and leaping into the air. . . . The case was frighteningly reminiscent of the cat death a month earlier near the Whitedog Indian reserve, farther west. That cat, too, danced.[57]

Tests on the cat's carcass showed the mercury levels far exceeded the levels of cats in Minamata, Japan.

Hutchinson and photographer Dick Wallace travelled to Japan with representatives of the two First Nations to meet with a research team from Japan's Minamata Disease Patients Alliance. Medical and scientific monitoring estimated that 90 per cent of residents in Grassy Narrows First Nation were experiencing disabling neurological symptoms from mercury poisoning. After the London Free Press stories, governments promised action, but like the situation in Japan, industry and government were slow to accept responsibility and make changes.

In 1976 when Hutchinson stepped forward in a low-key ceremony at Rideau Hall to accept the Michener Award, he found himself face-to-face with His and Her Excellencies Jules and Gabrielle Léger, "mindful that high-school dropouts aren't meant to mingle with governors general." Almost fifty years later, the memory remains clear: "They were most gracious. He was from my perspective at that time in life, very austere and fitted the position.

She was engaging . . . a delight."[58] Returning to his seat, Hutchinson handed the trophy to his publisher, Walter Blackburn, who "was absolutely thrilled and very possessive about it after that. And for years it sat on his desk. . . . It was a lovely sculpture," Hutchinson recalled. Receiving the award at Rideau Hall was the validation the newspaper was seeking — a prestige payoff for the money and months invested in an exercise of public interest journalism.

Hutchinson and Wallace followed up with the book *Grassy Narrows* in 1977.[59] "It was an emotional experience because I couldn't come up with answers," Hutchinson said. "It struck me that the people of the North, both white and native, had difficulty dealing with the enormous pressures that are upon them regarding the environment. The white population is dependent on resource extraction. The native people are involved in resource protection. And there's a tremendous clash of interests. It takes a great deal of political acumen to bridge those differences. It takes time, and it still hasn't happened. It's closer than it was."[60]

Change in Grassy Narrows has since come incrementally. In an article for the *Toronto Star* in April 2017, on the fortieth anniversary of the Grassy Narrows, Hutchinson's post-mortem was grim. "If it wasn't so tragic, you'd be excused for saying *déjà vu* all over again; Scientists flagging Minamata disease in the northern wilderness. Native protesters marching on Queen's Park. Politicians feigning concern or denying culpability. Industrialists mute. The public wringing its hands."[61]

The intensive media coverage of Grassy Narrows in the 1970s waned as journalists moved on to other stories. However, that initial coverage by the *London Free Press* and other media provided a foundation for the two First Nations communities in the region to organize and hold successive governments accountable to clean up the toxic mess and to financially compensate residents for their loss of livelihood and debilitating health from mercury poisoning.

It has been a fifty-year fight for recognition and compensation. In that time, the work of community activists has kept the issue in the media: court battles,[62] hunger strikes,[63] sit-ins and rallies.[64] The results have been compensation for some residents, $85 million towards clean up[65] and almost $20 million to build and operate a specialized care home for people suffering from mercury poisoning.[66] The story of the Wabaseemoong Independent Nations and Grassy Narrows First Nation will never be over as long as the toxic mercury remains in the waterways. "It's going to be in the sediment of that river system for a hundred years, and we're only halfway through that," Hutchinson said in 2022. "Now they are talking about remediation. Well, I am still waiting for science to explain how they're going to do that. There are hundreds of square miles of water and sediment. How are they going to clean up is beyond me."[67]

As with many other Michener award-winning stories, the story of mercury poisoning of communities pointed to a bigger, deeper and more complex problem that could not be remedied by any series of news reports. In the case of Grassy Narrows, the *London Free Press*'s dogged reporting kept the issue on the front page, forced incremental change and gave the Indigenous community a platform and opportunities to continue to hold those in authority to account.

And of the other 1975 Michener Award winner? A *Montreal Gazette* series exposed abuse and inhumane conditions in detention centres for young women run by the Québec government. When Québec's Ministry of Social Services twice turned down Gillian Cosgrove's request to do interviews, she went undercover and took a job as an *éducatrice* in Maison Notre-Dame-de-Laval, a major detention centre in Montreal for girls between the ages of twelve and eighteen.

"I had this image of being a crusader for change. . . . I really wanted to effect change and I wanted to effect it for people who were helpless to do it for themselves," she said in an interview.[68]

Many of the girls had been taken from their homes because of abuse or neglect, and they needed protection. Others were kids who had run away or skipped school too many times. Suddenly, these girls found themselves living nose-to-nose with juvenile delinquents, psychiatric patients and special-needs youth. In the first installment of her Michener Award-winning series, Cosgrove wrote:

> It was my fourth day working as an "educator" at Maison Notre Dame de Laval detention centre for juvenile girls, where I witnessed the plight of many of Québec's estimated 40,000 children in substitute care. . . .
>
> After 24 hours in "ice" a chastened Stephanie (not her real name) returned to the living unit upstairs and told me more about her experience in solitary confinement.

"I couldn't stand it. I went crazy. I was screaming at them to let me out," she said in a subdued tone, fidgeting with the hem on her skirt.

It was then the guards entered her cell, handcuffed her, and tied her on her back with leather straps.

"It's mean to handcuff a kid," she said. "And when they lie you down, you can't move, you can't itch, and you have to pee and shit in your pants and lie in it."

Stephanie [age 14] is just four feet, 10 inches tall and barely 90 pounds.

. . .

"These girls have done nothing wrong," a senior educator told me on my first day of work. "Most of them are protection cases, many of them runaways. They are not delinquents and should not be treated as such." Then he added with a sardonic chuckle. "Most of us did more things wrong in our youth than these kids ever did."[69]

Cosgrove said she couldn't believe this was happening in a provincial institution funded by taxpayers' dollars. "This was Québec, it wasn't the Québec of Duplessis, it wasn't the dark ages."[70]

Her three-part exposé in the *Montreal Gazette* of harrowing abuse moved 45,000 people to sign a petition demanding reforms and an end to the mistreatment. Then Minister of Social Affairs, Claude Forget, promised to reduce the use of solitary confinement. On February 1, 1975, the government called a provincial inquiry into youth protection and detention services and appointed Manuel G. Batshaw, *Directeur Général, Services Communautaires Juifs*, a respected Montreal social worker, as chair. The eleven-volume *Comité d'étude sur la réadaptation des enfants et adolescents placés en centre d'accueil* (known as the Batshaw Commission report), was released on December 22 of the same year. It recommended special care for youth with developmental problems, improved treatment and programs and better-trained childcare workers. The report also recommended each child's case be reviewed after six months in an institution.[71]

Cosgrove's 1975 series shed some light on the closed world of Québec's children and youth services. Those stories contributed to a process of change that included the introduction of the *Youth Protection Act* in 1979 and the closure of juvenile protection centres such as Marian Hall in Beaconsfield, a community west of Montreal. Cosgrove remembered the feeling. "I said, 'Oh my God, I won the Michener Award, and I changed the law. Aren't I wonderful?" She believed that "the kids are going to have love and guidance, not horrible punishment" and she said she "went on her merry way."[72] Cosgrove and the *Montreal Gazette* moved on to other stories, as media tend to do.

Forty years later, in 2019, a group of women, survivors from the Québec detention centre, "Marian Hall" on Elm Avenue in Beaconsfield, found Cosgrove on social media and invited her to join their private Facebook group. Cosgrove was a legend with the former residents. One woman told her, "We were in the hole, and we heard that this girl had snuck into an institution and you became our beacon of hope, you spoke for us. We didn't have any voice. You were our voice,"[73] Cosgrove said. For those girls in detention it was evidence that even if nothing much had changed, someone cared. The abuse and solitary confinement continued long after the release of the Batshaw report, even after Marion Hall closed in 1979 and the girls moved to other facilities.

Cosgrove said these revelations "shattered" her confidence in the power of journalism to effect meaningful change. The law changed, but they didn't demolish the cells or hire specialists. "So, I look back in sadness thinking that I had done something, but I really hadn't," Cosgrove said. "I should have gone back to the exact same cells and just done that proper follow-up," not just rely on the assessment of experts.[74]

Cosgrove is still trying to make it right, "so it doesn't happen to another kid." She appeared in a CBC *the fifth estate* 2019 documentary "The Forgotten Children of Marian Hall"[75] and is supporting the survivors in their class-action lawsuit seeking compensation from the Québec government.[76]

Journalists want their stories to change the world. But change inches forward slowly. Problems persist. Tragedies happen. The Québec government has been forced to revisit the ongoing issues with its youth protection policy and practices. In October 2019, the government of Québec appointed yet another special commission to look into the rights of children and youth in protection following media coverage of the death of a neglected seven-year-old girl in Granby, southeast of Montreal, earlier that year."[77] The Québec government has created a national director of youth protection to review youth protection services and the law. The Laurent Commission's final report, released in May 2021, called for a major shift and sweeping changes to the child protection system.[78]

Gillian Cosgrove's Michener Award in 1975 brought the abuses to the public's attention. It was also a spur for reporters elsewhere to look at living conditions for children in their government-run centres. Two years later, the *Globe and Mail* published a comprehensive look at Ontario's child protection laws through the story of fifteen-year-old Michael. The series won the 1977 Michener Award for its concentrated campaign — seventy news stories and sixteen editorials — aimed at reforming child protection laws. The judges noted that coverage disclosed shortcomings in provincial and federal legislation. The series brought about proposed legislative changes and, in some jurisdictions, official inquiries.

In 1979, the *Edmonton Journal* received an honourable mention for its forty-five stories that showed how youth at Westfield, a provincially run centre, were locked in solitary confinement — small, poorly ventilated "thinking rooms" — as punishment, even for minor misdemeanours. The province's social services department employees were ordered not to speak to reporter Wendy Koenig. The director of Westfield tried to prevent her from researching and writing the story. After publication, government staff filed libel charges against the newspaper. The Alberta deputy minister of social services even sent a letter to the publisher claiming that the series "amounted to character assassination of the worst sort."[79] The *Edmonton Journal* and Koenig were vindicated in a report by Alberta's Ombudsman, Dr. Randall Ivany, who credited the coverage for prompting the investigation. He recommended that provincial juvenile centres limit stays in solitary confinement rooms to no more than forty-five minutes.

Koenig kept digging into the story. The *Edmonton Journal* received the Michener Award the following year for her two-part series that exposed abuses in Alberta's child welfare and foster care system. The "moving and deeply sensitive" account of the mistreatment of children at a provincial institution in Peace River, Alberta, resulted in its closure and an inquiry.[80] The other story focused on children placed in the home of a man with a history of violence and mental illness. This story triggered an investigation and resulted in better screening of foster parents and monitoring of children in foster homes.

Reporters investigating provincial and Indigenous child protection services across the country continue to find a "sad record of failure."[81] In 1996, *Toronto Star* reporters Kevin Donovan and Moira Welsh gathered data from the provincial coroner's office that showed how children's aid workers, doctors and other professionals failed to protect children between 1991-1995. Their findings pressured governments and organizations to assess and change their practices and won the *Star* a Michener Award.

The passing of the federal *Young Offenders Act* in 1982 aimed to shift the focus in provincial courts from punishment to rehabilitation, but reform is slow. Stories from two Michener finalists from Canada's north in 2018 revealed ongoing abuses against children in facilities that were supposed to protect them. In the Yukon, a CBC North series documented continuing physical abuse and neglect of youth living in group homes. Research from APTN found that Indigenous youth are overrepresented in foster care and six times more likely to die by suicide than the non-Indigenous population.[82]

In 2020, APTN won the Michener Award for its series "Death by Neglect," an investigation led by Kenneth Jackson and Cullen Crozier into a First Nations child welfare system and the deaths by suicide of three sisters. The teens — Sasha Raven Bob, Shania Raven Bob and Arizona Raven Bob — had spent their lives in the care of the Weechi-it-te-win Family Services First Nations protection agency in northern Ontario. "There is no reason why Sasha Raven Bob [the last surviving sister] shouldn't be alive today but if not for neglect by everyone who ever knew her," said Jackson in his acceptance speech.[83] Crozier and Jackson's search for answers and accountability uncovered a culture of silence and fear along with a trail of neglect that permeated Indigenous, provincial and federal child-protection agencies across the country.

The APTN coverage resulted in profound changes, said Pierre-Paul Noreau, president of the Michener Awards Foundation. "Within weeks of APTN's broadcasts, several investigations were launched into individual cases; several families were reunited; new funding was announced for on-reserve child welfare; and a pandemic moratorium was imposed on Ontario youths aging out of care. And, while this humanitarian crisis continues unabated, it is this kind of wide-ranging impact that makes this series undeniably Michener-worthy."[84]

Stories like these revealed the immense changes in the journalism industry, which was increasingly pursuing hard-hitting investigative stories that pushed the boundaries of reporting. The Micheners recognized these stories, but their profile in the industry was still low enough that many worthy local or regional stories were not submitted for awards. As a result, big and medium-sized media outlets dominated the nominations — mostly newspapers, and mostly from southern Ontario. In the first ten years, the award's champion,

Bill MacPherson, would work diligently to make the Michener Award more inclusive and national. But to ensure that more media outlets — big and small — knew of and submitted their best work to the Micheners, the awards needed something that would make people notice them.

The Missing Ingredient

The Michener Award rewarded media organizations for their journalism that instigated change. Recognition of public interest reporting of this quality and impact was, of course, precisely the intention of the Michener Awards from the beginning. The challenge for MacPherson and Chief Judge Fraser MacDougall was how to get buy-in from Canadian publishers and broadcasters. They needed convincing that the Michener Award was not a flash in the pan. It should be considered the big prize, the one all media outlets should aspire to win. The support of the governor general and the ceremony at Rideau Hall were crucial to building the status of the award.

The judges were satisfied with the quality of the submissions but not with the number of entries. Was it that too few journalism organizations cared — or dared — to do the kind of stories the Micheners wanted? Or was the trouble closer to home? The Federation of Press Clubs of Canada was having trouble engaging its members — journalists affiliated with local press clubs in cities across Canada. In 1974, the Federation changed its name to Press Club Canada to give the disparate press clubs a sense of united purpose. The name change had little effect. When delegates met in Saint John, New Brunswick, two years later for its ninth annual meeting, Bill MacPherson repeated the grave misgivings of the judging panel about the organization's support for the award. As before, he appealed to local press clubs and the regional vice presidents to encourage entries.[85]

Delegates showed little enthusiasm for his appeals and suggestions to help the Michener Award. Instead, they complained that some of the press clubs had not received notice of the entry deadline for the Michener Award. Once again, Press Club Canada delegated MacPherson and chief judge Fraser MacDougall to keep the show on the road. It was becoming clear that if the Michener Award was to survive, it would be up to them, with help from Rideau Hall.

With little support from the organization, the four members of the judging panel made a few changes. In addition to honourable mentions, in 1979, they introduced a runner-up category, the Award of Merit "with the hope of stimulating wider interest in the award," chief judge Fraser MacDougall explained in his report to the board of Press Club Canada.[86] Changes of some sort were essential to stimulate interest. That year the panel received twenty-six entries — the highest in its history. However, all but four came from newspapers. Three others were from radio, and one was from a magazine. Only one entry was French and two came from community newspapers. Evidently, the Michener Award was typecast as a newspaper award even though in the first nine years broadcasters received one-third of all commendations and won three Michener Awards.

MacPherson was increasingly worried that Press Club Canada was splintering and had reverted to city-based social clubs for journalists to grab lunch or get a beer after work. He sensed that the umbrella group had lost the drive to build the institutional structure necessary to support a professional award of the calibre of the Michener Award. In 1979, MacPherson wrote to W. R. Anderson, president of Press Club Canada: "The difficulties I, as chairman of the award, have confronted, have been increasing by the year to the point that I feel they are overwhelming." He went on to say these difficulties were connected to "the very great problem involved in keeping the Press Club Canada itself alive and vigorous. . . . Now, it seems to me, Press Club Canada is either dying or dead, not having had a board meeting since 1977," the Club's tenth anniversary. He noted that members were not submitting their dues and "this has created problems periodically in keeping the Michener Award project afloat."[87] Money was so tight that MacPherson was worried about finding $200 for the trophy and expenses of judging, printing and postage.

It is not known how Anderson responded to MacPherson. But, at the awards ceremony later that year, MacPherson announced with no fanfare: "The Federation, later renamed Press Club Canada, has unfortunately fallen into some disarray in recent times, but the task of administering the Michener Award has been taken up gladly by the National Press Club of Canada." Some rescue! The awards found a new home with the Ottawa Press Club in name only. In practice, MacPherson and his chief judge were on their own. It was an increasingly unsustainable model. But that night was the tenth anniversary of the awards, and no one was dwelling on the problems. Hope for the future of the awards was at hand. There was a new governor general who would play an important role in giving the Michener Awards the boost it needed to gain wider recognition in the industry.

Prime Minister Pierre Trudeau likely wanted to shake up Rideau Hall when he recommended the appointment of Edward Schreyer as Canada's twenty-second governor general in 1979 to succeed Jules Léger. Schreyer was forty-three years old and the youngest governor general since Lord Lorne, the Duke of Argyll, appointed at thirty-three years old in 1878.[88] A mere three years earlier, Schreyer had made his first visit to Rideau Hall to receive the Governor General's Vanier Award as an outstanding Young Canadian of the Year.[89] Schreyer's list of achievements was long. He had four academic degrees, taught international relations, and at twenty-two, had become the youngest MLA elected to the Manitoba Legislature. Later, he was elected federally and, in 1969, he returned home to win the provincial NDP leadership contest and form the first NDP provincial government in Canada.[90]

Despite their divergent political roots — Michener, the Conservative, and Schreyer, the NDP — the two men formed a deep friendship. After taking office, Ed and Lily Schreyer welcomed the Micheners as guests to Rideau Hall for every Michener ceremony. The past and present governors general shared a conviction that they could use their non-partisan position to recognize and celebrate journalism at the highest level.[91] In an interview, Schreyer said, "I recognized along with him [Roland Michener] the importance in a democracy of a free press. . . . The fact that the awards are held to recognize and commend those journalists each year who have shown in their work that they have achieved a high standard of journalism."[92] Schreyer and Michener came from a generation that believed that independent media were necessary for a healthy democracy. Their support of the Michener Award was one way they could contribute.

It was in this light that Schreyer and his wife, Lily, transformed the awards ceremony from what had been a perfunctory afternoon stand-up event into a gala evening, with music, a sit-down dinner with wine and dancing. It was a night to remember. Journalists in evening gowns and black tie arrived at Rideau Hall on that clear, cool Saturday evening in November 1979. They were greeted by the soft music of the Canadian Forces central band's group Serenade of Strings at a reception in the long gallery with its blue and white Chinese carpets.

Their Excellencies Governor General Edward Schreyer and Lily Schreyer welcomed them. After the formalities of the receiving line, everyone moved into the ballroom with its neoclassical crystal chandelier and hand-carved columns for a four-course sit-down dinner. The menu was first class: "Le

Ramequin en gelée à l'Indienne, le vol au vent de crustaces à la crème, Le Gigot d'Agneau rôti <Les Baux>, Le riz du Manitoba, Les Zuchettes aux fines herbes, L'orange Norvégienne, les petits fours served with a choice of wines, Sylvaner, Château Bertin St. Juline and champagne."[93]

This was an awards night like no other before — one that appropriately recognized media organizations for their journalism in the public interest. Besides the introduction of runners-up, it was the first year that the winner of the Michener Awards had not been announced in advance, which added to the excitement of the evening.

In his opening speech, Bill MacPherson acknowledged the new format and its "overtones of the Academy Awards." He went on to say that "as one of the founding fathers, as it were, I feel like sort of the Gregory Peck of the Michener Awards."[94]

Over coffee and liqueurs, in true Academy Award style, J. J. Macdonell, the Auditor General of Canada, brought the sealed envelope with the name of the 1978 Michener Award winner and runners-up to the dais. MacPherson ripped open the envelope to announce the winner: the *Kitchener-Waterloo Record* for its series on unsanitary conditions in meat plants that were putting the lives of Canadians at risk. Farm reporter Jim Romahn was part of a new breed of journalists pushing for public access to government documents and data to add depth and context to their reporting.

The winner, it was true, had been selected from the disturbingly small intake of just nineteen entries that year, but the series had a huge impact. Romahn's stories resulted in changes to meat-processing inspections across the country. His investigation for the *Kitchener-Waterloo Record* into the Burns Ltd. plant in Kitchener, Ontario, began in 1975 after CBC-TV's *Marketplace* reported the cold cuts produced in the Kitchener meat plant had the highest bacteria counts in the country.

His big break came from a tip. "Not too long after that, one of the guys in the back shop [at the *Record*] was drinking at the Polish legion after work and he heard these guys who work for Burns Meats talking about American inspectors going through the plant and cutting off exports and I thought *ah ha*, I know what that is."[95] When Canada refused to release any information, Romahn went to Washington. Using the U.S. Freedom of Information law, he received 340 pages of inspection reports on the Kitchener and other Canadian meat processing plants. They showed that in 1975 the U.S. Department of

Agriculture had condemned not just the Burns plant, but twenty-five other Canadian meat-packing plants.

Romahn's stories included a shocking list of safety and health violations in Canadian meat-packing plants:

> Carcasses and vats of meat are contaminated; Sick animals and diseased meat could slip through lax inspection procedures before and after slaughter; Equipment is dirty and contaminated; Buildings are decrepit; Effluent is being discharged directly into a river; Toilet facilities in a wood plant are on a second story and urine could leak into meat-processing areas . . . [96]

The processing plants were ordered to close and to fix the problems before they could regain their right to export to the U.S.

Romahn kept pounding away at the issue, and his stories in the *Kitchener-Waterloo Record* series created a huge sensation. They were bad for business. "The labour union was really upset, the public was upset, and the city council passed a motion of censure against the *Record*," said Romahn. "We never were threatened with a lawsuit because the company knew that what we wrote was accurate, true." [97] There was more than anger and censure.

At one point a source in the U.S. Agriculture Department called Romahn to say, "Someone's on your tail." Under U.S. Freedom of Information regulations, he discovered it was Burns Security and he tracked down the guy. When Romahn called, the guy said, "Jim you're the most boring person. We were looking for dirt to get you off the case and there's just nothing there. I said, who hired you? He said, I can't tell you, and he asked, how did you find out? I said, I can't tell you," [98] Romahn recalled with a laugh.

But then the threats became dangerous. In the middle of the contaminated meat plant series, Romahn recalled the terrible day when his wife, Barbara, picked up the phone to hear a man's voice. "The guy said, your husband either comes off those stories or we will rape your daughters, who were three and five years old at the time. She [Barbara Romahn] was terrified and I kept saying to her, look, they're just trying to frighten you. If they're intending to do that, they would certainly not warn you." [99] Romahn never found out who made that hate call. He swallowed his fear and pursued the story until he got action. While this was shocking at the time, by the 2020s, journalists would experience harassment and threats both on the job and online on a daily basis.

Investigative journalism is not for the timid. It requires this kind of courage and persistence to uncover and reveal the truth that leads to change in society. When Romahn stood at the podium at the Michener Awards ceremony in November 1979, he used his speech to criticize the lack of freedom of information laws in Canada and how that hampered his investigation. "The government had a copy of the report in Ottawa, but they wouldn't release it," he told the hundred people gathered at Rideau Hall for the black-tie gala.[100] At that time Nova Scotia was the only province in Canada with Freedom of Information legislation; it would be another four years before Canada's *Access to Information Act* would become law in 1983.[101] It had been a long fight — first championed in 1965 by NDP MP Barry Mather, a former journalist and secretary-treasurer of the Federation of Press Clubs Canada, who had unsuccessfully introduced the Administrative Disclosure Bill, a private members bill, at every session of Parliament until he retired in 1974.

In 1979, the *Kitchener-Waterloo Record* series was credited with initiating the reorganization of the entire Canadian meat inspection system.[102] Nearly five decades later, Romahn isn't so sure. "The second in command of the Canadian Food Inspection Agency said, 'We were like an ostrich with our head stuck in the sand until you came and gave us a swift kick in the butt.' Well, that made a story, that made the award, but in practice, I don't think it changed. So they talk a good line, but they just carry on."[103] He says the promised reforms never materialized.

Romahn would win a second Michener Award in 1983 for revealing quality control problems in animal feed and fertilizer — a story he just will not let drop. Romahn still is writing about the fertilizer industry and how the lack of independent quality control is hurting farmers. "Of course, you always hope that you bring transformation. My hope was that the meat packing industry would improve, the Canadian Food Inspection Agency would improve, and the fertilizer and seeds [quality control], these things would improve. You always hold hope. You know, if I hadn't done it, it probably would've gotten worse. But the main thing I think is that the public gains an insight. They learn something they didn't know before about the way the system is failing them or needs to be reformed or fixed or whatever."[104]

The *Kitchener-Waterloo Record* would go on to win two more Michener Awards, proving that size is no barrier to meritorious public service journalism. Its second Michener was in 1981 for exposing a land swindle in which more than a thousand Canadian, American and European investors lost millions of dollars. The stories resulted in new regulations and the first-ever conviction and jail term under the *Securities Act* in Canada. In 2001, the *Record* received a Michener Award for its stories about the misuse of public funds in municipal leasing financing.

For all its back-room limitations, the very existence of the Michener Award was having the intended effect. The *Kitchener-Waterloo Record* was the poster child for improvement. Just a dozen years earlier, Senator Keith Davey had lambasted the daily and five other local media in *Maclean's* magazine for their "paternalistic" decision in 1971 to withhold a story involving a multi-million-dollar development plan until council approved it. Davey wrote that the publications "have damaged not only the public they serve but Canada's press as well."[105]

In May 1985, the assistant publisher of the *Kitchener-Waterloo Record*, K. A. (Sandy) Baird, wrote to chief judge Fraser MacDougall a letter of thanks. "Members of the public as consumers of information benefit because the Michener competition prompts the media to strive for improvement, and it helps the wider public understand how excellence in the media benefits society. . . . We like to think that our newspaper has improved because of our participation in the Michener competition. It has encouraged newsroom staffers to set their sights and standards higher."[106] The Micheners had been established exactly for this reason — to encourage media organizations to invest in journalism that exposed injustices and held power to account in stories that resulted in change for the better. As the award's reputation grew, media organizations like the *Kitchener-Waterloo Record* were encouraged to up their game.

Young, ambitious reporters were no longer content to follow in the foot-steps of their predecessors — many of whom had been described in the Davey report as mediocre, boosterish and content to cover the Rotary Club or chase fire trucks. With the energy and enthusiasm of the 1970s inspiring them, a new generation of journalists embraced their public watchdog role. In addition to larger organizations, the enterprising journalists found a home reporting in smaller outlets such as the *Kitchener-Waterloo Record,* the *London Free Press*, and *The Scotian Journalist*. They embraced new technology such as hidden cameras, pushed for freedom of information laws, and went under-cover to bring to light dysfunctional systems, institutional wrongdoings, and injustices among marginalized groups. Their reporting spurred institution-al and policy changes. That in itself brings professional satisfaction, but the

Michener Award was then as it is now the proverbial pot of gold validating the work of reporters and the media organizations that support them. And what better way to do that than with the endorsement of the governor general at a gala ceremony at Rideau Hall? Ed Schreyer's timely intervention boosted the award at a critical point for its survival.

3

The Michener Dream Takes Shape

The Michener Award came into its own in the 1980s as journalism organizations ramped up hard-hitting reporting in the public interest. Up to this point, the award had been run primarily by two postwar Ottawa newspaper veterans with support from former governor general Roland Michener. Despite annual money problems, they had made the Michener the top journalism award in Canada, coveted by both media managers and reporters. "It's the highest level of journalism award in the country," said the *Toronto Star*'s John Honderich. "The fact that the public service journalism part has an impact, that it's in fact done something and brought about change and is something journalists feel very proud about, something we think about. So when you put that all together to get to that place, it is the highest honour a journalist [and organization] can have to win a Michener or be nominated for a Michener."[1]

As the award entered its second decade of operation, the number of entries started to grow. Investigative journalism was maturing, resulting in higher quality and more hard-hitting Michener-type stories in the public interest. A nomination would mean an invitation to Rideau Hall and the prestige that the gala ceremony brought.

In 1981, a record forty-nine entries were submitted, up from thirty the previous year. "The striking increase in numbers and the equally striking improvement in quality vividly reflect the award's success in fostering and developing meritorious and disinterested service in Canadian journalism," wrote Fraser MacDougall, now in his tenth year as chief judge of the award. "The judges, all with long experience, found special merit in every entry, agreeing upwards of a dozen could easily have won the award itself, and still others would have achieved honourable mention or citations of merit."[2] The ceremony that year showcased investigations into land swindles, double-dipping on farm equipment fees, mismanagement of funds for *la Fête Nationale du Québec*, and fraudulent studies into the safety of pesticides, drugs and other chemicals. All were important and valuable stories for audiences and their communities.

This trend continued throughout the 1980s. The number of entries for the year 1986 hit an all-time high of seventy-four, a year before the 1987 stock market crash. The Michener Award was not only for big media such as the CBC, *The Globe and Mail*, the *Toronto Star* and *Le Devoir*. Smaller outlets like the *Manitoulin Expositor* (1982) were competing and winning Michener Awards for their community journalism. "For a small newspaper to present something for this award requires guts. It requires a darn good story, the conviction that it's of national importance," said Pierre Bergeron, president of the Michener Foundation from 2000 to 2004.

The growing participation and excellent entries were a testament to the dedication of founder Bill MacPherson of the *Ottawa Citizen* and Fraser MacDougall of the Canadian Press. Under the auspices of the National Press Club, these two firekeepers kept the Michener flame lit. Working out of MacPherson's spare bedroom, they single-handedly ran the Micheners — organizing the annual call for nominations, coordinating judging, planning the ceremony at Rideau Hall and handling communications — all on a shoe-string budget. But it was unsustainable, especially as the stature of the award grew and entries continued to multiply.

The Michener Awards would soon find a firmer footing. Its longevity and expanded scope were born out of profound internal and external uncertainty. Consolidation and concentration in the media industry, and the consequent release of the 1981 Royal Commission on Media put the spotlight on the quality of journalism. The Michener Awards presented an avenue for media executives to address the report's concerns. The awards were widely respected in the industry but lacked sustainable infrastructure and financial support. Under the leadership of Maclean-Hunter vice-president Paul Deacon, leaders in the industry created a charitable foundation for the Michener Awards to give the organization stability, the ability to raise money and opportunities to think bigger.

At the tenth celebration of the Michener Award in 1980, there was plenty of competition and an excellent slate of finalists from Alberta and smaller centres in Ontario. Three of the five finalists were Alberta newspapers — the *Edmonton Journal, Calgary Albertan* and *Calgary Herald*. They had written about crooked cops in Calgary, military families on welfare, and solitary confinement for children in detention centres.

The Michener Awards gala ceremony had become noteworthy enough to capture the attention of Ottawa political columnist Allan Fotheringham, who devoted his widely read Monday morning *Toronto Sun* column to "the western invasion" of Rideau Hall. "The black-tie affair was absolutely awash with publishers, editors and reporters from alien Alberta, assessing the grape and noshing the pheasant as if (as the Liberals apparently don't believe) they were full-fledged Canadian citizens." With acid wit, Fotheringham had fun at the expense of the central Canadian elite as he mused about how "the absolute absence of the heavy journalistic hitters of Toronto and Montreal in the envelope category might indicate a certain lassitude, a weary decline, in their attitude toward innovative work at the typewriter — and evidence, perhaps, of other symptoms of the Family Compact."[3]

One might almost have heard Fotheringham, after a good feed and watering at Rideau Hall, clucking dyspeptically at the absence of the big hitters as he penned how the award went "to the *Whig-Standard* of Kingston, a sleepy town reputed to be even more paralyzed than Ottawa (presuming that unlikely state to be possible)."[4] But there was nothing sleepy or paralyzed about the *Whig-Standard*'s series about the devasting effects of fluoride poisoning on the Akwesasne lands of Cornwall Island (Kawehno:ke) and Wolfe Island from aluminum smelter plants across the St. Lawrence River in nearby Massena, New York.

Journalist Sylvia Wright along with Karl Polzer and Penny Stuart exposed an "environmental nightmare and bureaucratic scandal."[5] The toxic fluoride pollution four times the legal limit, coming from a ring of chemical plants in the United States, was killing livestock and making farmland infertile.[6] Federal and provincial officials had known about the threats for five years yet had ignored the requests for studies and action from the Indigenous community — a community which had been isolated geographically and linguistically, as most residents at the time spoke Mohawk (Kanienkeha).

The *Whig-Standard*'s Michener Award-winning stories put a human face on the science. In this article, Penny Stuart profiled long-time farmer Elijah Benedict:

> All Benedict knows is that since Reynolds opened in 1959, he has been watching cattle and vegetation die. . . . "What usually happens on Cornwall Island is a calf is born stunted. The proportion

of the head to the body is smaller and the head is elongated be-cause of the accelerated bone growth," says Henry Lickers.

Lickers, a Mohawk biologist in charge of the St. Regis Environmental Division, an Indian-financed research centre, has seen a lot of cattle, including cows on Benedict's farm, die.

"With fluoride ingestion over a long period of time, maybe three years, the teeth start to wear down. The animal loses condition. It won't be able to eat as much food. It loses weight.'

In its final stages, three or four years later, the teeth fall apart, the enamel seems to dissolve, and the teeth become like chalk.

In time, all the nerves are exposed. The cow can't chew. Benedict carries warm water to the barn. It is less painful to drink. . . .

"They can't drink. They lap like a cat," said Lickers. "I have seen animals lying down on the top of the hill, knowing water is just down the hill and crawl on their knees to drink and then crawl up again to sit on the field."

Instead of 10 to 12 years of life, a newborn calf has a life expectancy of about four years.[7]

The Michener Awards judges wrote that the *Whig-Standard* series "jarred a lethargic Canadian government into action on a problem it had known about for five years, embarrassed the Ontario government into clumsy acts of secrecy, and shocked an apathetic public into an awareness of the dangers posed by an industrial pollutant usually looked on merely as a beneficial tooth decay preventative for children."[8] Through a "first-class pursuit" the *Whig-Standard* brought to the public's attention scientific research that had been shelved by governments on both sides of the border. It forced authorities to compensate the community and begin the long process of remediation.[9] This was enterprise journalism that not only uncovered wrongs but got action.

The *Whig-Standard* was on fire with the Michener values during the fourteen-year tenure of editor-in-chief Neil Reynolds, a person with "cool intelligence . . . and a sense that he was three chess moves ahead of his opponents."[10] Under his leadership, no issue was too big for the small daily. "Hearing of an injustice with or without some local implication, the paper would investigate in such a way as to provoke other, richer journalists and shame and embarrass some arm of government into correcting what it, the poor little *Whig*, could only bring to public attention."[11] That zeal resulted in another Michener and two honourable mentions for national and international stories.[12] This was the kind of enterprise journalism that the Michener Awards wanted to stoke among media organizations.

At the ground level, journalists were delivering stories that exposed, informed, changed laws and improved the lives of Canadians. But that kind of journalism was under threat. A series of economic recessions starting in the mid-1970s led media managers to cut newsrooms and consolidate their holdings. Companies closed papers such as *Montréal-Matin* in Québec in 1978 and the *Montreal Star* in 1979, and merged others. For example, on Vancouver Island, the *British Colonist* and the *Victoria Daily Times* became the *Times Colonist* in 1980.

This trend of "takeovers, mergers, agreements, and closings"[13] took on national importance only when it hit Ottawa and slapped parliamentarians in the face. On August 27, 1980, just three months before the tenth anniversary awards ceremony, four major cities lost competing English-language newspapers. In Winnipeg, the Southam newspaper chain shuttered the ninety-year-old *Tribune*. Within hours, the Thomson newspaper chain closed the almost ninety-five-year-old *Journal* in Ottawa. Instantly, the capital of Canada and a major western city became one-newspaper towns. On the same day, Vancouver and Montreal became newspaper monopolies. Southam News bought out the *Montreal Gazette* and the *Province* in Vancouver from owners Thomson and Pacific Press respectively.[14] The closures and takeovers were sudden and unexpected for Ottawa MPs, the public and many in the industry. This "rationalization of 1980"[15] foreshadowed enormous challenges media would face in the 2000s from the Internet and social media.

"Black Wednesday," as it was called, set off a chain reaction. Deprived of two competing daily newspapers, Ottawa politicians of all stripes were suddenly crying foul. The Ministry of Consumer and Corporate Affairs launched an investigation into Canada's two largest newspaper chains, Southam and Thomson (both entities no longer exist), that led to eight charges of conspiracy under the *Combines Investigation Act*. The chains were acquitted in 1983, but in the House of Commons, the Liberal government of Pierre Trudeau faced cries of collusion and demands for action. Within a week, Governor General Ed Schreyer signed an order-in-council to form a Royal Commission on Newspapers. Its mission was to look at the condition of the country's newspaper industry and make recommendations.

Tom Kent, a lanky, well-connected former newspaper editor and Liberal mandarin turned academic, was appointed to head the investigation. Kent was known as "an elitist reformer, no fan of corporate concentration, and a proponent of government intervention."[16] He was not about to sugar-coat the growing concentration of media ownership in Canada. The report found that in Québec, Québecor, Gesca and UniMedia controlled 90 per cent of French-language newspaper circulation.[17] The situation was not much better in English Canada. Southam, Thomson, the Sun group and smaller chains such as Irving in New Brunswick and Armadale Corp. in Saskatchewan controlled more than 74 per cent of newspaper circulation. "Chains accounted for 77 per cent of all copies of newspapers published in Canada in September 1980, an increase from 58 per cent 10 years earlier" when the Davey report was released.[18] Such data contributed to Kent's grim conclusion that "newspaper competition . . . is virtually dead in Canada," which "is clearly and directly contrary to the public interest."[19]

In the pre-social media world of 1980, the extent of public engagement in the issues addressed by the Kent Commission was impressive. Over the eight months of hearings, hundreds of citizens, community groups, media workers and municipal officials submitted briefs about the quality of news and information in their local media. At the public hearings, they lined up to complain about the shortcomings and stress the value of a vibrant local media. Everyone had something to say about the need to preserve a multiplicity of media and diversity of news and opinion.

The Commissioners grilled media executives, some of whom appeared with their lawyers. The executives defended the independence of the media and their businesses, arguing against any government intervention. The Kent Commission's focus, however, was to protect the interest of the public, not business.

The final report recommended legislation to limit monopoly and cross-ownership between newspapers and broadcasters. It suggested the formation of an independent national Press Rights Panel to oversee the industry, similar to the Press Ownership Review Board suggested by the Davey Commission ten years earlier. In 1983, Jim Fleming, minister of multiculturalism in the Liberal government, incorporated those recommendations into a private members bill — *The Daily Newspaper Act*. Bill 226 faced vehement opposition from both the industry and Conservative members of Parliament because it would limit media consolidation and cross-ownership. The bill never made it past second reading in the House of Commons and died with the election of the Conservative government of Brian Mulroney in 1984.

With the free market firmly in control, publishers promised action to ensure the quality of journalism. The Ontario and Québec press councils increased their membership, and new councils were established in Atlantic Canada, Manitoba and British Columbia.[20] While the press councils adjudicated citizen complaints, they did nothing to address the fundamental concerns raised by the 1981 Kent report (and the previous 1970 Davey report) about the decline in diversity of news sources from the spate of takeovers and closures. The race to consolidate would continue unabated through the next four decades.[21]

The release of the Kent report made media executives from Southam, Thomson and Maclean-Hunter sensitive to criticism and eager to prove Kent wrong. The newspaper chains were suddenly keener to invest in investigative journalism — and it was at this point they started to take a direct interest in the Micheners. It would be another way to allay fears that a smaller, more concentrated media pool would lead to a lack of diversity and public service journalism. Involvement in the administration of the Michener Award could be their public service — evidence that media conglomerates were committed to encouraging excellence in journalism.

Their involvement turned out to be a good fit — one that came just in time. In its first ten years, the Michener Award had established itself as the premier journalism award and was an incentive for newsrooms of all sizes to set their sights higher. But by 1981, Michener administrators MacPherson and MacDougall desperately needed support, structure and firm financial footing. Each year was a struggle to pay for new trophies, travel for the judging panel to meet in Ottawa, printing and postage. The award was heading towards a premature death.

At the end of 1981, a group of influential, high-powered media executives from Southam News, Thomson News, Canadian Press, CBC and CTV — many of the same outlets criticized in the Kent report — swooped in to save the Micheners. The award and its focus on public service journalism had become too important to fail. It also provided a way for media executives to show that, despite all the cutbacks and consolidation in the industry, media organizations were prepared to give reporters the time and resources to produce investigative journalism in the public interest. For these executives, it was a matter of professional pride that they were still producing important journalism that had an impact. It was also good business. Big stories attracted bigger audiences and advertisers. Reporters and editors regarded the journalism that the Michener Awards prioritized as their highest calling.

Media executives met with MacPherson and MacDougall in 1981 to begin the process of setting up a charitable foundation to ensure the survival of the Michener Award. While the 1980s were by no means smooth sailing, the creation of The Roland Michener Foundation/*La Fondation Roland Michener* provided the structure necessary to sustain the award and expand its public service mission for journalism.

The catalyst in this intervention was Paul Deacon, vice president of Maclean-Hunter. He had been editor and publisher of *The Financial Post* when the *Post* won the first Michener Award in 1970. "So I know how much they mean to everyone involved," he said in a speech at the 1983 ceremony.[22]

"Paul Deacon was a lifesaver," recalled Clark Davey, founding director and former *Globe and Mail* editor and publisher with Southam News. "The thing was very close to expiring. There was a feeling that if we didn't do something about it, it was going to die."[23] Deacon was a visionary who saw possibilities for the Michener Award that went beyond an awards gala and self-congratulations at Rideau Hall, and he was prepared to work hard to realize that vision.

The executives gave Fraser MacDougall — "a pillar" and defender of public service journalism — the responsibility to lead the transformation.[24] MacDougall was the perfect choice. He had been a Michener judge since year two and was known at Canadian Press to be a stickler for detail. A hard-bitten journalist with ink in his blood (MacDougall's father was a printer at the daily *Beacon Herald* in Stratford, Ontario),[25] MacDougall junior started as a cub reporter for a small daily, *The Sault Star,* in Sault Ste. Marie, Ontario, before joining the Canadian Press in 1941. He quickly rose to the position of Ottawa bureau chief, where "he was instrumental in building the news wire's key service: quick and accurate election coverage."[26] In 1972, at age sixty-five, MacDougall retired from the *Canadian Press* and threw himself into setting up Ontario's first Press Council, where he became known as the "journalistic father-confessor,"[27] a reference to his early years as a student minister at Baptist churches on the north shore of Lake Huron.[28] He brought that same zeal to the role of the chief judge of the Michener Awards for 18 years.

A New Beginning

On September 20, 1982, six lawyers met in a law office where John Manley, later a Liberal cabinet minister, assumed the chair and presented the Letters Patent. The document set out the mission of the Foundation: "to foster journalism which promotes the public interest and demonstrates high social values," to award "meritorious and disinterested public service in journalism" and "to advance education in the field of journalism.[29] The first act was to elect officers. MacDougall would be the founding president, a nod to the tedious backroom work he had put into creating the Foundation. He presided as the lawyer-directors passed bylaws and set up the structure and operations for the Foundation's governing body. In April 1983, a board representing the stalwarts of Canada's media industry — publishers of newspapers and magazines, national broadcasters, wire service editors, independent journalists and journalism educators — took over.[30] Their ongoing support would be crucial to the success of this new foundation.

With the endorsement of Roland Michener, now long retired, the new board of directors immediately changed the name from Roland Michener Foundation/*La Fondation Roland Michener* to the Michener Awards Foundation/*La Fondation des Prix Michener.* The board understood the value of keeping the Michener name while at the same time putting the journalism award front and centre. On August 31, 1983, Fraser MacDougall stepped down from his caretaker president role. According to plan, Paul Deacon was elected president. Over the next eight years, Deacon would lead the Foundation through tumultuous times, never losing his singular vision to build a culture of public service in the industry.

Deacon was regarded by his colleagues and competitors as "soft-spoken, mild-mannered, and elegant."[31] Starting as a reporter in 1947, he rose through the ranks of *The Financial Post* to become investment editor in 1952 and FP editor in 1964. Deacon had worked his way up to vice president of Maclean-Hunter in 1979. At that time, it was the biggest media conglomerate in Canada, with broadcast and print interests across North America and Europe. Deacon was a master juggler, keeping up with and moving forward on many disparate projects. "He had a comfy chair in the bedroom where he'd sit after dinner and before going to bed," recalled his son James. "It had loosely sorted stacks of paper and files piled on either side — what he called his 'homework'."[32] He was known as "a nut for accuracy and a believer in objectivity."[33] His leadership was exactly what was needed to propel the Michener Awards forward.

The first annual meeting of the newly expanded board of the Michener Awards Foundation was held in Ottawa on a cold, cloudy Saturday morning on November 12, 1983. Roland Michener travelled from his home in Toronto to join the media executives gathered in the boardroom at the National Press Club on Wellington Street. The minutes from the annual general meeting record Michener's pleasure that he was "the 'inspiration' for the award in 1969, and that he had served a sound and useful purpose in its encouragement of the journalistic media across the country."[34] After twelve bumpy years, Michener said he was encouraged by the creation of this new charitable foundation. "I now think that the organization might outlast me!"[35] He also paid tribute to his successors as governor general for their continued support for the award. The endorsement of the award by the Office of the Governor General sent a strong message to Canadians about the pivotal role of journalism in democratic institutional life.

At the awards ceremony in November 1983, the newly formed Michener Awards Foundation broke out champagne to celebrate a new beginning. It was a night for another first. A small family newspaper from the north shore of Lake Huron, the *Manitoulin Expositor,* had defied the odds to become the first weekly to receive a Michener Award for its reporting in the public interest, "proving that bigger isn't necessarily better," said Fraser MacDougall, chair of the award jury.[36] The win was evidence to the hundreds of smaller news organizations across Canada that they, too, could win a Michener.

The *Expositor* took on the sensitive topic of suicide and the lack of social services on the island. In such a small, tight-knit community with a year-round population of around 10,000, the number of suicides was about two times the national rate of twenty people per 1,000. Suicide on Manitoulin Island was endemic. For over a decade, the *Expositor* had hammered away, week after week, at the problem. Back in 1975, the publisher had faced scathing criticism from Indigenous leaders of Wikwemikong First Nation over the *Expositor*'s coverage of a rash of suicides of young people. "The Council were really angry that we were drawing attention to this," publisher emeritus Rick McCutcheon said.[37] When another cluster of suicides happened in 1982, this time in white communities, the *Expositor* gave the issue the same attention as in 1975.

The paper's dogged coverage stirred the community to action. An elementary school teacher started talking about the issue with her students. "They all wrote letters to the editor expressing empathy with the families of the people left behind and we ran them together," said McCutcheon.[38] Mary Nelder, "a Haweater" as the locals call themselves, led a campaign to get a toll-free twenty-four-hour distress phone line. "She should get an award, too," said Peter Carter, a former editor and reporter at the *Expositor*.[39]

In Manitoulin, the *Expositor* team was thrilled to be invited to the ceremony at Rideau Hall. Carter and his girlfriend Helena, who later became his wife, took the seven-hour bus trip to join publisher Rick McCutcheon for the ceremony and "to meet all the people I looked up to," said Carter. During a bathroom break, Carter recalled running into Ottawa journalist John Fraser, who asked if Carter had his acceptance speech ready. "Yeah, right, Mr. Fraser," Carter replied and laughed. Both Carter and McCutcheon were so convinced the paper was not going to win that neither had prepared a speech. After all, the *Globe and Mail* had the Donald Marshall story. Carter said he thought the nomination was tokenism, "throwing a bone to the community newspaper world."[40] They were wrong.

McCutcheon and Carter ended up ad-libbing their acceptance speeches that night. When Carter, a gangly twenty-three-year-old, got up to the podium, he found the words. "I guess we got this award for community service in journalism. It's not pleasurable reporting suicide rates, but I think we did something by reporting them, and that's what journalism can do."[41] McCutcheon said it was "very, very cool" to receive the Michener Award, but maybe a little too cool for some of the big boys. Before the announcement, he said, "Everybody was quite chummy, and all of a sudden, they weren't, they were quite cool. They [the *Globe and Mail*] stopped speaking to us."[42] Hurt egos mended quickly. The following week, the *Globe* sent a reporter to Manitoulin Island to do a feature story on the *Expositor*. The story was published the following March.[43]

The Michener win didn't hurt Carter's career. At a celebratory breakfast the next day, the publisher of the *Ottawa Citizen* tried to lure Carter away with an offer to work in the big city, but Carter turned down Russ Mills. "It would have been a game-changer, but I went back to the Island," Carter said. "I like working for Rick. I like being on the Island. I liked my life."[44] McCutcheon enjoyed the congratulatory notes, but "the next day you've got to go to work and prove you're doing a good job all over again, just like always."[45]

The *Expositor* win was an example to other smaller outlets. It showed the value of courageous reporting on sensitive and often taboo topics, and how sustained reporting about uncomfortable issues like suicide can lead to measurable change. In the case of the *Expositor* coverage, the suicide helpline brought the issue to national attention. In the first few weeks of operation, the helpline was credited with saving two lives. The win also showed the value of not letting a story drop. Over ten years, the paper's ongoing coverage of mental health issues connected to suicide activated the community and resulted in more social services becoming available in the area. It was a prod to small publications to dig deeper and do more than the routine reporting of police reports and sports scores. If the story was good enough, it could win the top prize in Canadian journalism.

The tiny *Expositor* had shut out five other larger media outlets who went home with honourable mentions and citations of merit. Every story nominated that night had impact. For example, the *Globe and Mail*'s exclusive interview in 1982 with Donald Marshall, a Mi'kmaw man from Membertou on Unama'ki [Cape Breton Island] who spent eleven years in prison for a murder he didn't commit. The judges wrote that five days after the *Globe and Mail* interview, the federal justice minister instructed the Nova Scotia Supreme Court to hold a hearing. "The succeeding *Globe and Mail* stories gave Marshall the support he urgently needed to deal with the transition to civilian life. The climax came in February 1982, when Marshall won acquittal and became a fully free man," read the citation of the judges.[46]

The success of the Michener Awards tempered concerns about media concentration. It was evident that the system was working just fine. Smaller independent media were producing investigative stories and competing with larger media outlets, and both had not abandoned their watchdog role. They were exposing pressing social issues and holding those in authority to account. Journalism was making a difference. It was a matter of professional pride. The Michener Awards tapped into that ethos.

For example, *Toronto Star* Sunday features writer Frank Jones thought he was going to the Yukon to do a cut-and-dried story about a twenty-three-year-old former cross-country ski champion who had shot and killed her husband after a night of excessive drinking and violence. Khristine Linklater lived in Old Crow, an isolated fly-in community. She had been convicted of second-degree murder and was in the Whitehorse jail waiting to be shipped south to serve a minimum ten-year life sentence in the Kingston Penitentiary for Women.

When Jones arrived in Whitehorse, he found the pages of the local daily newspaper filled with angry letters from Yukon women. They were outraged at the guilty verdict by an all-white jury because the women "had experienced what it was like to live with booze and violent husbands in remote communities, a lifestyle almost impossible to escape."[47] Being sent to serve time in the South was like a double punishment, Jones said in an interview.[48]

While he was in Whitehorse, two courageous women — one, an Indigenous court worker, the other, the wife of Yukon's health minister — pulled strings and got Jones into the jail. He interviewed Linklater in the laundry room with two guards listening to every word. She was pining for her ten-month-old son Norman. "I'm scared stiff," Linklater whispered to Jones. She was convinced she "would never live to do the 10 years."[49] Jones's sensitive, thoughtful account of Linklater's night of tragedy resulted in an outpouring of offers to fund the appeal and pay for her to go to Toronto for addiction treatment at the Donwood Institute. Civil rights lawyer Clayton Ruby helped her lawyer prepare the appeal.

The story took an unusual twist. Jones was vacationing in the United Kingdom with his family when the Yukon Supreme Court released Linklater on $10,000 bail with the condition that she be under the supervision of Jones. "Without being consulted, I came back to find out that Khristine was my charge. I was responsible for her, which is a bit unusual when you're doing the story," Jones said.[50] Linklater flew south to live with Jones, his wife and six kids until a place opened at the Donwood Institute. When she finished addiction treatment, Linklater moved to an Indigenous-run residence. As her guardian, Jones kept an eye on her. Jones wrote that when the word came that Justice W. A. Craig of the Court of Appeal had reduced her conviction to manslaughter, Linklater "sobbed and threw her arms around me."[51]

Linklater was returned to the Yukon for the sentencing hearing. The same judge who released her into Jones's care gave her a suspended sentence and probation. She went free.[52] It was one of the most unusual stories Jones ever covered because it became personal. "It certainly committed the paper [*Toronto Star*] to being right on the story and following it all the way through," he said.[53] Jones said the story put spousal abuse on the national stage and contributed to overall changes for women in abusive relationships. Today the

Star would trumpet such a story on the front page with the sub-head: *"The Star gets action."*

Michener Award nominees were often the first to identify emerging trends and under-reported issues. A nomination alone was enough recognition to catapult stories onto a national stage and engage citizens and decision makers in a discussion. For media executives, it was a demonstration that they had not abandoned their public service role and were putting time and money into stories with impact. A Michener nomination or win also offset criticism that media concentration and cross-ownership diluted the quality and diversity of news and information.

In the 1980s, the Michener Award-winning journalists drew attention to changes involving immigration and multiculturalism, trends that would become hugely political and socially important for Canadians. These stories emerged as the country welcomed people fleeing natural disasters, conflicts and violence, persecution, and political and humanitarian crises. Refugees came from Sri Lanka, Uganda, Chile, Vietnam, Cambodia and Laos. Others migrated from Jamaica, Haiti, Trinidad and Tobago and Bermuda.[54] Most made their homes in Toronto, Montreal and Vancouver. These new communities signalled a marked change from past patterns where newcomers had come mainly from the United States, Europe and the Eastern Bloc countries.

The national adoption of multiculturalism within a bilingual framework in 1971 meant that Canada, unlike the United States, was no melting pot, but rather a country that aspired to celebrate differences. The influx of newcomers was changing Canadian communities. In 1985, Toronto's two largest newspapers — the *Toronto Star* and the *Globe and Mail* — each received a Michener Award for their investigations into problems refugees and immigrants faced getting into and staying in Canada and how new ethnic communities were changing the culture of cities like Toronto.

The *Toronto Star* "explored the rewards and disappointments of life" among the seven largest ethnic communities — Black, Jewish, Italian, Chinese, Portuguese, East Indian and Pakistani — in Canada's biggest city. Reporter Olivia Ward interviewed 1,400 people over three months in 1985. She discovered the city had moved light years in just fifty years, from a city of two solitudes, who greeted Jewish immigrants with signs that said, "No dogs or Jews." In her final installment, Ward observed:

It's Sunday morning at the Mars Cafe and taxi drivers of assorted shapes and sizes are carrying on their verbal war against "young guys."

"Ever notice you can't get a decent bagel anymore?" one adds. What kinda town are we living in?"

Nearby, a Japanese waiter serves coffee and muffins to a young black woman and her French-Canadian boyfriend. Behind them, a dark-haired student dips a donut into his tea and bookmarks his homework with a page from a Chinese newspaper.

"Merry Christmas," an elderly man shouts.

"Happy Chanukah," Somebody calls back.

This is Toronto in the 1980s. A multicultural metropolis striking an uneasy balance between integration and suspicion, where open doors and closed minds exist in inverse proportion. A city that brings a unanimous verdict from visitors and residents: "It works."[55]

The series was used in schools and by community service and research organizations. "When you look back at it, the series was in its infancy of covering multiculturalism. It was doing the snapshot and we gave a lot of effort and we felt very proud of leading the way on what was obviously to become a huge issue," said John Honderich. "It was way, way ahead of its time, cutting edge and carving out what matters, and what this city is about."[56]

Since 1985, coverage of diverse communities has evolved. Newsrooms have hired racialized journalists, added columnists who write about equity, diversity and inclusion in communities and created reporting beats focussing on newcomers, diversity and immigration.

The other 1985 Michener Award winner was the *Globe and Mail*. Investigative reporter Victor Malarek documented the government's inability to process a flood of illegal immigrants and refugees seeking to stay in Canada. Malarek, who prides himself on being a "crazy guy who is not afraid to take people on,"[57] unmasked dodgy lawyers and immigration consultants and exposed government refugee detention centres in Toronto for violating United Nations human rights laws:

There is no privacy; doors to the rooms must stay open. "It's a depressing situation to be in detention for a long time," an Immigration official said. "We don't want a suicide." The main activity is watching television. There were no books or magazines and an exercise bicycle stood unused.

When a few detainees said they get only a half-hour of fresh air time when the regulations call for an hour, a security guard said, "The reason you get a half hour is because it is cold outside and we are concerned about your health." One detainee from Liberia said he doesn't go out at all because he has no winter coat.[58]

After the stories came out, the refugees in detention were released to church groups and the centre was shut down.

The win propelled Malarek to dig deeper into the problems immigrants to Canada face. Three years later, the *Globe and Mail* received another Michener Award for a series of stories that included Malarek's investigation into a federal entrepreneurial immigration program, designed to fast-track wealthy immigrants wanting to move to Canada. The goal was to entice "economic migrants" to start businesses and create at least one job. Malarek's Michener Award-winning stories debunked the government's claim that the program was a success:

Two Hong Kong brothers, Philip Kwok-Po Lee and Kenneth Kwok-Hon Lee, said they would inject $500,000 into a Toronto knitting mill. They received their landed-immigrant status, returned to Hong Kong shortly after their arrival in Canada and did not follow through with their business proposal.

Louis Hin-Kuen Chan said he would invest $300,000 in a beauty supply company outside Ottawa. The investment was not made.

Joseph Shao-Kong Wu said he would set up a shipping company at Pearson Airport in Toronto with an initial investment of $150,000. The business venture was never realized.

None of the landed immigrants could be reached at their Canadian addresses.

> Entrepreneurs are under no obligation to follow through with their proposals unless such a condition is imposed by immigration officials on the applicants' visas. . . .
>
> The federal Immigration Department has yet to prosecute or deport any entrepreneur who has not established any kind of business venture in Canada.[59]

Malarek's sources led him to one of the top Bay Street law firms — Lang Michener. Immigration lawyers there came under RCMP investigation for "allegedly creating false Canadian residences and bogus business intentions so that as many as 149 of their wealthy Hong Kong clients could get landed status and, eventually Canadian citizenship."[60] One lawyer faced criminal charges and nine partners in Lang Michener faced disciplinary action from the Law Society of Upper Canada. As a result of the *Globe* series, the Law Society adopted stricter oversight and transparency rules, and the Canadian government tightened its control of the immigration entrepreneurship program.

Paul Palango, an editor at the *Globe and Mail*, accepted the 1988 award. With Roland Michener sitting in the first row, Palango did not shy away from noting the story's connection to the law firm Michener had founded. "It's more than a little ironic that we have been recognized by the Michener Award Foundation for our work on Lang Michener. The audience laughed."[61] Victor Malarek recalls his conversation with Michener at the stand-up reception after the ceremony. Michener said, "You know it's a different group of people working there now. I don't understand them. It's very embarrassing and I am glad that I am no longer there." Malarek said he gave Michener no quarter, reminding him, "Well, they carry your name on the masthead."[62] The fact that an exposé of a law firm with ties to the principal benefactor of the Michener Awards could be nominated — and win — attested to the independence of the judging panel from external influences, including the Foundation board and Rideau Hall.

The two other finalists that year also looked at issues surrounding legislation and policies that affected refugees and immigrants to Canada. The *Calgary Herald*'s special report that revealed the Alberta government was not enforcing labour laws prompted a major review. The *Vancouver Sun* produced an in-depth look at Canada's immigration laws and refugee policies with a particular focus on the Sikh community, since 90 per cent of India's immigrants to Canada came from Punjab in India, and many had settled in the Vancouver area.

In successive years, Canada welcomed victims of conflict, religious persecution and climate from such countries as Bosnia, Burma (Myanmar), Syria, Iraq, Nigeria and Afghanistan. While the faces and names had changed, the horror stories of exploitation had not. CBC-TV's Toronto and Winnipeg investigative unit received the 1991 Michener Award for reports that "exposed how the director of immigration in Manitoba was in league with an immigration consultant in various practices."[63] After the story aired, the manager was fired, and new processes were adopted. Global News, a 2017 Michener Award finalist, reported on how Canada's Department of Citizenship and Immigration was using faulty criteria in considering permanent resident applications for newcomers with medical conditions. Following the news reports, the Standing Committee on Citizenship and Immigration found "overwhelming evidence" to repeal Section 38 – 1 (C) of the Act. Instead, the government revised financial thresholds, which came into effect on June 1, 2018.[64]

Evidence-based journalism such as that recognized by the Michener Award defends those who have no voice, holds those in authority to account, and exposes and pursues issues and problems to get action and change. This is the kind of enterprise journalism that the Davey and Kent Commission reports in 1971 and 1981 feared would shrink in the face of increased cross-ownership and concentration.

The Lustre of Rideau Hall

The creation of the Michener Awards Foundation in 1983 had given the award some administrative and financial stability. This hard-won stability and new initiatives depended on the involvement and support of the governor general and staff at Rideau Hall. The annual ceremony presided over by the governor general at Rideau Hall sent a clear message to media outlets that this award was different from other industry-based recognition. It elevated "disinterested and meritorious" journalism that resulted in measurable change. Moreover, the state recognized the essential role of journalism as a pillar of democracy. Any threat to that relationship with Rideau Hall was a threat to the Michener Award.

The appointment of Jeanne Sauvé, a Saskatchewan francophone and first woman governor general, in 1984 had garnered wide praise among media pundits and the Michener Awards Foundation. They expected another smooth five-year term. After all, Sauvé was one of them. She had spent more than 20 years as a broadcaster and political analyst with the CBC and Radio-Canada. She had freelanced for CTV, American networks and major Canadian newspapers before following her husband Maurice into politics.[65] As a Liberal MP, Madame Sauvé held several cabinet posts, including Communications. She followed in Roland Michener's footsteps and was serving as an effective Speaker of the House of Commons when she received the call from Prime Minister John Turner to succeed Ed Schreyer.

Her first Michener Award ceremony in November 1984 was promising. Like her predecessor, Sauvé and her husband Maurice opened the doors to Rideau Hall and picked up the tab for journalism's social event of the year. She had invited about 120 journalists and media executives to honour and celebrate journalism in the public interest. The event brought together big names and journalists from big and small media outlets. It was the place for small-town print journalists to meet national journalism icons. "Among the guests at the dinner were author Doris Anderson, busy in Toronto writing another book, *The Journal*'s Barbara Frum, glittery in a black sequined dress, and her husband Murray, Global TV anchorman Peter Truman and his wife Eleanor, and sculptor John Matthews who created the original Michener Award," wrote columnist Margo Roston in the *Ottawa Citizen*.[66]

"Hobnobbing" was an unofficial but very appealing aspect of the award ceremony. Once a year, in a most auspicious setting, it was an opportunity for top-notch journalists, editors, producers and publishers to put aside linguistic, geographic and professional barriers to share in a celebration of their best work. This was not lost on any of the governors general who had experience working in the media. For one of Sauvé's successors, it was close to being an underlying purpose of the awards. "It provided a place for engaging with other journalists from across Canada," recalled Michaëlle Jean, the Radio-Canada journalist who served as governor general from 2005-2010. "So for networking it was quite important. It was for a moment among us."[67]

Sauvé would have understood this dimension. She regarded the award as "our Canadian Pulitzer Prize for Journalism."[68] But in year three her enthusiasm for the gala Michener ceremony appeared to cool. In 1986, Rideau Hall proposed a scaled-back ceremony. Paul Deacon appealed to Esmond

Butler, secretary to Her Excellency, reminding him that "The presentation ceremony has become an important vehicle for recognizing and encouraging, at a national level, high standards in journalism."[69] For media organizations and their employees, the ceremony at Rideau Hall not only validated the public service role of journalism but also served as a demonstration to reporters and editors that their work was important and made a difference. "It's a very powerful moment, a very powerful signal," said David McKie, journalism educator and deputy managing editor of the *National Observer*. "I think it's an important symbol and a recognition of how important our work is, like what we do matters. To me that is the ultimate recognition of that as far as awards and ceremonies go."[70] Rideau Hall acquiesced. Deacon won a reprieve for the 1986 ceremony, but for the last three years of Sauvé's tenure, the ceremony was a modest affair that harkened back to the days of Roland Michener and Jules Léger — the presentations, followed by a brief reception.

Rideau Hall gave no reason for the change except that Her Excellency wanted a simpler ceremony. Could it have been financial restraint or health issues?[71] Before taking office, Sauvé had suffered a severe respiratory illness. Her health remained a topic of media interest. Sauvé refused to comment after an Ottawa television station reported on the six o'clock news that according to "informed sources, she was receiving treatments for Hodgkin's disease," a treatable form of cancer.[72] Later, she told her friend Shirley Wood "I don't want sensational stories in the press — I'm not a sick person and I don't want the country to have that kind of image.[73] No doubt that helped to chill her enthusiasm for celebrating.

Another possible reason for the change in ceremony was that over the years, going back to the mid-1960s, Sauvé had weathered and deflected her fair share of media criticism. A Conservative MP accused Mme. Sauvé of conflict of interest because she was working at the CBC and Radio-Canada when her husband was a Member of Parliament and held a cabinet post as Minister of Forestry in the Liberal government of Lester B. Pearson. After becoming governor general, she faced criticism over what was termed an extravagant expenditure of $700,000 for kitchen renovations at Rideau Hall,[74] a criticism other governors general would face.

The attitude of the Rideau Hall staff could have influenced Sauvé's cooling toward the Michener Awards ceremony. Her secretary, Esmond Butler, a retired naval officer who had served the previous five governors general, had no love for the scribbling class. In a note to Her Excellency, he advised

Sauvé that "The media is traditionally sophist in philosophy. . . . Good news is no news. Bad news is good news for them. Thus, it's a constant game for the media to try and embarrass the government, no matter the political stripe. And what better way to do this than through the governor general."[75] With support from her staff, Sauvé decided to host the Michener Awards ceremony in 1987, but there would be no gala.

Her Excellency Jeanne Sauvé opened the late afternoon scaled-back ceremony in 1987 by acknowledging the finalists. Still, her speech hinted at the sting from the media scrutiny over her health. "This occasion obliges each governor general once a year to stand before you and sing the praises of our national media pundits, a chorus which does not, as a rule, roll easily off the tongues of those in public life who rarely find such accolades being issued in the opposite direction. But I'm happy to acknowledge your talents. Through the example of these acclaimed articles, there is established a standard of journalism and a goal towards which each journalist can strive in their pursuit of professional excellence."[76] Sauvé set aside personal grievances and focused on the purpose of the Michener Award and recognized excellence in journalism, She took time to commend Roland Michener "for having perceived the need to establish some system of formal recognition of the print media in this country and for affording us an occasion to reflect on the positive and constructive service which is rendered to the Canadian community through the efforts of those whom we honour here this evening."[77]

After a brief reception, everyone went on their way. It was a huge disappointment to Peter Moon, the lead reporter for the *Globe and Mail*'s Michener Award-winning story. While he was impressed at the ceremony in the ballroom at Rideau Hall, he had anticipated a lavish gala dinner in the style of former governor general Ed Schreyer to celebrate the newspaper's aggressive and groundbreaking series. Moon left Rideau Hall disappointed that the Sauvé had not done more to recognize journalism in the public interest.

The *Globe and Mail* had devoted its news and editorial pages throughout 1986 to a court challenge against a December 1985 amendment to the Criminal Code of Canada that denied journalists and the public access to information in police search and seizure raids — one of investigative journalism's most important tools when it came to covering the police and courts. Section 487.2(1) made it illegal for media to identify search locations, people in the premises and "the identity of anyone named in a search warrant as a suspect in the offence under investigation."[78] The only way around this was if "the publisher obtained the permission of those searched or named as suspects — an unlikely scenario . . . " wrote legal media historian Dean Jobb.[79] Privacy was about to butt heads with press freedom.

In January 1986, the *Globe and Mail* and other media outlets launched a challenge to the amendment. "It was intended. It was planned," said Moon, the story's lead investigative journalist.[80] Toronto lawyer Clayton Ruby eagerly took on the case to get the Criminal Code amendment thrown out in the Supreme Court of Ontario as a violation of Canada's *Charter of Rights and Freedoms*. The Winnipeg *Free Press* had launched a similar challenge in Manitoba.

The *Globe* tasked Moon to hit the streets and find a search warrant that had not been publicized. His managing editor Geoffrey Stevens wanted an example of how this amendment curtailed press freedom and stood in the way of Canadians receiving information about an important part of the criminal justice system. It was a fight for journalistic freedom and citizens' rights.

Moon says he lucked out. "I stopped to have a coffee with Gerry McAuliffe, who was working for CBC Radio at the time, and I told him what I was doing. 'Oh fuck,' he said, 'look at this.' He went to his drawer, and he pulled out a search warrant to seize his home telephone records and his work telephone records because he was exposing a lot of things involving the Niagara Regional Police," Moon recalls. "It was perfect. The [Ontario Provincial] police executing search warrants against a CBC reporter who was investigating the [Niagara Regional] police."[81]

McAuliffe and the CBC gave Moon permission to write about the warrants. So did a businessman from St. Catharines who had had his business records seized. But the Criminal Code amendment required the consent of all parties. Moon still needed permission from Bell Canada to use the phone records before he could legally publish the story. When Bell refused, "we jumped up and down with joy," Moon said. "This meant we had a great story."[82] It also meant the *Globe and Mail* would willfully defy the search warrant section of the Criminal Code and risk prosecution and a fine of up to $2,000 and/or six months in jail.[83] The stories started to roll out in February 1986, with Moon writing the news stories and the editor-in-chief, William Thorsell, the editorials. In a front-page story Moon wrote:

> "I would be very surprised if the Attorney-General of Ontario were to charge us with breaching this new provision of the

Criminal Code," Globe managing editor Geoffrey Stevens said in an interview.

"Any law officer of the Crown would be embarrassed to have this provision in the code. It's so obviously at odds with the Constitution, particularly in this instance. I think this is a particularly clear-cut case.

"I don't think we are breaking the law in any way publishing this story. In fact, publishing this story is entirely legal and constitutional. Section 2 of the *Charter of Rights and Freedoms* guarantees the public's right to know through the device of the freedom of the press. You cannot separate the freedom of the press and the public's right to know."[84]

In June, the Manitoba Queens Bench ruled that the amendment was "much wider than necessary." Two months later, based on the warrants Moon received from CBC, the Supreme Court of Ontario struck down the amendment as unconstitutional under the *Charter*. "The big thing is newspapers very rarely get to change the Criminal Code or any major legislation the way we did. And then we went up to the Michener Awards ceremony and we won. We were all ecstatic."[85] For Moon, the Michener Award remains the single outstanding moment in his journalism career. "I won the Michener Award, as did the *Globe* and [William] Thorsell. It was a big event in my career, and I've used it."

Geoffrey Stevens used his acceptance speech to send a message to Rideau Hall about the importance of the ceremony. The following day, he wrote a letter to Sauvé to thank her and reminded her that "The continued patronage of the governor general distinguishes the Michener Award from all other journalistic honours and prizes in Canada."[86]

Relations with Governor General Sauvé never warmed. For her final three years, 1987-1989, after the Michener Award ceremony there would be no gala dinner at Rideau Hall for the finalists and winners. After the disappointment of the 1987 ceremony, where journalists left feeling unrecognized, the *Ottawa Citizen* stepped in. Its publisher, Clark Davey, a founding director of the Michener Awards Foundation, hosted a dinner and dance at the National Arts Centre for the last two years of Sauvé's tenure. But an industry-hosted dinner was anti-climactic for the Michener Award winner and finalist nominees who had come to expect an evening at Rideau Hall. That gala would return with the appointment of Ramon Hnatyshyn in 1990.

Twenty years after the *Globe and Mail*'s win, the importance of the story still resonated. William Thorsell reminded readers that the *Globe* "fought against the 'secret knock on the door in the middle of the night.' If the police were going to use that power against citizens of any ilk, we argued, they should use it in public. We won."[87] While section 487.2(1) remains in the Criminal Code, Dean Jobb writes in *Media Law for Canadian Journalists*, "the ban is no longer considered to have the force of law." This is journalism at its best and clearly deserved the top Michener Award.

While the annual Michener Awards ceremony at Rideau Hall was the Foundation's *raison d'être*, the Foundation was committed to outreach and education — to build capacity through elevating exemplary people and educational opportunities for working journalists.

4

Expanding the Mission: Special Awards and Fellowships

The creation of the Michener Awards Foundation was borne of tumult in the industry and media executives' desire to respond to the critique from the Kent Commission report. Deacon and the directors were committed to expanding the Michener mandate into the journalism community through education and outreach. Out of that came the Special Award to recognize an individual for their journalistic contribution and study fellowships for mid-career journalists.

One of the first acts of the new Michener Awards Foundation in 1983 was a special award to recognize journalists who are exemplars when it comes to encouraging and producing journalism in the public interest. At the Foundation's first annual meeting, Murray Chercover, the president of CTV News Network, pitched the idea. The network was still mourning the loss of its London correspondent Clark Todd , who had been killed two months earlier while covering the civil war in Lebanon.[1] Chercover suggested the Foundation bestow a special award to honour Todd's journalism.

Foundation president Paul Deacon ran with the idea. It fit with his vision. It sent a clear message that journalism in the public interest was not just stories produced by media outlets; it also involved the highest standard of professional practice or service. At the 1983 awards ceremony, Deacon announced the creation of a Special Award for individuals "whose efforts exemplify the best in public service journalism."[2] He went on to say that at the next awards ceremony the first recipient of the special award would be given posthumously to Clark Todd.

Deacon used the platform to praise Todd's courage, his coverage of conflicts in Poland and Belfast, his many awards for economic reporting, and his documentaries on Eurocommunism and the Pope in Poland. "One of my personal heroes in journalism, the late Kenneth R. Wilson, used to say that our job as journalists was to alert people to the important issues of the day, to give them some understanding of the pros and cons, and let each individual decide what to do about them," Deacon concluded. "Clark Todd lived that kind of journalism — and died in its service."[3] That was the standard that Deacon set for this new special award.

Tim Kotcheff was head of CTV news at the time. "Clark had an insatiable urge to cover action stories and sometimes he'd go without asking. I was always against that." This was the case when he flew off to cover a civil war in the hills of Lebanon which Kotcheff described as a local war between Druze and Phalanges militias. "He's up in the middle of nowhere and they're shooting each other and he's in the middle. And he caught one here [Kotcheff points to the heart] and he bled to death over three days and he wrote a letter to his wife saying how much he loved her." Kotcheff flew to Lebanon and drove into the Chouf Mountains through an artillery barrage to retrieve Todd's body. "I found it. I had to get it back to London. It was horrific," he said.[4]

At the awards ceremony in 1984, Todd's widow, Ann Carmichael Todd, travelled from her home in Hertfordshire, England, to accept the trophy for her husband's "exceptional contribution to public service and journalism," from Roland Michener himself. The new trophy, designed by sculptor John Matthews, is a circular bronze disc sitting on a white marble base. One side sports an old typeface that spells out the name of Michener, and the other side has a map of Canada.[5] This Special Award was smaller and, at three pounds, it was much lighter than the Michener Award trophy.

In those early years, the Special Award did not become a part of the annual Michener Awards ceremony. The award may have been so 'special' that nominations from the board were sporadic, even tightfisted. Between 1984 and 2020, only eight individuals were honoured; each had made a unique contribution through exemplary practice or volunteer service to further the Michener values of journalism in the public interest and inspire a new generation of journalists.

In 2009, the board recognized the journalism and service of Clark Davey, who had "worked tirelessly" in newsrooms across Canada and as a founding director with the Michener Awards Foundation. He served as Michener president from 1993 to 1998 and then as executive secretary, a position he held for eighteen years, until 2016. Davey was a shrewd and steadying force for the Michener Foundation, as he had been throughout his career as a reporter in the Parliamentary Press Gallery, as managing editor of the *Globe* and *Mail*, and as the publisher of the *Vancouver Sun*, the *Montreal Gazette* and the *Ottawa Citizen*. Many reporters and editors owed their success to Davey's tough-love mentorship. Heads in the ballroom of Rideau Hall nodded at the 2009 Michener ceremony when the incumbent president David Humphreys said, "Clark Davey's contribution to investigative journalism is inspirational."[6]

Over the years, the board also honoured three of its directors — Tim Kotcheff, Alain Guilbert and David Humphreys — with a special award for their exceptional service furthering the mission of the Foundation.[7] The efforts of the volunteer board members were crucial to the success and survival of the Michener Awards Foundation. They spent countless hours building websites, overseeing the administration, marketing, fundraising and promotion, organizing the awards ceremony and maintaining cordial relations with its patron, the governor general and Rideau Hall, which at times required the skills of a diplomat.

The award was renamed the Michener-Baxter Special Award in 2009 to recognize and honour the contributions of the Baxter family. Clive Baxter was an award-winning journalist with the *Financial Post* who received the first Michener Award for the 1970 series "The Charter Revolution." The Baxter family were also generous benefactors, especially in the early years when donors were few and money was tight. His widow Cynthia Baxter served as a Michener director for twelve years. Their son James, a third-generation public affairs journalist and the founding editor and publisher of *iPolitics*, has served on the Michener Board since 2010. James Baxter recalled how the Michener Award was a big deal in his family. He was about six years old when his father received the Michener Award in 1971. The photograph of his smiling father shaking Roland Michener's hand "was front and centre in my house for all the years that I was there. I think it's probably still on my mom's picture table in a frame. So, I was ready to understand that it was an important and seminal moment in his life, but also an important thing in journalism. So, when I was asked to replace my mother on the board, I was thrilled." Baxter says he's trying to "help make journalism in Canada better one step at a time. And I do think everyone involved in the Micheners over the years has had that same goal."[8]

The Michener-Baxter Special Award was another step in that direction. The laureates are exemplars in journalism. The 2010 posthumous award to Michelle Lang was both inspiring and heartbreaking. Lang was the first Canadian journalist to be killed while covering the operations of Canadian soldiers in Kandahar as part of the Canwest News Service rotation to Afghanistan. The *Calgary Herald* reporter was with a Canadian military reconstruction convoy on December 30, 2009, when the armoured vehicle she was riding in drove over an improvised explosive device. Lang and four Canadian soldiers died in the explosion.

Governor General Michaëlle Jean recalled with great emotion attending Michelle's repatriation ceremony at CFB Trenton four months earlier. "Michelle Lang wanted to report on the efforts being made by the Canadian Forces to improve the security of the Afghan people on a daily basis, and to focus on the changes being made as a result of the military presence in this troubled region of the world," Jean said.[9] Her parents, Arthur and Sandra Lang of Vancouver, dressed in black, still heavy with grief, walked up to the podium to receive the Michener-Baxter Special Award from Her Excellency. As they returned to their seats, everyone stood and applauded.

While Lang's posthumous award for her ultimate service to journalism in the public interest was front-page news, the Michener-Baxter Award also was mindful to recognize those behind-the-scenes journalists and editors who work quietly in the service of the Michener values. In 2013, the Michener Awards Foundation honoured Bryan Cantley, a week before he died from pancreatic cancer, for his commitment and outstanding contribution to journalism and the newspaper industry. Cantley was a superhero in the newspaper business.[10] He was respected for his roll-up-the-sleeves and let's-get-to-work attitude in his service as vice president of the Canadian Newspaper Association, secretary of the National Newspaper Awards and executive director of the Commonwealth Journalists Association. Cantley was too ill to attend the awards ceremony on June 19, 2013, so his close friend, Michener past-president Pierre Bergeron, accepted the award on his behalf from His Excellency Governor General David Johnston. Cantley embodied the Michener Award values that its founder, Roland Michener, and the Foundation saw as fundamental to journalism in the public interest. "He believed in news and the value it brought to a stronger democratic society," said Scott White, then chair of the National Newspaper Awards and editor-in-chief of The Canadian Press.[11]

The Michener-Baxter Prize recognized many sides to journalism in the public service. Due to the COVID-19 pandemic, the vivacious "icon of Canadian journalism"[12] John Fraser received the Michener-Baxter Special

Award at a pre-taped fiftieth anniversary ceremony broadcast in December 2020. In an acceptance speech recorded in his living room, Fraser — wearing his signature bow tie — beamed as he looked into the camera and spoke of his beginnings in journalism as a sixteen-year-old copy boy at the *Toronto Telegram* on Melinda Street.

Unlike many watching the virtual ceremony, Fraser was one of the few journalists who could say that he had spent time with Governor General Roland Michener. He was a young summer reporter with the *Evening Telegram* in St. John's in 1968 when he was assigned to cover Michener's tour of Newfoundland and up the coast of Labrador. Fraser, a self-professed monarchist, described Michener as a "modern model of a governor general, the epitome of what we can do as a country."[13]

Fraser spent six decades as a "reporter, columnist, editor, ombudsman, academic and benefactor."[14] In his address, he proudly proclaimed that he's "still in the game" as the executive chair of the National NewsMedia Council of Canada, "a voluntary, self-regulatory ethics body for the news media industry in Canada" that mediates complaints and promotes ethical practices in the industry.[15] In a reflective moment, Fraser observed how everything seems so changed in the world of journalism from when he was that kid standing beside the pneumatic tube at the *Toronto Telegram*, but in some ways, it has not changed at all. "It's just the technology. Some things have simply not changed, and that is the core values in journalism, the ones that I learned a long time ago, the ones that I learned on the streets of Beijing, that I learned in Sherbrooke, Québec, in St. John's, Newfoundland, Toronto, up North and wherever I got sent, and that is the old cliché — to report without fear or favour."[16]

The Michener-Baxter Special Award was a way to expand the mission of the Foundation beyond an annual awards ceremony. It says that journalism at its best is more than just a job; it is a vocation on behalf of the public. While the industry had an eye for profits, it also cultivated a measure of excellence. Each laureate offers a unique example of what it is to be a role model. The board hoped that the Michener-Baxter winners would inspire journalists to aim high in their professional practice.

Back in 1983, Paul Deacon had his eye on using the awards and the journalism recognized to inspire cub reporters to do more than chase the proverbial fire engine or monitor the police scanner. In the early years, the Michener board organized panel discussions on the day of the awards ceremony with finalists at Carleton's School of Journalism in Ottawa, but attendance was lacklustre, and without a champion, it fizzled. For a few years, the board recorded the annual ceremony and sent CDs to journalism schools, but the packages often remained unopened. The recording just could not replicate the sparkle and excitement of the live ceremony.

When Adrienne Clarkson became governor general in 1999, she was quick to notice that the Michener Awards invitation list contained a lot of old familiar journalism faces. She insisted that the Foundation invite journalism educators and their students from Carleton University and Algonquin College in Ottawa. It was building capacity among journalism students and recent graduates entering the business. Clarkson eventually expanded the invitation list to journalism schools across the country and her successors continued the practice.

Every year a handful of aspiring senior journalism students and recent graduates in suits and long sparkly dresses walk into Rideau Hall to spend an evening with some of their journalism heroes and to hear inspiring stories about journalism that makes a difference. Ken Ingram had just graduated with a Bachelor of Journalism from the University of King's College in 2015 when he was invited to the awards ceremony at Rideau Hall. "I imagined the evening as a culmination of outstanding public service in journalism, not one of new beginnings," recalled Ingram.[17]

That night the *Globe and Mail* won the 2014 Michener Award for a series that resulted in compensation long denied to victims of thalidomide — a drug widely prescribed in the late 1950s and early 1960s for severe morning sickness. The drug company claimed it was safe, but thousands of babies were born with severe physical malformations, and those who grew to adulthood struggled with health challenges.[18] In 2014, the survivors began a campaign with the *Globe and Mail* to get government compensation.

Editor-in-chief David Walmsley said, "Thalidomide in some ways structurally was a conscious move by me to go after what was a completely non-controversial argument about making change."[19] But even Walmsley was astounded at the impact. When Ingrid Peritz and Andre Picard were doing the stories, "I didn't know that the thalidomide stories would create a unanimous decision in the House of Commons. I didn't know that the Prime Minister himself would move the bureaucracy fast and give the survivors funding. Basically, everything that we could have dreamt of if we'd sat down and created a line item of things we wanted, we achieved, I couldn't have known any of that."[20] When the winner was announced, the ballroom erupted in applause and gave a standing ovation for Mercédes Benegbi, the executive director of the Thalidomide Victims Association of Canada (TVAC).

It was a night of surprises for many. After the ceremony, Ingram said he was waiting for a taxi when he recognized the star of the evening, Ms. Benegbi. As a good Nova Scotian, "I felt compelled to introduce myself to Mercédes and I exchanged contact information in what felt like a chance encounter. I didn't anticipate the incredible year that would soon follow," Ingram recalled.

Something about the sincere young man moved Benegbi. She hired Ingram to create a "behind the scenes" documentary. Ingram said the video project paid tribute to "the Survivors, their journeys, and countless lives affected by this tragedy and triumph in Canadian history." That chance meeting at Rideau Hall made a huge impact on Ingram. "However minor my role was, it was an honour to be part of such an incredible story."[21] Building a culture of public service journalism was what the Michener Foundation was set up to do.

As part of the Michener mission, Deacon was determined to help build a culture of investigative public service journalism among working journalists through study fellowships. For a small, underfunded volunteer organization it was a tall order that would take persistence, time and money.

Financing the Fellowships

In 1983 the critical issue for the new Michener Awards Foundation was all too apparent. If it was to expand its mission beyond the awards ceremony, it needed to build a financial nest egg. Paul Deacon was of the vintage that believed that when you agreed to serve on the board, you pulled your load. He set the gold standard when it came to volunteering.

His son James liked to tell the story of when his parents served on the board of the National Ballet of Canada. "After Rudy Nureyev joined the National, Dad supported a motion requiring all board members to make substantial contributions to help build a set and costumes worthy of Nureyev's debut staging of *Sleeping Beauty*. He didn't have anywhere near the cash, but he knew you couldn't ask the world's greatest ballet dancer to fit his sparkling new choreography onto the tattered old set the company had been using for previous productions. So, he and my mother — who years previously had to drag him reluctantly to his first ballet performance — made their contribution by remortgaging the family home."[22] Deacon brought that same commitment to the Michener Foundation in time and money.

Deacon saw his role was to ensure that the mandate of journalism in the public service found full expression in the activities of the new foundation. His vision was to build a culture of service in the profession that went beyond an annual awards night. At the first awards ceremony of the newly formed Michener Awards Foundation in 1983, Deacon announced both the creation of the special award and plans for study fellowships: "In this and other ways, the Foundation seeks to go beyond the annual award to encourage far more Canadian journalists to take an interest in meritorious and disinterested public service journalism."[23]

The idea of study fellowships had been kicking around since the Federation of Press Clubs of Canada passed a motion, ten years earlier, to look into "setting up a major fund to provide a sabbatical or some other recognition of journalistic merit funded by any donor."[24] Nothing happened, but in 1977 minutes show that Ford Canada was interested in funding a $15,000 scholarship for mid-career journalists, but there was no one to champion the idea. Bill MacPherson and Fraser MacDougall had their hands full just keeping the award going. With no budget, no resources and no time to think big, the proposal was put on the back burner.

Before the rise of journalism schools in the 1970s, many journalists learned their craft from older experienced reporters and editors in a guild-like system. Employers provided little in the way of professional training, giving rise to the establishment of professional associations like the Centre for Investigative Journalism in 1978, which offered its members advocacy, training and workshops at annual conferences.[25]

The formation of the Michener Awards Foundation with a volunteer board and executive revived the discussion of educational opportunities for working journalists. A mid-career sabbatical? A term studying? Whatever the Foundation landed on, Deacon emphasized that these fellowships would take real money. The directors had confidence in Deacon. He was known as a "pioneer of financial journalism" at the *Financial Post*, and if anyone could do it, Deacon could assemble a powerhouse team to raise the money.[26] He threw himself into the presidency with enthusiasm and dedication that would turn around the Foundation's meagre fortunes.

That first meeting of the new Michener Awards Foundation was a financial reality check. With a bank balance of $4,596.80, the directors quickly turned their attention to the need for some serious fundraising. Deacon proposed a goal of $500,000. If invested, a return of 10 per cent per annum (in 1983) would provide an annual budget of $50,000, enough to cover expenses for the award competition and an education scholarship for a mid-career journalist. The key was getting the right person to chair a fundraising campaign.

The board tossed around names such as Allan Taylor, president of the Royal Bank, Hal Jackman of E-L Financial Corp., and Conrad Black, founder of Hollinger Inc., an investment holding company. In the end, Deacon enlisted Robert J. Wright, a founding partner in Roland Michener's law firm, Lang, Michener, Cranston, Farquharson & Wright (the firm is now known as McMillan) to chair the first campaign. Wright, a graduate of the University of Toronto Schools, Trinity College at the University of Toronto and Osgoode Hall Law School at York University, knew his way around the monied of Toronto. Wright's practice included commercial, intellectual property and criminal law.

Meanwhile, the Michener Award Foundation's bank balance was dwindling as money went to pay for an audit, judging, a new letterhead, stationery and brochures. By April 1984, the treasurer's report showed a bank balance of $1,858.82. Deacon wrote a personal cheque for $1,000, and MacDougall threw in $200 to cover the costs of the November 1984 ceremony.[27] The Foundation closed 1984 with a bank balance of $110.66. A retired Roland Michener came to the rescue by writing a cheque for $2,000 "to help us over the next six months."[28] Donations from Deacon, MacDougall and Michener "helped keep things going for the first two years."[29] Michener continued to support the Foundation through television appearances, interviews, letters to donors and financial contributions. "I don't ask for money, but I thank people for giving it," he said.[30]

When it came to fundraising, Deacon and the board were starting at ground zero. It was a challenging time to be looking for money. The country was just coming out of a severe economic recession that had cut into the advertising revenues of newspapers and broadcasters. In 1983, Statistics Canada recorded prime interest rates of 11.7 per cent, unemployment of 11.8 per cent, and inflation at 5.8 per cent.[31] As the economy improved, so did the industry's financial fortunes, though never to the pre-recession profits of 20 per cent or more that some newspapers experienced, and that their shareholders continued to expect. Little did the media barons realize that within twenty years the biggest threat to profitability and its very existence, the Internet, would hobble newspapers by siphoning off classified advertising and readers.[32]

A year into the campaign, chair Robert J. Wright wrote that after a series of meetings in Toronto in 1984, "It is clear it will not be possible to raise the kind of money . . . originally contemplated." He suggested Deacon scale back the $500,000 campaign goal to a modest $50,000 or $60,000 "to properly fund the award side." Another disappointment was Wright's advice to Deacon to put sabbaticals for mature journalists on hold. Potential donors, Wright wrote, were not interested in funding a fellowship. Neither was Roland Michener. "I think it's fair to say that while he has very strong enthusiasm for the continuation of the awards . . . he is not nearly as supportive of the concept of raising a substantial sum of money and granting bursaries or sabbaticals," Wright wrote. He went on to say that Michener shared the views of other funders "namely, that the primary responsibility for raising monies of this kind should rest on your industry rather than on a general appeal of any kind."[33]

This view became evident to Paul Deacon in a meeting with Beland Honderich, publisher of the *Toronto Star* and chair of Torstar Corp. Deacon got an "unenthusiastic reception" for the idea of Michener study fellowships.[34] The Honderich family and the *Star* were at the beginning stages of establishing the Atkinson Foundation "to fund a $100,000 year-long fellowship for a Canadian journalist to pursue a research project on a topical public issue."[35] Furthermore, the Michener Awards Foundation was not the only organization raising money to elevate the quality of journalism.

The Canadian Journalism Foundation (CJF) was about to be launched in 1991 by a Toronto-centric group of business, government and media executives with excellent money connections. The CJF vision with its focus on lifetime achievement awards, education and research into journalism ethics was eerily similar to the Michener Awards Foundation. The Michener directors may have been confident of their position as the guardians and promoters of journalism excellence, but they knew that, without money, the award's status was in jeopardy.

At the 1985 meeting, the board drew up a three-page list of more than sixty potential donors. Banks. Insurance companies. Airlines. Printers. Pulp and paper companies. Broadcasters. Daily and weekly newspaper groups. Magazines. Advertising companies. Foundations. Breweries. Developers.[36] With the help of the advertising agency Bertram, Peacock and Bush, Wright crafted a pitch letter for potential donors. The directors set the target of this "one-time" campaign at a more modest $150,000. The pitch letter highlighted the cachet of the Foundation's founding patron. "Roland Michener, truly one of the most distinguished and well-loved Canadians of our generation, has agreed to associate himself with us in this manner."[37] It also laid the groundwork for the expansion of the Michener mission. Despite the advice of Wright and the obvious reluctance of Roland Michener and the corporate sector, Paul Deacon had included a line that stated one of the goals was to "eventually establish an annual scholarship or fellowship for mature journalists interested in improving the quality of their work in the public service area."[38] Deacon understood far better than Michener that a study fellowship was a grass-roots investment in the future of journalism in the public service. He also knew that the fellowship was contingent on raising enough money.

It must have been a satisfying moment for Deacon at the November 1985 annual meeting to report that the Foundation's cash flow "is vastly improved over the previous year." The bank balance of $110 had swelled to $12,000. The campaign was starting to produce results, with another $16,000 pledged for 1986. The good news is exactly what Roland Michener wanted to hear. "We haven't had to declare bankruptcy," he said. "It seems to me the award is viable now, and that it will go on." Deacon attributed much of the campaign's success to Michener's strong personal and financial support, to which he replied. "Don't expect that to stop soon. I have no intention to retire."[39] Michener, eighty-five years old, was good on his word. In the autumn of 1986, he gave the Foundation a donation of $12,000 to be retained as capital for ten years.[40]

Paul Deacon was "anxious to increase the momentum" of the campaign. He arranged a lunch with Roland Michener and John Fisher, chairman of the Southam newspaper chain, who agreed to lead round two of the fundraising campaign. Fisher set up a five-person committee, each with a special assignment: George Currie, founder of accounting firm Coopers and Lybrand and former president of Bowater Corporation, directed corporate projects; Michael Davies, owner and publisher of the Kingston *Whig-Standard*, the media; Clark Davey, publisher of the *Montreal Gazette*, corporations; Robert J. Welch, lawyer, politician and Ontario deputy premier in the Bill Davis government, foundations; and Lisa Balfour Bowen, Québec political journalist and art critic, special names.

Balfour Bowen sent the pitch to thirty-seven media, government and businesspeople withstanding in the community. It raised $4,500 from twenty-three individuals, a success rate of 60 per cent. In a memo to John Fisher, she observed that the Michener "isn't everybody's favourite charity" as "many donors continue to perceive the Michener as an award for big newspapers — not small magazines and electronic media" and as a result, they had little interest in giving. It was especially evident in francophone Québec, where her appeal to potential donors such as Pierre Trudeau, Paul Demarais, Gerard Pelletier and Claude Ryan was declined or ignored.[41] The lack of interest from potential francophone donors mirrored the paucity of French-language Michener entries and pointed to a need for some serious long-term bridge-building.

Deacon kicked off the fundraising campaign with the announcement that his employer, Maclean-Hunter, would contribute $50,000 — $10,000 a year for five years.[42] Other media corporations fell in line. By 1987, John Fisher and his team had raised enough money to endow the Michener Award and to cover two annual study fellowships for five years. If the Michener Awards encouraged media organizations to pursue stories in the public interest, the Michener study fellowships, as they were initially called, would be an investment in the education and development of journalists. It was all about building capacity in journalism that creates change to improve the lives of Canadians.

The Michener fellowships were late to the scene. Harvard University had been awarding the Nieman Fellowships since 1938 "to promote and elevate the standards of journalism."[43] The Southam Fellowships at Massey College, started fifteen years earlier, funded mid-career journalists to study at the University of Toronto.[44] Both these fellowships were competitive and ran an entire academic year. In 1987, the Michener fellowships offered journalists $20,000 for four months away from the newsroom — an academic term — and the opportunity to develop expertise, investigate, and write.

Investigate and Educate

Her Excellency Jeanne Sauvé presented the first two Michener fellowships in 1987 to Moira Farrow, a reporter with the *Vancouver Sun*, and Roger Bainbridge, an editor at the *Kingston Whig-Standard*. No two fellowships were the same. Farrow, a visiting scholar at the University of Western Ontario, studied Third World issues. Bainbridge used the time and money to travel and study business magazine models at *Harrowsmith* and *Equinox*.

The fellowship winner the following year, Québec journalist George Tombs, interviewed reporters and editors about their ethical knowledge and practice. His findings showed that journalists think about ethics from time to time "but generally don't have time for it." He found a home for his research in journalism publications, broadcasts and newspapers such as *Le Devoir*. "The prestige of the fellowship has given me greater visibility and has allowed me to be more frank in my judgements. I think I can help a broader debate get started, at least in Québec,"[45] Tombs wrote. In 1995, fellowship winner Sue Rideout revisited the topic. She examined the role culture plays in the ethical decision-making of journalists when it comes to privacy. She concluded that it was "past time" for journalists to learn more when reporting on Canada's multicultural communities.

Jim Romahn of the *Kitchener-Waterloo Record*, the 1988 fellow, was no stranger to the Michener Awards. Reporting by the veteran agriculture reporter had garnered the paper two Micheners and two citations of merit.[46] Romahn spent his term studying at the University of Guelph and wrote articles about the funding and politics surrounding the emerging science of biotechnology. Years before Dolly the sheep, Romahn was learning about cloning and its potential for agriculture. "For example, Dr. Bob Stubbings told how he's taking eggs from unborn calves, fertilizing them in a test tube to create embryos and transplanting the embryos into dairy cows; when he perfects the technique, the purebred cattle industry will probably die because there will be no market left for anything but the absolute best — i.e., only one bull and one cow in 100,000 will be genetic parents."[47] The time and money from the fellowship gave journalists like Tombs, Rideout and Romahn a chance to deepen their knowledge and reflect on their day-to-day practices, which was reflected in the journalism they produced.

The recipients cast a wide net and produced original research and articles of interest and value to audiences. The fellowship allowed internationally focused journalists to study politics in countries such as Italy, the Soviet Union, Catalonia and Slovenia, and human rights in Southeast Asia. Some fellows photographed people and landscapes ravaged by developers and acts of nature.[48] Others looked at the roles of Canadian institutions such as the public broadcaster,[49] the federal public service[50] and the developing ethical relationship between universities and drug companies.[51] In the late 1990s and early 2000s, the fellowship bought time to write books that ranged from the history of investigative journalism to genetics and web porn.[52] Many of the investigations are stories that continue to make headlines, such as the crisis in children's mental health[53] and Canadian aid to Afghanistan.[54]

For working journalists, the fellowship proved to be "an exceptional moment"[55] in their careers. Jean-Pierre Rogel, the 1998 Investigative Fellow, said that the four months this award gave him away from the pressures of daily reporting allowed him to learn and write a book, *La Grande Saga des Genes,* about human genetics. "I would not have been able to write this book without this award. I now have a more profound concept of science and a renewed interest towards journalism," he wrote in his report. "At a time when newsrooms are being downsized and budgets cut, this fellowship allows journalists to continue the tradition of investigating subjects that need to be written about." The fellowships would evolve to meet the changing needs of journalism and the industry.

Incubating and Reinventing Journalism

For the first twenty-five years of the study fellowship program, the Foundation supported individual journalists to build specialty expertise and produce investigative stories. While that was still important, in 2012 the board recognized that journalism education was an untapped area that could help to encourage a culture of public service journalism among students.

Alongside the fellowship for investigative reporting, a second one with an education focus allowed experienced journalists to partner with a university to research and teach cutting-edge newsroom developments in journalism schools. This expansion gave scope for mid-career journalists to reflect on and even intervene through their research and teaching on the state of their industry.

The first 2012 Michener-Deacon fellow, Melanie Coulson, a senior editor at the *Ottawa Citizen,* conducted research about community newsrooms and citizen journalism, and she taught a multimedia journalism class to third-year undergraduates. "I fully submerged myself in a community that means so much to me: at Carleton's journalism school, with students who will be on the vanguard of change in our industry," she wrote.[56] In subsequent years other recipients developed courses in entrepreneurial journalism, big data and social media for journalism students.[57]

Matthew Pearson remembers the muggy June night in 2017 when he received the fellowship. Pearson, a municipal reporter and editor at the *Ottawa Citizen,* proposed developing an education module for students and journalists about trauma and journalism. He was surprised by what happened at the reception. "Almost immediately I was being taken aside by journalists and hearing their stories and hearing them say, we've never talked about this, there's no support for this and getting the sense that wow, this is something that is needed."[58] The fellowship acknowledged it was time for journalists to shine the spotlight on themselves. In the performance of their public interest role, journalists were becoming burned out. They were also becoming targets for threats, harassment and verbal abuse. They needed one of their own to step back, give them advice and arm up-and-coming journalists.

The fellowship led Pearson out of day-to-day reporting at the *Ottawa Citizen* and into the classroom. He says the time to step back gave him a research agenda and was the "springboard" to a tenure-track teaching job at Carleton's School of Journalism in 2021. "The fellowship opened my eyes to research in a journalistic space and allowed me to see how I could expand my horizons through research that is still connected to and informed by journalistic practice in Canada. And it's really exciting," Pearson said. "I would not be where I am today if it weren't for that fellowship because I wouldn't have had that initial taste." The work he did as a Michener fellow became a "launch pad" for his latest research project, "Taking Care," "the first of its kind and national research survey on mental health, wellbeing and trauma in Canadian journalism."[59]

Pearson's Michener certificate is on his office wall at Carleton for students to see. "My degrees aren't there, but the Michener one is, and I do recognize that that was such a turning point in my professional life and, and really helped me see that there was a different avenue to explore in journalism that is still quite powerful because it is a really hard thing to leave a job as a practising journalist. Many of us love our work. And this allowed me to see how I could do both."[60]

The second fellowship in education also opened doors for journalists to develop new models for practising journalism in the public interest. In 2015, *Toronto Star* reporter Rob Cribb used his fellowship to create the framework for a National Investigative Reporting Project, a network of journalism schools that harnesses the energy and enthusiasm of students to work with media outlets on in-depth stories of national public interest. It was something that had never been done before in Canada. Cribb's vision was to give young reporters "the unique experience of contributing to ambitious, aggressive journalism alongside seasoned professionals. And media organizations who take part are distinguished by the stories, the resulting public debate and the opportunity to see emerging young talent up close."[61]

Cribb says the genesis of the idea came from his teaching at Ryerson University (renamed Toronto Metropolitan University in 2022). He found it impossible to finish student projects in twelve weeks because "investigations don't work on an academic timeline." There was no mechanism to move them forward. At the time, newspaper editors were not interested in student work that needed more fact-checking and interviews and could be fraught with potential legal problems.

For Cribb, that changed in 2011. The work that his class did was too important to let moulder. Their investigation into academic "credit mills" at private for-a-fee provincially licensed schools revealed, "a two-tiered education system that allowed those with the lowest grades to get the highest grades and get scholarships."[62] So when the term ended, Cribb worked nights and weekends checking facts, doing more interviews and hiring students to help. In September, the *Toronto Star* published the first of the series: "Cash for marks gets kids into university."[63] Cribb said it was an experiment with moving an in-depth piece from the classroom into the newsroom and then onto the front page.

"It was dynamite." There was an investigation, and the students saw their bylines on the front page of Canada's largest circulation newspaper. Cribb spent the next four years refining the Ryerson-*Toronto Star* collaborative model and went into his Michener-Deacon fellowship, convinced it could be scaled up to involve other journalism schools and media partners across the country.

The following year, Patti Sonntag, the newly appointed "journalist in residence" at Concordia University in Montreal, used her 2016 fellowship to test drive a prototype of Cribb's model. Students and professors from four universities and journalists from the *Toronto Star, National Observer* and *Global News* teamed up to produce the series "The Price of Oil."[64] In a series of stories in various media, they documented toxic emissions from oil and gas facilities in Saskatchewan and Ontario.

Buoyed by that success, Concordia University created the Institute for Investigative Journalism (IIJ) with a founding grant from the Rossy Family Foundation and named Patti Sonntag its first director.[65] The IIJ was a consortium of newsrooms and universities based at Concordia University in

Montreal, Québec, modelled on a blueprint Cribb developed as a Michener fellow in 2015.

The IIJ's first project led by Sonntag and Cribb, "Tainted Water," involved 120 people — journalism students and faculty from nine post-secondary institutions and journalists from six media outlets: *Global News*, *Le Devoir*, the *Toronto Star*, the *Star* Halifax/ Vancouver/ Calgary/ Edmonton, the Regina *Leader-Post* and the *National Observer*. The series took an in-depth look at lead and other contaminants in drinking water. "What we found is that Montreal, Gatineau, Saskatoon, Regina, Moose Jaw and Prince Rupert had lead levels comparable or higher than those of Flint, Michigan, during its 2015 lead crisis,"[66] Sonntag said.

The series racked up a string of awards, including a nomination for the 2019 Michener Award, the first non-traditional media outlet ever to receive a nomination. "Tainted Water had swift impact, with Canada-wide commitments to replace lead pipes and test water more rigorously. More importantly, it represents a new way forward; a new way to produce great public-service journalism," noted the Michener Awards Foundation news release.[67] "It was amazing," Cribb said, his eyes sparkling. "We just gave birth to this thing. And the first project is . . . is magical." The success led to subsequent investigations into drinking water on Indigenous reserves and, when COVID-19 hit, "Project Pandemic."

Cribb has taken the model one step further with his Toronto-based Investigative Journalism Bureau (IJB) at the Dalla Lana School of Public Health at the University of Toronto (2020).[68] Young journalists, media outlets, law students and academic experts from multiple universities work together in what Cribb says is an independent non-profit newsroom. Cribb credits his fellowship for the success of the IJB and its inaugural project, "Generation Distress"— an investigation into rising anxiety, depression, suicidal ideas and self-harm among young people.[69]

5

The Foundation Sets Its Course

By 1987 the Michener Awards Foundation was on a roll. In five years, it had achieved a modicum of financial stability to endow the Michener Awards and fund the creation of new fellowships. Journalists and media executives coveted the award. Industry respected the Michener judging panels for their impartiality and independence in adjudicating both the awards and the inevitable disputes. All this arose from an understanding of the place of the Michener Awards in Canadian journalism.[1] It was a vision shared and promoted by industry volunteers, inspired leaders and successive governors general. But these developments did not necessarily guarantee success for the organization or the award, given the flux in the industry.

The predictions of the Kent and Davey commissions were being realized. Media organizations had ramped up buying, selling, mergers and closures. Readership was in freefall. Advertising had shrunk following the 1987 stock market crash, known as Black Monday. The poor economy, limited fundraising and the formation of a new, well-funded rival — the Canadian Journalism Foundation — were all reminders to the Michener Award Foundation volunteer board members that they could not take the claims to be Canada's premier journalism award for granted.

As the Michener Foundation approached its twentieth anniversary, the directors were presented with an interesting proposition — an offer to be part of the new journalism organization. The proposal would create an existential moment for the Michener Foundation and everything the award represented.

In 1986, the journalism community in central Canada was abuzz with news that the country's top business leaders, politicians, journalism executives and educators were forming a new journalism organization — the Canadian Journalism Foundation. The CJF, as it's now known, had connections, money and ambitions to bring the National Newspaper Awards and the Michener Awards under its umbrella.[2] Toronto businessman Eric Jackman, the driving force behind the CJF's creation, wanted "to have the same kind of distinction and style the Pulitzer Prize does in the U.S." Jackman's vision was "to create an award which would be so prestigious — money and recognition-wise — that journalists receiving it would say, 'I don't have to feel bad about myself because of my profession, I'm not really an ink-stained wretch.' And young journalists would say, 'What did that person do to get that award, how can I emulate him — what judgement, sensitivity and responsibility did he bring to his writing'."[3]

A CJF partnership proposal in 1989 forced the Michener board to take a hard look at who it was, what it wanted and how much it was prepared to give up. It raised tough questions about how the Foundation would negotiate its independence: resisting Jackman's overture would have consequences. It would mean giving up substantial grants from Jackman's foundation and forgoing other well-placed donors who would have provided ongoing financial security for the Michener Awards Foundation. Ultimately, however, the Michener founders would take no step to jeopardize the Foundation's relationship with Rideau Hall or its reputation for independent adjudication. In a sense, this decision sacrificed one form of independence for another, as the Foundation gave up potential financial stability to maintain its ethical and professional autonomy — an important stand, but one that would require ongoing negotiation and grit in the face of economic and legal challenges.

Judging: Preserving the Reputation

From day one, the reputation of the Michener Award had rested on the quality of its journalistic judgement. The administrators of the Michener Award understood the quality of the judging was crucial for the success and credibility of the award. If it was going to be the best, then the award and those judging it would have to be above reproach — independent of the industry, funders, Rideau Hall and even the Federation of Press Clubs. It would not be an award judged by peers, as with other industry awards. Its judges would be arm's-length and experienced former reporters, editors, publishers and journalism educators.

It had taken some time for Bill MacPherson to assemble the first panel to judge the 1970 entries. But the roster sent a clear message that the Michener Award was above partisan self-interest. It would not be beholden to any media outlet or other interests. The all-white male panel looked like an old boys' club — a common sight in the senior echelons of journalism back then — but each member had heft. They came to the judging table with years of journalism experience but were no longer affiliated with or involved in the day-to-day operations of a news organization.

The first chair, Davidson Dunton, was president of Carleton University. He had started as a reporter at the *Montreal Star* and went on to become editor of the *Montreal Standard*, a national pictorial weekly newspaper. At the age of thirty-three, he became the first full-time chair of the Canadian Broadcasting Corporation. Dunton oversaw the creation of a national CBC network before taking the top job at Carleton in 1958 and serving as the co-chair of the Royal Commission on Bilingualism and Biculturalism in 1963.

Dunton was joined on the judging panel by George Ferguson, editor emeritus of the *Montreal Star* and a former Rhodes scholar, Yves Gagnon, director of Communications at Laval University, and Sam Ross, a journalism lecturer at Vancouver's Langara College and retired Parliamentary Bureau Chief for the All-Canada Mutually Operated radio group. Together they assessed the 1970 Michener submissions for their impact and contribution to the public interest. Over the years, judges would come and go — some would sit on the judging panel for a year or two, most for longer. Dunton left after two years, but Ross sat as a judge for five years and Gagnon for seven.

There's a rhythm to the judging process. At the start of each year, anticipation builds as the chief judge waits to see how many applications from the previous calendar year will arrive by the February deadline. A lot depends on the media outlets. Their financial health often dictates the investment in investigative journalism and submissions to the Michener Award. The 1987 stock market crash saw entries fall to thirty-nine after an all-time high of seventy-four the year before. The pandemic of 2020-21 from the COVID-19 virus created a firestorm of breaking news and updates unsuited to a Michener-worthy investigation and resulted in the number of Michener entries bottoming out at sixteen. The churning of the world's powerful forces combined with the internal storms in each media organization made predicting the number of applicants each year akin to trying to forecast the weather in Nova Scotia, where conditions change by the hour.

It was an analog world for the first forty years of the Micheners. The chief judge and a board member would meet at the *Ottawa Citizen*, the collection point for the entries. Then the sorting would begin, hours spent ripping open envelopes and boxes, checking to make sure each outlet sent five copies of the submission, with supporting material and then divvying up the submissions destined for the judges. Five boxes, each stuffed with tear sheets from news-papers and audio and video tapes are then shipped to the judges.

With that, the judges could begin the real work of the Michener Awards Foundation. Whether there are seventy-four or sixteen entries, singling out the top six finalists and then the award-winner is a daunting task. Judges spend hours and hours over many weeks in the privacy of their homes watch-ing, listening and reading each entry. They're looking for professional, un-biased, arm's-length reporting. But that's not enough. Judges seek evidence of outcomes — stories that have had an impact on the public or helped to change public policy or practices. The effects can be local, provincial, national or a community of people or interests. The judges are sensitive to an organiz-ation's resources and staffing. That makes it possible for small media outlets such as the *Prince George Citizen* in B.C., the *Nunatsiaq News* in Nunavut and Cogeco's Montréal radio station 98.5 FM to compete with well-resourced national media such as the *Globe and Mail*, CBC or *Toronto Star*. In short, the Michener Awards Foundation's criteria and judging system were developed not just to honour the industry's biggest and most powerful media actors, but also to nurture the values of public service in all media outlets across the country.

In year three of the award, Fraser MacDougall, the executive secretary of the Ontario Press Council, took over as chief judge, a position he held for eighteen years. With the precision of the Canadian Press wire service editor he had been, MacDougall set out criteria in a memo to guide his fellow judges in selecting a Michener winner. Number one was the importance of public ser-vice intended. MacDougall explained the process: "Theoretically this might range from a design to save mankind — physically or spiritually or both — to local promotion of a remedy for dandruff in cats. Practically, in the Canadian context, the goal of an equitable federal tax system, or elimination of partisan influence from a province's administration of justice, or by securing of a safe water supply for a village, might reasonably be given high scores."[4]

Next on MacDougall's checklist was the "validity of factual material" presented in a clear, forceful and persuasive manner. "Measurable, probable or potential impact" of the entry was also significant, as was the "sweat quo-tient" involved in the piece of journalism. He gave this example of how to rank effort. "A low benchmark here might be the simple reprinting of material prepared by others. The high might be a brilliant analysis of a constitutional issue or a high-powered piece of journalistic advocacy." The last criterion on

MacDougall's list was disinterestedness, defined as "above and beyond what the medium should normally be doing in the way of public service." For a group establishing its reputation, the criteria provided a valuable framework to guide the judges in determining the best journalism with impact.

By the early to mid-2000s, the formal weighted judging system would disappear. Somewhere along the way, it had morphed from a formal set of guidelines to an informal ethos. Carleton University journalism professor Chris Waddell sat at the judging table for nine years, until 2017. He brought to the judging table seventeen years of experience in print and broadcast, as well as academic rigour. "I don't recall there being any sort of rubric at all." But he said the judging mandate was clear. "It was always stories that had an impact and had some demonstrated results" that would lead to action to remedy the situation so it wouldn't happen again. In most years, four or five entries would stand out from the rest. Waddell explained, "Of the five judges, about six [entries] would be the same by all of them. Then each of them would have a couple of others that they like, maybe because they were from that region of the country or they knew a bit more about that issue or something else. So even if there wasn't a rubric, people seemed to agree on what story should be important."[5]

Until the COVID-19 pandemic hit in early 2020, the Michener judging panel met in person to select the finalists and the winner. The process could be compared to picking a pope. Go into a room, close the door, pitch, listen, discuss and eventually reach a consensus. Daily and weekly newspapers, television and radio broadcasters, online publications and magazines from all corners of the country. English, French. There was even an Italian entry in the days before Google Translate. When the judges leave the room, they have a winner and finalists. When the news release goes out a few weeks later, most publishers, editors and reporters nod with approval at the finalists, especially when they see their organization on the list. In the beginning, the judges would announce the winner months before the ceremony, but since 1978, the winner remains a tightly guarded secret until the night of the award ceremony.

The integrity of the Michener Award rests on the work of the judging panel. The Foundation does everything to ensure it is separate and independent from the board and its membership. The only job of the panel is judging. The chief judge is the one who reports to the board. The firewall is respected so much so that, in 1996, the judging process was a revelation to newly elected president Clark Davey when he helped chief judge Arch MacKenzie sort and catalogue fifty-seven entries. Davey was captivated by an entry from the *Telegraph Journal* in Saint John, New Brunswick, all thirty-one pages about the plight of Canada's salmon streams. It "gave me an insight into the daunting tasks the judges face each year, but I was gratified to hear when I had lunch with them . . . that they had a remarkable convergence of opinion on which were the top entries," Davey reported. "Arch's organization and direction of the judging process for both the award and the fellowships is a major job of work which we should all appreciate."[6] The president and directors of the Foundation might appreciate the work of the judges — and they might help with administrative tasks, like sorting the entries — but they had no role or say in deciding which entries were the best.

It has been the practice to select judges with extensive journalism experience, who are no longer in the news business and have stellar reputations. "The Michener Award was considered then as it is now to be the top journalism award in Canada. It has preserved that reputation with the quality of people. People looked behind the screen and see the names associated [with judging] are good people," explained Russ Mills, chief judge 2004-2009.[7]

The judges have spent their lives immersed in the practice, management and, in some cases, teaching journalism. They're no longer affiliated with a journalism outlet, which gives them an independence not found in industry-run awards in print, magazine and broadcast. Four-time Michener Award winner Victor Malarek says that makes all the difference. "These are people from the outside who look at a whole body of work and determine whether your investigation merits public service journalism. And that to me means more than a bunch of people from the journalism community voting or not voting with you because they like you or dislike you."[8]

The independence of the judging process is a point of pride for the Michener Foundation — one that the board has protected at all costs. This principle, and how far the Michener Foundation was willing to protect it, came to the forefront when the backers of the Canadian Journalism Foundation came calling.

Merger or Independence: An Existential Crisis

The rumblings of a new journalism foundation had been on the Michener radar for some time. Three years earlier, in January 1986, an exploratory overture had been made when Paul Deacon was on the hunt for money to fund Michener study fellowships for working journalists. Deacon and Roland Michener thought the Jackman (family) Foundation, with its focus on education, would be a good fit for funding. They met for lunch with Dr. Frederic L. R. (Eric) Jackman, the Foundation's chair, on January 29, 1986. In the discussion, Deacon found Eric Jackman to be "super confident that he understands what's needed."[9] But it quickly became clear to Deacon that Jackman had something else in mind when it came to supporting journalism. His vision made Deacon bristle.

The next day Deacon wrote his concerns to Michener. "Our discussion with Eric Jackman on Wednesday continues to bother me a bit. My interpretation of his approach is that he's selling a 'be kind to politicians' education program." Deacon recognized that Jackman's vision would find a sympathetic audience, especially among those with money. "There'll be lots of bruised businessmen as well as bruised politicians who would love to find some way of making journalists more compliant." Deacon was concerned that he had come on too strong at the meeting with Jackman. "I found it hard to contain my horror," he wrote, and then asked Michener if he was overreacting, before concluding, "I suspect we should keep our distance and not get tied in with him in any way."[10] Michener gave Deacon his full support. "I concur in the suggestion you made about keeping distance. He [Eric Jackman] and I are good friends. I enjoyed his company at lunch recently. He pursues his program on his own and we may hear from him again. He is not getting much encouragement from the media."[11]

But three years later, in 1989, as word spread about the creation of the Canadian Journalism Foundation, some journalism educators and reporters shared Deacon's earlier skepticism about the motivations of this new alliance of elite industry, government and media managers. That's because its genesis was a research project about Canada's media — initiated by the Niagara Institute for International Studies, a business-focused think-tank, and funded by the Jackman Foundation. The Institute's director, W. C. Wilton, had conducted more than seventy confidential in-camera interviews with executives from media, business and government. There was an emphasis on the latter two sectors "that are generally suspicious of the media," according to Alberta newspaper executive J. Patrick O'Callaghan, who represented the Southam newspaper chain at the early planning meetings.[12]

O'Callaghan wrote in his memoir, *Maverick Publisher*, that the Niagara report "Canada's Media," released in July 1988, raised "concerns about the media's balance, accuracy, professionalism, ethics, agenda-setting, scarce resources and accountability." From O'Callaghan's point of view, the undertone of the Niagara report was that "these cynical critics wanted a tamed and subservient media."[13] The report's findings had a similar ring to Deacon's conversation with Jackman in 1986.

O'Callaghan, never shy with his words, butted heads with other members of the tony Canadian Journalism Foundation's media advisory committee.[14] "From the start I was not on the same wavelength because I believe a free press should steer clear of all those who want to bring it under the Establishment's heel," O'Callaghan wrote.[15] Once he divined the group's direction, O'Callaghan left the committee in the spring of 1989 to devote his energies to the Michener Awards Foundation, where he had been a director since 1984. O'Callaghan brought an insider perspective of the CJF media advisory committee to the Michener table. His presence on the Michener board proved crucial when the CJF made a second overture.

In 1989, Bill Dimma, president and CEO of major realtor Royal LePage and former Torstar executive and York University dean of business, reached out on behalf of the CJF to broker an association with the Michener Awards Foundation. It was easy to see how the Michener Awards — a well-established and respected organization — would be a huge boost to the nascent CJF. For almost twenty years, the Micheners had honoured Canada's best journalism in the public interest. While not monied, the award had the prestige of the Michener name, continued vice-regal patronage, and an annual gala ceremony at Rideau Hall. But the CJF was also well aware of the Foundation's financial ups and downs.

This time, Paul Deacon didn't bristle. He responded with cautious enthusiasm. While he didn't necessarily agree with the CJF's philosophy and approach, he was pragmatic. There was value in the financial stability that the CJF could offer, as he explained in a memo to the Michener board of directors in October 1989. "It's hard to tell at this stage whether the Journalism Foundation will get the funding it will need to do all the things it plans, and whether, if we joined forces in some way, they could help our problems of continuity, permanence and money. But I believe it's worth pursuing."[16] Deacon then wrote to Dimma, who was working with Trevor Eyton, president and CEO of Brascan, a resource-based holding company, and Eric Jackman to set up the new organization. The group already had start-up funding of $100,000.[17] This kind of money was inaccessible to the Michener Foundation.

John Miller, chair of Ryerson's School of Journalism and a judge for the Michener study fellowships, shared O'Callaghan's concerns about the agenda of the new Foundation. After meeting for lunch with Eric Jackman, Miller came away with the impression that Jackman "had a very low opinion of journalists and that's what set off the alarm bells for me." As Miller recalled, "He wasn't interested in public service at all. He was interested in hardworking businesspeople who got bad press."[18] Miller was alarmed when he caught wind of a possible partnership between the CJF and the Micheners and wrote to Deacon, advising caution. "Meritorious public service in journalism often is not compatible with what businessmen see as good journalism, and for that reason, I think you should be wary."[19] Deacon replied, "Unless they can assure us that the independence and objectivity of the Michener Foundation can be continued, I'm afraid there may not be much point in pursuing the matter."[20] Still, Deacon left the door open.

During a discussion of the Michener Foundation's future at the annual meeting of November 1989, Deacon raised the idea of a possible affiliation. "The CJF's final organization pattern isn't settled, but its discussions to date have visualized it being an umbrella organization that would try to heighten public awareness of existing awards and programs and possibly help fund them,"[21] Deacon explained. Some board members could see benefits to sharing administrative costs and fundraising. Not O'Callaghan, a self-described "token dissident."[22] At the board meeting, he actively opposed any "take-over by the CJF" and argued strongly to maintain "our independence."[23] His view prevailed. Deacon delivered the message to Bill Dimma at a dinner meeting the following week. "I told him that the Foundation board feels the Michener program should maintain its name and its independence."[24] Deacon did offer to explore ways to cooperate with the CJF to raise the profile of the program and to promote good journalism, but for the most part, the two organizations went their own ways for the next 29 years.[25]

In the 1990s, the Canadian Journalism Foundation attracted corporate donors that had eluded the Michener Foundation — donors such as Senator Trevor Eyton, Bill Dimma, Eric Jackman and Mickey Cohen (Molson Brewery). The Jackman Foundation donated $100,000 in 1990 for the CJF's first interim budget on the condition that the CJF could raise another $500,000. It seems that the CJF had no problem gaining funding. By 1994, it was sponsoring a series of seminars on how to improve Canadian journalism and raising serious money.

Clark Davey reported to the annual meeting of the Michener Awards Foundation that the CJF had established an office and raised $250,000. The knock-on effect was that the Micheners and the National Newspaper Awards were having trouble signing on new donors. With prospects for new donors looking grim, Davey, now president of the Michener Foundation, expressed concern about an exodus of longtime donors.[26] Davey had written to "45 major suppliers of electronic and printing equipment" and received only one positive reply.

The Michener board must have been aghast when Governor General Roméo LeBlanc opened the doors of Rideau Hall to the Canadian Journalism Foundation. On May 31, 1996, the CJF held its first awards ceremony with co-chairs Knowlton Nash of the CBC's *The National* and Roger Landry of *La Presse*. The first CJF lifetime achievement award honoured Toronto journalist and author Robert Fulford. Neil Reynolds of the Irving-owned Saint John *Telegraph Journal* and *Evening Times Globe* in New Brunswick received the Excellence in Journalism award. After the ceremony, LeBlanc hosted a stand-up reception.

There was good reason for the Michener Awards Foundation to be a wee bit territorial. For twenty-six years, Rideau Hall had hosted the Michener Awards, upon the initiative of former Governor General Roland Michener. The Foundation was not keen to share the venue and the prestige that went with it. By rejecting the CJF's partnership proposal, it put the two organizations in an unstated competition. For the Micheners, the stakes were high.

The concerns were amplified when the CJF awards ceremony was back at Rideau Hall the following year. It appeared to the Michener board that the CJF was "building it in as a permanent part of their program."[27] The board could not quell the fear that the CJF wanted to swallow up the Michener Awards, and they seemed to have support from Rideau Hall. In 1997, when the Canadian Journalism Foundation approached Government House about its Rideau Hall ceremony, "the initial response was a strong suggestion that the CJF and Michener Awards should be handed out at the same occasion," Davey reported. "I have also been told that I will get an invite to lunch with the Governor General [LeBlanc] to discuss the Michener Award, so I expect the pressure to continue," Davey wrote in a letter.[28]

To nip the CJF initiative in the bud, Davey proposed that Rideau Hall support an umbrella organization or event such as the Governor General's Journalism Awards modelled on the awards for literature and the arts. But

His Excellency Roméo LeBlanc showed no interest.[29] His attention was focused on his newly founded Governor General's Caring Canadian Awards which celebrated ordinary people doing extraordinary things. The Michener board must have breathed a sigh of relief in 1998 when the CJF decided to move its awards ceremony to Toronto, the centre of its funding base.

After that close brush with the CJF and partnership, the Michener executive kept a close eye on what was going on in Toronto. A tinge of resentment could be seen in the minutes over the CJF's financial success "with its annual budget of $280,000 from the corporate world."[30] In a letter to a board member, Clark Davey remarked that the CFJ "pays its part-time director $90,000!!!"[31] This was in contrast to the Michener Awards Foundation with its operating budget of less than $30,000, volunteer labour and no paid staff. Davey did not miss an opportunity to gloat when the CJF's competition for the second annual award for newsroom excellence had attracted only a single entry several weeks after its deadline. "We had 44," wrote Davey.[32] The robust number of entries seemed to affirm the board's decision eight years earlier to say no to the CJF to guard the independence of the awards, even if the move shut out new sources of funding and stunted opportunities for growing the Foundation. Relations with the CJF over the next thirty years remained polite but cautious.

Over the years, the Michener Awards Foundation's independence gave judges the freedom to break from the pack and make bold decisions. For example, in 2013 the Michener judges paid no regard when the National Newspaper Awards (NNA) failed to nominate the *Toronto Star*'s entry for its extensive coverage in 2013 of Rob Ford's disgraceful behaviour as Mayor of Toronto. Maybe NNA judges dismissed the municipal series as "just the traditional Toronto media blowing a Toronto story out of proportion," mused Chris Waddell, a former judge for the Michener Award and the Canadian Journalism Foundation's Excellence in Journalism Award.[33] Others suggested the series was overshadowed by more important newspaper stories. It had been a banner year for hard-hitting stories.

So, when the *Toronto Star* entry made the list of six finalists for the Michener Award, there were raised eyebrows. The Ford series was competing with CTV for its exposé of the Senate scandal, the *Canadian Press* for its coverage of Ottawa's shabby treatment of veterans, the *Globe and Mail*'s investigation into the Lac-Mégantic rail disaster, the *Edmonton Journal* and *Calgary Herald*'s examination of the deaths of Indigenous children in foster care and the *Windsor Star* for issues with Cancer Care Ontario and thoracic surgery procedures. The ballroom at Rideau Hall crackled with tension on that June evening.

The judges' citation got to the heart of why the series was Michener-worthy — the *Star*'s tenacity and courage that led to measurable change in Canada's largest city.

"Despite intimidation and an organized campaign trying to undermine the credibility of the reporting, the *Toronto Star* exposed Ford's public drunkenness, boorish behaviour, abuses of his office and existence of a video of him smoking crack cocaine accompanied by members of a drug gang. *The Star* did not waiver [sic] as the mayor countered every story with vehement denials and attacks. Behind the scenes the Toronto police launched an investigation that proved all the *Star*'s allegations to be true. Going to court to win the release of details about the police investigation, the *Star*'s work led the council of Canada's largest city to remove all powers from the mayor, leaving him just a figurehead."[34]

When Russ Mills announced the *Toronto Star* as the winner of the 2013 Michener Award, the newspaper's publisher, John Honderich, shot up out of his seat, threw his arms up in victory and, with an ear-to-ear smile, bellowed, "Yes!" It was vindication. Later, Honderich would say that the Rob Ford story "was probably one of the greatest threats to the paper because they [supporters of Rob Ford, the Ford Nation] wanted to launch a full boycott of advertisers and readers. But the moral corruption and behaviour was so egregious that to let it sit there unchallenged would have been awful."[35] The *Star*'s coverage helped defeat Rob Ford and elect a new council in Toronto.

"Rob Ford was the right decision to make. Absolutely," said Waddell who sat on the judging panel that year. "In retrospect, it was even a better decision to make than it looked like at the time. *The Star* pursued Ford very aggressively. Everything they said about Ford turned out to be true. . . . And what more can you ask for in an era of misinformation, disinformation."[36] The collective experience of the judges, combined with their distance from the industry, gave the Michener judges a unique perspective on entries. Moreover, it allowed them to be guided by the Michener values of public service and impact — enabling them to nominate, and reward, stories that other organizations overlooked.

Judging: Complaints and Intimidation

Experienced judges need the distance and experience to deal with thin-skinned publishers, editors and reporters — and to maintain their independence. Many a judge over the years has found warm, chummy encounters before the awards ceremony turn rather frosty at the reception and dinner that follow. It is not unusual for a bruised publisher, editor or reporter to corner the chief judge to pronounce how the panel got it all wrong, while eyes are fixed on their rivals celebrating across the room. Complaints and calls to rescind nominations, and even awards, have come from business and community leaders stinging from the bad publicity. They have also come from other journalism outlets suffering from a case of self-righteous sour grapes. Over the years, media outlets with grievances have tried to sway the independent judging panel's decisions.

For example, in April 2001, *the fifth estate* was on the list of Michener finalists for its six-part series on "how police and justice officials approach their jobs, the techniques they use and the way they respond to mistakes."[37] Within days, chief judge David Humphreys received a fax, as did the *Globe and Mail*, the *Toronto Star* and the *National Post*, complaining that the same story about the Saskatchewan justice system had appeared in the Saskatoon *Star Phoenix* a year earlier. This was not, of course, the first time a publication had claimed to have broken a story that another entry would pick up, develop in much greater detail, and then submit as a Michener entry. The *Globe, Star* and *Post* likely saw the complaint as groundless because none of their papers published the complaint. As Humphreys reported at the May annual meeting, "Since the issue did not become public, no action was taken." At the awards ceremony that night, a beaming David Studer, executive producer of *the fifth estate,* stood beside Her Excellency Adrienne Clarkson to receive the Michener Award.

Any journalistic awards organization can expect whinging, complaints and threats; some deserve more than a shrug. As head of the Michener Awards judging panels, a respectful reply was appropriate for a complaint in 2016. Société Radio-Canada's *Enquête* received the 2015 Michener Awards for its coverage of allegations from Indigenous women of ongoing physical and sexual abuse by Quebec's provincial police (SQ) in the northern community of Val d'Or. "And together, with one voice, they denounced for the first time publicly the abusive behavior of Val d'Or police officers. Sexual assault, abuse of power, intimidation, 'geographic cures' (a police tactic which consists of punishing an individual by transporting him several kilometers from home and forcing him to return on foot), from police officers who should normally protect them," wrote Jean Pelletier, editor-in-chief of *Enquête*.[38]

After an investigation announced no charges would be laid against the accused officers, a competitor emailed to ask if the Michener Foundation would be rescinding the award. After consulting the panel, as chief judge, I responded that the decision of the judging panel stood because *Enquête*'s broadcast had resulted in important outcomes — including an investigation and a $6 million assistance program for Indigenous women in the community — and was not contingent on subsequent legal decisions.[39] The complaint deserved a response, but ultimately the board felt that the judges had done their job — and supported their independent decision.

Sometimes complaints come from Michener board members who are not at arm's length and who have a direct interest in the outcome of the Michener Award. In one case, it was John Honderich, a long-serving Michener director and editor of Canada's largest newspaper, the *Toronto Star*. Honderich challenged the judges' decision to give the 1993 award to the *Ottawa Citizen*. The story involved the Mulroney government's plan to privatize the Toronto Pearson airport.

In a three-page letter to the Michener Awards Foundation, Honderich called for a decision review. Simply put, his letter argued that the *Citizen* did not "break this story" as was stated in the Foundation's press release and repeated several times during the awards ceremony. He could "only assume that the judging panel made its decision on a false premise." That's something no chief judge wants to hear. While *The Star* did not enter its coverage, Honderich included a folder of clippings that showed the *Star* was at least two weeks ahead of the *Citizen* on this story. His letter requested action "for the prestige of the awards." [40]

Honderich also sent his letter to the *Ottawa Citizen*. Its editor, James Travers, took the initiative and wrote a stiff letter to chief judge Arch MacKenzie demanding "to put the record straight."[41] He stated that the *Citizen* did not claim to have broken the story. Travers wrote its only claim was that by revealing confidential cabinet information, it "turned an existing story into a national scandal" that prevented the privatization of the airport. With no love lost, the *Citizen* then made the *Star*'s complaint public. An article by Chris Cobb, the *Citizen*'s media writer, quoted liberally from both letters. Soon, the story was on the national wire service Canadian Press, and newspapers across the country ran the story of the *Toronto Star* taking on the *Ottawa Citizen*. When reminded of the brouhaha in a 2019 interview, Honderich responded with a big grin, "I loved that, you know."

With all this material in hand, Chief Judge Arch MacKenzie wrote a confidential memo to the judging panel. First off, "we are agreed that who got what first isn't really relevant, especially when the complainant didn't enter." Then MacKenzie fell on his sword. "I think we may agree that I as writer of the news release erred in saying that *The Citizen* 'broke' the story. . . . I should have said something like 'break open' and I will carry the can on that one."[42]

Two days later, the Michener Awards Foundation issued a news release confirming the *Ottawa Citizen*'s win. It stated that the *Citizen* stories, "based on internal documents from the Conservative government, broke the Toronto airport story wide open in the middle of an election campaign" and were "key to exposing secretive developments adversely affecting the flying public, the taxpayer, the air industry and Pearson as a hub of the Canadian airline system."[43] *The Star* ran a story based on the news release and Arch MacKenzie wrote to John Honderich saying that he assumed the matter was closed. It was for the Foundation, but not for Honderich, who for years remained willing to defend his reporters and argue the *Star*'s case.

Complaints of a different order arrive in white envelopes, with no signature, no return address, just a typed note, news article and an affidavit to remind the Michener judges that the publisher, editors and reporters of a certain entry could be facing a lawsuit. The correspondence is intended to influence the judging process, and maybe even convince the judges to withdraw a nomination. One case involved the *Daily Herald* in Prince Albert, Saskatchewan, a finalist in 1994 for its "tenacious enquiry into spending practices by municipal politicians and officials . . . All but one of the incumbent city councillors seeking re-election lost his job."[44]

The City Commissioner, who also lost his job, had filed an intention to sue the *Daily Herald*, its publisher and editors.[45] Threats of a libel and slander lawsuit against the *Daily Herald* did not deter the Michener judging panel or the newspaper, which proudly published the announcement of its Michener nomination on the front page.

Investigative journalism, by its very nature, can spark threats of legal action, some serious, some nuisance, some to intimidate. For example, the *Toronto Star* faced a $2.7 billion libel lawsuit by the Toronto police union when it won the 2002 Michener Award for its series on racial profiling. The *Star* was vindicated in January 2005 when the Supreme Court denied the Police Association leave to appeal an earlier court ruling.

Far more controversial among the Michener finalists at the 1995 awards ceremony, however, was CKNW/98, New Westminster, and its incandescent program host Rafe Mair. The nomination of Mair's year-long on-air campaign against the massive Kemano hydroelectric project in northern British Columbia raised all the vexing questions about the role of advocacy in public interest journalism. At issue was the proposal by the Alcan corporation to redirect 20 per cent of the flow of the Nechako River to provide more power for aluminum production in Kitimat. Mair, a devoted fly fisherman and environmentalist, was having none of that.

He was a well-known figure in B.C. Whether as a lawyer, municipal councillor, provincial politician or broadcaster, Mair was a self-professed "noisy one."[46] In the 1980s and 1990s, he ascended to become the grand inquisitor of private broadcasting. The airwaves were his pulpit, British Columbians his faithful congregation. More than 100,000 people tuned in each day to hear Mair dissect guests with caustic and razor-edged questions. "I have been a contrarian all my life. From childhood on, I never liked being told what to do and challenged authority at every turn. I would argue any politically correct proposition from the opposite side at the drop of a hat," he wrote in his memoir, *Rafe*.[47] The Kemano fight was no exercise in rhetoric.

In his attack, Mair released secret government research that showed the project threatened the environment, including salmon and other fish stocks. Then he opened the airwaves. As he later wrote, "native bands, labour unions, fish biologists, professionals, environmentalists and people from every other walk of life joined in the fray."[48] Alcan fought back with a letter-writing campaign throughout 1994 to CKNW and other media outlets such as the *Georgia Straight*, *Equity* and the *Financial Post*.[49] With the heat rising, NDP Premier Mike Harcourt decided in January 1995 to cancel the Kemano dam project. Within weeks, former Conservative federal fisheries minister Tom Siddon slapped CKNW and Mair with a defamation and libel lawsuit for making allegations of dishonesty and corruption in the "fever pitch" of the on-air battle.[50]

The announcement on March 25 that CKNW/98 was a finalist for the 1994 Michener Award inflamed the counter-attack by opponents in British Columbia. Suddenly, Chief Judge Arch MacKenzie was flooded with letters from Alcan, former employees, supporters, and even the District of Kitimat demanding the Foundation withdraw the nomination.[51] Alcan's director of Corporate Information and Public Affairs, Les Holroyd, wrote that he was "appalled to hear of this nomination."[52]

With hundreds of potential jobs down the drain, Kitimat town council passed a motion strenuously objecting to Mair's nomination. The motion claimed Mair was "an unsuitable candidate for such a prestigious award" because he had failed to provide "listeners with a balanced reporting of all sides."[53] One Alcan employee, C. H. Whicher, complained that the show represented "everything sensational, sleazy and dishonest in journalism" and was appalled that it "could even be mentioned in the same breath as a gentleman such as the late Mr. Michener." In a subsequent letter to Clark Davey, Michener president, Whicher further suggested the award be renamed "The Joseph Goebbels Award, particularly appropriate on the 50th anniversary of VE Day!"[54] Passions ran high, and the gloves were off.

The Michener board could not ignore the furor. Chief Judge Arch MacKenzie raised the issue at the annual general meeting on the morning of the awards ceremony in May 1995. Clark Davey read some of the letters and said he had responded to the complaints. His message was clear. "Advocacy journalism as practised by Mr. Mair was not excluded from the competition and that obviously the judging panel had been impressed by Mr. Mair's ability to influence public opinion."[55] In other words, the complaint that Mair had failed to provide balanced reporting did not mean CKNW had not conducted public service journalism worthy of a nomination. At that point, only the judges knew that CKNW/98 Westminster would receive the 1994 award later that night.

That year's awards ceremony was the first for Governor General Roméo LeBlanc, but if he knew about the buzz around the nomination, he gave no sign. LeBlanc knew the media business. He had travelled the world as a political correspondent for Radio-Canada and reported from bureaus in Ottawa, London and Washington between 1959 and 1967. He left journalism to take on the job of press secretary to Prime Minister Lester B. Pearson, and later, Prime Minister Pierre Elliott Trudeau, but LeBlanc never forgot his time in the journalism trenches. His welcoming speech praised media organizations for investing in public service journalism. "We celebrate our good fortune of living in a country where investigative reporting is not only tolerated, but positively encouraged."[56]

Looking across the ballroom, LeBlanc picked out two of his contemporaries, Chief Judge Fraser MacDougall and Bill MacPherson, as "role models" and "front page legends."[57] The tribute had particular poignancy for long-hauler MacPherson, sitting in his black suit with his battery-powered electronic larynx at his side. He had been with the Micheners from the beginning and was not going to miss the twenty-fifth anniversary. He had survived surgery to remove his larynx and esophagus, and, with typical grit, he was fighting leukemia caused by earlier throat cancer treatments. It would be MacPherson's final trip to Rideau Hall.[58]

At the front of the room, the next act of a more contentious drama began to unfold with LeBlanc's presentation of the 1994 Michener Award trophy to a beaming Shirley Stocker, executive producer of CKNW's public affairs programming. The judges' citation recognized the coverage of the Kemano Completion project as a "potent force in the British Columbia government's decision to kill the billion-dollar completion of the Alcan power project."[59] The impact was measurable, but for some, it stung.

The Foundation received another downpour of letters from Alcan and such groups as the Kitimat Community Coalition, the District of Kitimat, former Alcan employees and individuals who questioned the judgement of the judges.[60] "Alcan tried to get this award taken away from me because they said that I had libelled fisheries minister Tom Siddon,"[61] Mair wrote.

Siddon's Writ of Summons and Statement of Claim pointed to Mair's on-air comments made eight years earlier about the Kemano 1987 settlement with Alcan. "He hit us with a long list of one-liners to which he had taken offence."[62] Siddon's lawyer, Eric Rice, even tried to drag the Michener Awards Foundation into legal action.

In August 1995, Rice requested details of what information the judging panel had used in February to base its decision.[63] Ever-cautious Clark Davey was in no rush to reply. Davey sat on the documents for two months before seeking legal advice from Ottawa lawyer Anthony P. McGlynn at Perley-Robertson, Panet Hill & MacDougall. As Davey's letter to McGlynn revealed, "Earlier this summer Senator Findlay McDonald approached Arch MacKenzie, chairman of the judging panel and a member of our board and executive, seeking a copy of the CKNW/Mair submission. When asked, he said he was acting on behalf of Tom Siddon who was suing Mr. Mair for defamation, Mr. MacKenzie and I agreed that we should not give up this submission, at least in this way."[64]

Davey's response to Rice in October 1995 was clear. "As a third party to the Siddon/Mair dispute, we have no wish to become involved particularly when the documents we hold, or copies of them, would be available to you from the other party to the litigation."[65] However, in December 1995, the Foundation succumbed and handed over "The Rafe Mair Program Michener Submission," including three audio cassettes, to Siddon's lawyer.

A key issue became what the Michener judges knew, and when they knew it. Based on what Davey reported, McGlynn's legal letter a week later assured Siddon's lawyer that "Mr. MacKenzie and the other members of the judging panel had no idea at the time they considered the submissions and made their decisions that the defamation action was pending or had been commenced against CKNW, its owners or its on air personalities."[66] He noted the practice of the judges is to consider submissions based on the material submitted by the applicants. With a possible jury trial, Davey even swore an affidavit "affirming that our judges did not know at the time of their selection of CKNW for the award that a libel action had been started" at the time of judging.[67] Later CKNW would take issue with Davey's account, noting that the award submission "specifically referred to [the lawsuit] in at least one of the documents submitted by CKNW."[68] A look through the CKNW's original submission to the judges shows not one, but three references to a lawsuit. Siddon's legal team did not pursue the alleged oversight.

Supporters of Alcan and Siddon refused to let the issue drop and pressured the Michener Awards Foundation to rescind CKNW's award even after Mair settled out of court with Siddon in March 1977 for a reported sum of almost $300,000.[69] When the board met two months later, directors supported the executive's decision to resist pressure. Davey issued a press release affirming the decision of the judges and "emphasizing that while the board recognized the seriousness of the libel complaint, the material giving rise to the complaint was not crucial to the CKNW/Mair campaign against the second phase of the Kemano project."[70] Davey went on to explain that, "In any event, a suit for defamation should not, of itself, be grounds for barring an entry from competition."[71]

The Price of Independence

Typically — as in the battle over Mair's Kemano campaign — legal threats from outraged parties are usually directed to the media outlet that produced the story. Not so in 2018, when a legal challenge in Alberta threatened both the Michener Awards Foundation and the judging panel. The case involved a series of broadcasts and online stories produced in 2017 by reporters Charles Rusnell and Jennie Russell of CBC Edmonton. "Private Health, Public Risk" examined the actions of Alberta politicians concerning a private health foundation funded by a wealthy Calgary philanthropist. CBC Edmonton had disclosed in its submission that it was facing legal action, but, given the public interest and significance of the outcome, the judges selected the series as one of the eight finalists. Days after the announcement, as chief judge at the time, I received a registered legal-sized brown envelope. When I looked at the first page I took a deep breath, sat down, and read the 33-page document. The title on the first page read "Journalistic errors must disqualify CBC nomination."

Lawyer Michael Flatters, the secretary of the board of Pure North S'Energy Foundation, had a list of allegedly "factual" objections to the 133-word *précis* of the CBC story in the Michener Awards news release.[72] He included supporting documents: a terse letter from a public health official qualifying his comments to CBC, and a defamation lawsuit against the Dieticians [*sic*] of Canada, another source in the CBC story. There was also a twenty-page complaint Pure North had sent to CBC Ombudsman Esther Enkin a year earlier. I had barely acknowledged receipt of the first letter when a second one arrived four days later. This one, from lawyer Grant Stapon of Bennett Jones Ltd. representing Pure North S'Energy. His letter gave notice of additional defamation charges against CBC, including the *précis* published on the Michener Awards website and made a formal request: "Take down or rewrite the summary."[73] The letter threatened legal action against the Michener Awards Foundation. A first.

The first reaction among the judges was that this was a nuisance suit. Even so, a few inquiries showed the complainant, Allan Markin — businessman, philanthropist and the founder of Pure North S'Energy Foundation — had a reputation for being litigious, and he had deep pockets. The Michener Awards Foundation was in a bind. If the Foundation refused the request to change the write up, it could expect a prolonged and expensive legal proceeding, most likely in an Alberta court. The directors had no appetite for a fight and the cash-strapped Foundation had no war chest to bankroll a prolonged lawsuit. The Micheners had maintained their independence over the years, but it left them vulnerable to financial threats such as this lawsuit. Furthermore, the Foundation did not have liability insurance, so the volunteer judges and board members could find themselves bankrolling a costly legal battle.

A chill descended, as Pure North had hoped. The CBC nomination stood but rewrites of the *précis* vetted by Halifax *pro-bono* media lawyer David Coles flew back and forth across the country. Pure North's legal team kept requesting more "appropriate factual corrections" with the promise that "If that was done Pure North will regard the matter as resolved in so far as the content of the summary of the CBC story published by your organization is concerned."[74] It galled to have to pare the write up and then pare some more. With Pure North's stamp of approval, the news release and citation for the awards ceremony in June 2018 became a mere two sentences that said nothing and everything: *"Canadian Broadcasting Corporation Edmonton: Private Health, Public Risk?* The CBC Edmonton is being recognized for its investigative series focusing on Pure North, an alternative health foundation of a Calgary businessman. They have continued to publish stories while facing a defamation lawsuit."[75]

On June 8, the letter from Stapon arrived "absolving the Michener Awards Foundation."[76] A letter from Pure North S'Energy Foundation's lawyer Michael Flatters followed. It was to "affirm our appreciation for the rewrite of the summary of CBC Edmonton publications."[77] The threat was over for the Michener Awards Foundation, but if Pure North's goal was to threaten the Michener Awards Foundation into submission, it worked. Even the national Cable Public Affairs Channel (CPAC) got cold feet. Its president, Catherine Cano, sat on the Michener board and was party to the Pure North deliberations. The broadcaster taped the awards ceremony, but CPAC decided not to broadcast it after CBC reporter Charles Rusnell's speech. Another sad first. The Michener board bought liability insurance that autumn to protect the directors and judges. This was an unhappy example of how independence has to be negotiated in the face of financial pressures and powerful forces.

As anticipated, four years later, in May 2022, Pure North discontinued its claim against CBC Edmonton and released the two reporters from all liability. CBC retracted nothing and paid nothing to the claimants. It re-published the series "Private Health Public Risk?" in May 2022 with this update: "While CBC Edmonton stands behind the accuracy of its reporting, the CBC has agreed with Pure North to provide a link to a statement where Pure North provides an additional response to the article below and related coverage."[78] "We don't regret doing the stories because they were clearly in the public interest. But we do regret losing weeks of time that could have been devoted to investigative reporting,"[79] Rusnell wrote later. He and Jennie Russell left

CBC in December 2021 to start their own freelance unit and hope one day to finish the investigation.[80] The question for the Michener Awards Foundation's future panels will be how to deal with hard-hitting investigative stories facing libel lawsuits.

In its fifty years, there has been only one instance where the Michener board was compelled to update a decision of the judging panel — seven years after making the award. In April 1998, a blond, fresh-faced David Rodenhiser stood on the podium before 140 guests in the ballroom at Rideau Hall. He gave the camera a big grin as one hand gripped the heavy trophy, and the other clasped the hand of Chief Justice Antonio Lamer of the Supreme Court, who was standing in for an ailing Roméo LeBlanc.

The reporting team from the *Daily News* in Halifax had won the Michener Award for its three-month investigation into its exposé of abuse at a reform school for boys in Shelburne, Nova Scotia. Reporters had dug up and used information from a sealed government archive, unknown even to senior civil servants. As a result of the dogged coverage, the provincial government introduced an alternative dispute resolution to compensate former victims. More than 1500 former residents came forward, accusing some 400 current or former employees of physical and mental abuse.

The page three headline of April 29, 1998 "The *Daily News* wins national award" trumpeted its Michener win for public service journalism.[81] The news was met with "dismay, disbelief and resentment" by Cameron S. McKinnon, a lawyer from Truro, Nova Scotia. Steaming with fury, he sat down and typed a letter and faxed it to the editor of the *Daily News* and Arch MacKenzie, chief judge of the Michener Awards. From McKinnon's point of view, the series "System of Abuse" series was "one-sided reporting." He complained that the *Daily News* had never contacted employees or former employees he represented for the other side of the story. The coverage, he wrote, "overlooked the very thing that we as Canadians are guaranteed: the presumption of innocence." His letter claimed his clients had been denied the right to due process because the *Daily News* coverage was "judge, jury and executioner of all employees."[82] MacKenzie responded the next day to say he had distributed the fax to all the judges and promised that "Your concerns are being given the consideration they deserve."[83] There is no record of how MacKenzie responded to McKinnon's concerns.

Seven years later, Halifax lawyer Dale Dunlop — who had represented 180 employees and former employees at Shelburne — wrote to the Michener

Awards Foundation as a citizen "who is troubled that many years after the fact, your website continues to publish false and potentially defamatory information on what went on in Shelburne."[84] He was referring to the citation on the Michener Awards website that read:

> The Michener judges praised the *Daily News* for taking reporter David Rodenhiser out of daily news reporting in 1997 to spend three months investigating allegations of abuse in Nova Scotia's reform schools. "Grim details of beatings, molestations and rapes emerged," especially after Rodenhiser discovered a "massive, sealed archive" of government documents. Senior civil servants and even the RCMP, who had been investigating some 1500 allegations, did not know existed. As a result, "approximately 400 suspects are under investigation. The RCMP subsequently began investigating allegations of fraud against some complainants seeking provincial compensation, the Michener citation read."[85]

Then, in a lawyerly fashion, Dunlop started making an argument for amendments. He noted that an RCMP investigation and the Nova Scotia government had exonerated many of the accused. He pointed to the CBC's 1999 *fifth estate* documentary and a 2001 feature story in the *Ryerson Review of Journalism* which raised issues with the coverage. "It is troublesome enough that the Michener Foundation has not seen fit to review its 1997 recipient, but even more so that the lies propagated by the *Daily News* still find a place on your website,"[86] Dunlop concluded.

The executive consulted chief judge David Humphreys as it mulled over what to do. At its June 14, 2006, meeting, with consent from the judges, the executive decided the Michener Award to Halifax *Daily News* would stand as is. But on the website, at the end of the citation, they would add an "update" that read: "Two years after the *Daily News* reports were published, the Nova Scotia government appointed Mr. Justice Fred Kaufmann to conduct an inquiry into the government's handling of allegations of abuse. In his report, published in 2002, Mr. Justice Kaufmann said: "The plight of innocent employees, as well as the distress of true survivors, was greatly exacerbated by frequent stories in the press. I have no doubt that there were claimants who were truly subjected to physical and sexual abuse. Similarly, I have no doubt that there was a significant number of employees who were falsely implicated."[87] That clarification remained on the Michener Awards website until 2021 when the site was taken down as part of a website remake.

The mention of Shelburne can still polarize journalists, educators and media pundits. Stephen Kimber had a front-row seat for the Shelburne story. He was director of the School of Journalism at the University of King's College and wrote a column for the *Daily News*. He said the story of abuse at the Youth Centre would not have been told without the *Daily News*. "You had a very small news organization tackling a subject that was incredibly difficult," said Kimber.[88] He said if the *Daily News* was the mouthpiece for the youth confined there, the competing daily newspaper in Halifax, the *Chronicle Herald,* was the spokesperson for those in authority. Between the two newspapers, people got a pretty good sense of what was happening. Kimber said the problem was not the *Daily News* crusade, it was the government's decision to compensate the victims on an honour system that undermined the whole process. "So I think the *Daily News* did a public service by bringing this to the attention of the public."[89]

Judging public interest journalism is not a science. Perceptions change, new issues emerge, old definitions are challenged, and controversy is never very far offstage. From time to time, as the examples above show, various aggrieved parties have challenged the decisions of the Michener judging panel. Whatever their grounds, none has ever shown that industry pressure, political favouritism or private concerns affected the outcome of the selection process. In choosing from among the annual competitors for the award, the decisive question has always been "who has served best the public interest?"

This claim to integrity came with a cost, one that was fixed in the 1989 debate among the directors of the Michener Awards Foundation over a proposed partnership with the Canadian Journalism Foundation. What emerged on that snowy afternoon in Ottawa was a certainty among the directors that what they had created was special. Their collective determination was that the Michener Award would remain independent from any business or industry pressures to preserve its public service mission, its precious connection to Rideau Hall, and the independence of its judging panel. The decision also meant for its first fifty years the Michener Awards would be perpetually underfunded and operate with a volunteer board and no staff. Its ability to move with the times would be limited, especially when it came to outreach and social media. It would be obliged to rely on Rideau Hall to assist in organizing the annual awards ceremony and struggle to find funders to support its fellowships.

In contrast, the CJF would go forward to tap into big donors and form partnerships with corporate and media organizations. With substantial funding, the CJF established an office with full-time staff that allows it to offer events throughout the year, including an annual journalism awards gala in Toronto and a speakers' series that focuses on issues in the industry. Over the years, concern about the role of special interests in the CJF has abated with its active presence on social media and partnerships to fund education, training and research opportunities for emerging and working journalists. John Miller, an early critic, has come to change his views and sees the CJF as a valuable organization, different from the way it was set up in 1990. "I think there's a number of strong industry voices there that have probably swung it back towards a journalism focus."[90] While the early suspicions and concerns about corporate influence on the journalism recognized by the CJF have evaporated, wariness about the CJF lingered among some long-serving Michener directors and influenced potential collaborative ventures.

As for now, however, the Michener Award remains unique: the prize that reporters, editors, broadcasters and publishers want most of all. "The Micheners stand for something singular. It is the one," said David Walmsley, editor-in-chief of the *Globe and Mail* and a former chair of the Canadian Journalism Foundation. "It's the only award where you're up against everyone in broadcast, local print, both languages, and you've got a very clear set of criteria that you have to achieve: a public policy difference in a calendar year. . . . What I love about that is that the Micheners are clear as to what you have to do. And if everyone's rowing in the same direction, for public policy difference, it means it doesn't matter if you won or not because you get nominated. That's pretty special. It means everyone has achieved a certain standard already.[91]

For Walmsley, the other aspect that elevates the Michener Awards is the "pivotal role" the governor general plays. "There is nothing more humbling than to be allowed into Rideau Hall to see the head of state who takes a personal interest and commitment to understanding why journalism, as a central part of democracy, also represents the best of what Canada represents," said Walmsley[92]

It's not the prestige, not the ceremony at Rideau Hall, not viceregal status that gives the Michener Award its status. That comes from the independent stand and work of the judging panels. It stands apart from the board directors, many of whose news organizations regularly submit their work for a Michener Award, "So it's absolutely integral that the jury be impartial, unbiased and independent, and they have been all these years," said chief judge Margo Goodhand.[93] She pointed to the 2020 nomination of CBC News as a Michener finalist for its series, "Inside Rideau Hall" — "an investigation that truly precipitated or tore the veil off the culture in Rideau Hall and presumably precipitated Julie Payette's resignation." Goodhand said that, when she went to present the list of finalists at Rideau Hall, nobody questioned the fact that the series did not deserve to be on the list or that it should not be honoured. "So we [the judging panel] are unbiased, we are independent, and we curry no favours."[94]

That independence is a point of pride, and it is fiercely guarded in the decision-making process and in how the judging panels navigate the controversies and complaints of bruised reporters, editors and publishers. It would be the baton handed to a new generation of leaders who, in turn, would face no shortage of new tests of judgement and independence.

6

The Waves of Change

The twentieth anniversary of the Michener Award for meritorious and disinterested public service in journalism in 1990 was a time for reflection and celebration. It was the first Michener Award ceremony for Governor General Ramon (Ray) Hnatyshyn and his wife, Gerda, and they threw a gala that harkened back to the days of Edward and Lily Schreyer. Journalists, dressed to the nines in long gowns or black tie, received hand-calligraphed programs with a photograph of Rideau Hall on the cover, with the citations for the finalists and fellowships, and the dinner menu inside. Rideau Hall staff escorted guests into the ballroom. The tables were set with the finest china and silver. After the awards ceremony, the RCMP band played while journalists were served a lavish four-course dinner of *crème froide cressonnière, crevettes Fra Diavolo, tournedos gismonde, salade printaniere, vacherin estival* and *douceurs en bonbonnière* with the choice of wines *Clos du Château* 1986, *Pignan* 1985, or champagne, *Joseph Perrier* 1982.[1]

In a CBC interview to mark the occasion, Fraser MacDougall, who had been in charge of judging for eighteen of the first twenty years, explained the genesis of the Michener Award. It began in 1970 to "promote fearless, vigorous journalism, relentless probing for all the facts, particularly those deliberately hidden from the public eye, all without any thought of personal gain."[2] Inspiring words for a new decade that would see the Michener Awards Foundation lose its key founders — Roland Michener, Bill MacDougall and Paul Deacon — and welcome a succession of new leaders, including Gail Scott, Clark Davey, Norman Webster and Pierre Bergeron. Despite a fresh round of financial difficulties that emerged from the changing journalism landscape, these new leaders would work to expand the Michener Foundation's reach outside the golden triangle of Ottawa-Toronto-Montreal. They campaigned to reassure francophone and smaller media outlets that the Michener Awards Foundation was relevant and, like their journalism, it was making a difference. The Foundation was there to support media outlets and celebrate the impact of their journalism — which, in the 1990s, was often directed toward scrutinizing public institutions and agencies. Toward the end of the 1990s, the Foundation would step into the digital age with the creation of a bilingual archival website that showcased its history and award-winning journalism since 1970.

Passing of the Old Guard

In June 1990, Roland Michener, the self-professed "father of the award," had just turned ninety years old and was recovering from his first-ever surgery, but that did not slow him down.[3] He was as enthusiastic and playful as ever at the Foundation's annual meeting. After thanking retiring president Paul Deacon for his eight years of service, Michener quipped that the success of the award "makes me feel as if I can retire." Without missing a beat, incoming president Gail Scott responded, "Mr. Michener don't you dare retire. I need you."[4] She knew that his constant support in those first twenty years had deepened the award's connection to Rideau Hall and had served as an example to successive governors general who might not have been as keen on the awards as Michener was.

Scott also knew that Paul Deacon was a hard act to follow. The creation of the Michener Awards Foundation in 1983 had been his initiative. During his tenure, he had moved the awards out of Bill MacPherson's spare bedroom, created a charitable foundation with a board of directors and worked to put the organization on a firmer financial footing.[5] From his savings, Deacon had contributed more than $150,000, helping to build a modest endowment and pay the bills. He had put together a dedicated team of volunteer directors, introduced special awards and study fellowships to expand the mission of journalism in the public interest and ensured the independence of the judging panels.

Gail Scott was a timely appointment in two ways. As a well-known and popular national television personality, she broke the stereotype of the Michener Awards Foundation as a bastion of male newspaper publishers and editors. She was also the first female to take on the top executive job at the Michener Awards Foundation. She had impeccable credentials. Scott started as a local TV reporter in her hometown of Ottawa, became a parliamentary correspondent for CBC and then CTV, hosted CTV's *W5* and co-hosted CTV's *Canada AM*. She taught broadcast journalism at Ryerson Polytechnic Institute in Toronto (now Toronto Metropolitan University).

She was bilingual and knew her way around the organization. She had been a Michener Awards judge for three years and had sat on the board for two.

The twentieth anniversary of the Michener Award showcased journalism from across the country and demonstrated that the Michener Award was indeed national and bilingual. *Le Devoir* broke ground as the first French-language Michener Award winner with its bilingual — French and Inuktitut — "coverage of the issues and challenges facing the Inuit people in northern Québec" as they prepared to vote in the 1989 referendum on self-government. The forty-eight-page supplement, "*À l'heure du choix*" ("The Deciding Hour") involved working with fourteen communities in the high Arctic of Québec.

Associate editor-in-chief Paul Beaugrand-Champagne said the project presented a wide range of challenges for the small daily. Besides getting reports from and going to the isolated communities, the paper had to adapt letters and characters of the Inuk language for the electronic press. Then the paper faced the challenge of figuring out how to explain southern concepts and expressions for which there were no words in Inuktitut. The Michener judges commended the newspaper for "its enormous public service" and "the extraordinary effort made to communicate with the Inuit on an equal basis and for what it achieved."[6]

The stories of other finalists brought attention to emerging or systemic problems that would resonate from coast to coast for years to come. The "Donald Marshall Case," published in *Reader's Digest* in 1989, brought to the forefront the embedded racism against Indigenous and Black people in Canada's police forces, courts and prisons. The story documented how the white justice system had failed Donald Marshall, the Mi'kmaw teenager from Cape Breton, who spent eleven years in prison for a murder he didn't commit. The Marshall case would pave the way for the reexamination of other miscarriages of justice. For example, the case of William Mullins-Johnson, who spent twelve years in prison after being wrongly convicted of the murder of his four-year-old niece. The *Toronto Star* received a Michener citation of merit in 2005 for uncovering the "sloppy and incompetent work of a pathologist" and recovering the evidence that showed the child had died of natural causes. The coverage prompted Ontario's Chief Coroner to order a review of all autopsies involving murders and suspicious deaths of children.[7]

Another 1989 East Coast finalist, the weekly St. John's *Sunday Express*, put into print the whispers and rumours that members of the Congregation of Christian Brothers had sexually and physically abused boys in its Mount

Cashel orphanage. These revelations gave voice to others who experienced abuse in orphanages and boarding schools run by religious orders and private groups. More than forty years later, these organizations face new accusations and are providing apologies and financial compensation to victims.

These tough, important stories exposed ugly realities in society and, in doing so, led to incremental changes. However, societal problems are not remedied quickly; they persist and resurface with disturbing frequency. For example, a finalist at the twentieth anniversary celebration was from the *Kingston Whig*-Standard. The forty-eight-page article, "Rock-a-Bye Baby," focused on the failure of the criminal justice system. The investigation detailed the tragic life and death of Marlene Moore, the first woman in Canada to be deemed "a dangerous offender." Moore, aged thirty-one, was "a victim of incest and rape and of male violence" who died by suicide in the Kingston Penitentiary for Women after "a life of physical and mental pain inflicted on her by respected segments of society."[8] Shamefully, this was not a rare or isolated event in Canada's prisons.

Twenty-one years later, CBC's *the fifth estate* would win the 2010 Michener Award for its shocking account of the events leading to the death of Ashley Smith in 2007 at the Grand Valley Institution for Women in Kitchener, Ontario. "Ashley Smith's story is not about some hardened criminal but a mentally disturbed kid who got 30 days for pelting a postman with crab apples,"[9] journalist Hana Gartner said at the ceremony. When Smith died in 2007 at nineteen, she had been shunted from institution to institution and spent more than 1,000 days in segregation over four years.

CBC's *the fifth estate*, with the support of Smith's mother, challenged the Correctional Service of Canada to get access to the deeply disturbing video of Smith's final hours. Guards — ordered not to enter her cell as long as she was still breathing — watched and videotaped Smith, as she strangled herself on October 19, 2007.[10] CBC's legal challenge went all the way up to the Ontario Court of Appeal. The judges in a landmark 3-0 decision ruled "that media have the right to unfettered access to all exhibits before the court," Gartner said. "Journalists and the public now have another tool to hold public officials accountable for their actions."[11]

Along with the legal precedent, *the fifth estate* broadcasts "Out of Control"[12] and "Behind the Wall,"[13] played a pivotal role in widening the scope of the inquest into Smith's death. In 2013, Ontario Coroner Dr. John Carlisle ruled that Smith died from ligature strangulation and potential lack of oxygen (asphyxia), but her death was not a suicide; it was the result of homicide.[14]

It was Gartner's last big story before she left *the fifth estate*. "It was a good way to go out," she said. "The Michener Award meant a great deal to me. Along the way, you sometimes get Gemini Awards and all sorts of awards and it's very nice and you feel good for one evening and you forget. But this one, it was incredibly meaningful in that it was the story that got to me the most, in many ways, I still live with it."[15] The vigilance of media organizations in producing programs such as *the fifth estate* is vital to the health of our society. Investigative journalism brings systemic social problems to the attention of the public and those in authority, but change is slow, and issues are revisited.

Six years later, in 2016, the Michener Award went to the *London Free Press* for its two-year investigation into the death of Jamie High. The body of the forty-year-old father, athlete and successful real estate agent was found naked on a cell floor in solitary confinement at London's Elgin-Middlesex Detention Centre. Reporter Randy Richmond wrote to High's family:

> The reason the *Free Press* and I have been driven to tell Jamie's story, and stick with it, is because he never should have had a story like this.
>
> He never should have been "jail guy."
>
> He should have had the chance to become, at least, some guy who had some trouble once and got some help and moved on.
>
> He should have had the chance to become again some guy you played hockey with, or saw in a gym, or met in a bar watching football and liked because of his cockiness or didn't like because of his cockiness, maybe a good friend, or a business partner, maybe your brother, or son, or husband, or ex-husband, boy-friend or ex-boyfriend, or father.
>
> Jamie's last days should not have been spent naked and alone on the floor of a jail cell.
>
> His last words should not have been incoherent mutterings.

He never should have had a story written about him called "Indiscernible".

No one should.[16]

The Michener judges wrote the *London Free Press* series "exposed serious shortfalls that produced changes in policing, bail, community mental health care, hospital mental health care, the relationships between hospitals and police, the role of courts and the treatment of inmates. Their work exemplifies the critical value of local media relentlessly pursuing stories and seeking accountability to counter what too many others choose to overlook and let slide as simply indiscernible."[17] Three years later, in June 2019, Bill C-83, the *Corrections and Conditional Release Act*, passed. It was supposed to end the inhumane practice of segregation, but it is still happening in Canada's prisons, now under another name — structured intervention units (SIU).[18]

These stories cover thirty years. Combined, they show how Michener stories do not end on awards night. They have consequences. As Governor General Hnatyshyn said at the twentieth anniversary in 1990, all the nominated stories had a common focus: " . . . they were disinterested, meritorious and performed a public service. In my view, however, they are more: they are examples of how professional men and women use their intelligence and determination to meet the highest standards of journalism and how, if they are very fortunate, they work for organizations willing to bet on their talents and resourcefulness."[19]

Hnatyshyn, a former lawyer and politician, understood the importance of the message he was sending about the role of journalism in a democracy through viceregal support of the Michener Awards. His emphasis on the excellence of journalism was in keeping with the idea — painstakingly established over the previous two decades — that this night was only for the best. If he had any doubts when he received the annual request from the Michener Foundation, they were put to rest by his secretary, Judith Larocque. "Your participation in this event assures the prestige of the award and provides a great boost to journalists and media organizations interested in encouraging public service and high standards in journalism," she wrote to Hnatyshyn.[20] What's more, Larocque noted in her memo that the event earned good national media coverage that was well worth the expense.

Rideau Hall documents from 1990 estimated that an evening including the presentations and a formal dinner would cost $13,000. The other option from Larocque was that the Michener Award ceremony be followed by a reception and no dinner, which is what Hnatyshyn's predecessor Jeanne Sauvé had done in the last three years of her tenure. "This alternative is not advisable, however, as it would detract from the prestige of the award," she advised. Hnatyshyn followed her advice. It was welcome news to Michener president Gail Scott and the board. A ceremony and gala at Rideau Hall demonstrated that the State, through the office of the governor general, valued the journalism of the Fourth Estate as an essential pillar of a democratic society, precisely what Bill MacPherson and Roland Michener had intended twenty years earlier.

The Michener Awards Foundation's annual meeting in May 1992 was tinged with sadness as President Gail Scott remembered founder and patron, Roland Michener who had died in August 1991. "It was more than 20 years ago," she recalled, " that Mr. Michener had lent his name to a journalism award to honour those who were able to effect social change and had the courage to do so." At the awards ceremony that evening His Excellency Hnatyshyn paid a tribute to his predecessor. "Here was a man with unrelenting energy who did the most serious and significant kind of work on behalf of his country and did it all with a twinkle in his eye."[21] Before presenting a special commemorative plaque to Michener's daughter, Diana Michener-Schatz, Hnatyshyn praised Roland Michener's loyalty and advocacy that helped to make the Michener Awards an annual highlight of Rideau Hall.

Hnatyshyn reminded journalists and media executives that Michener appreciated journalism that made for a better society. "These awards celebrate content, depth and understanding. They become even more important as economic pressures squeeze at the heart of both our print and electronic media, and publishers and producers look desperately for every possible way to attract readers, listeners, viewers — and, of course, advertisers. If those pressures ever gather to the point that the custodians of the Michener Awards have trouble gathering journalists of the quality that we have represented in this room today — any of whom are worthy of this prize — then Canada will be the lesser for it."[22] Technological changes and an economic downturn were starting to erode media organizations. For the industry, this connection to Rideau Hall and the governor general's spotlight on journalism in the public interest became more valuable than ever.

Hnatyshyn surprised everyone that night when he stood up at dinner and called upon each of the six Michener Award finalists to talk about their stories. That was a first. Up to now, the tradition had been for the president to read the judges' report and citations, and then for the governor general to present the awards and announce the fellowship recipients. But that night, the audience heard moving accounts from the journalists on the front line of the most important stories of 1991. The Michener Award winner was CBC-TV's investigative team with a package of seven stories that focussed on corruption and failures in government administration.

Journalists Gloria Lowen and Susan Papp spoke about the abuses and malfeasance uncovered, including loopholes in federal tax law, abuses of Indigenous band funds, fraud and "blowing the lid off" widespread abuse of Ontario's health insurance by drug addicts in U.S. treatment centres.

Another CBC story in the package described "how the director of immigration in Manitoba was in league with an immigration consultant in various corrupt practices. He was removed after our story," recalled Cecil Rosner, then producer of the CBC Winnipeg I-Team.

In another story, the CBC journalists exposed a group of corrupt Winnipeg police officers who were stage-managing break-ins. "They would hire one criminal, in particular, to get all his buddies together, do a break and then they [the police] would burst in and arrest everybody since they had kind of instigated it and get all the accolades of having made a bust. They would let him go and charge the others. . . . This is not a script from a Netflix series, it was actually going on in Winnipeg," Rosner said, reflecting on the series years later.[23]

The other finalists shared heartbreaking stories about child exploitation, sexual abuse, and municipal and judicial injustices. L'Actualité's exposé about children as young as eleven years old working sixty hours a week for fifty cents an hour sparked outrage, especially in Québec, where the government had scrapped the minimum age requirement in 1974. The Globe and Mail's Paul Taylor explained how the series involving sexual abuse by psychiatrists and therapists in Ontario led to the creation of a task force and new regulations by the Ontario College of Physicians and Surgeons. Ruth Teichroeb's Winnipeg Free Press investigation into sexual abuse and exploitation of youth at Manitoba adolescent treatment centres prompted a public inquiry.

In response to city hall secrecy in St. Thomas, Ontario, radio station CKSL-Q103 took unprecedented action and allowed its reporter David Helwig to open a freedom-of-information advocacy service for citizens, which played a role in municipal elections. Stories written by Constance Sampson of the *Prince Albert Herald* forced the Saskatchewan government to review the sentence of a white supremacist who pleaded guilty to manslaughter in the shooting death of Leo LeChance, a Cree trapper. Sampson said it is "a case that won't go away."[24] Each speech brought the stories to life that resonated with the Michener values of public service.

"I thought the unscheduled, spontaneous introduction of the finalists for brief speeches was the best innovation I have seen in the course of attending Michener nights," Chief Judge Arch MacKenzie wrote in a thank-you letter to Hnatyshyn. "The fact that His Excellency became the impromptu Master of Ceremonies gave the proceedings a down-to-earth friendliness and informality that is impossible usually to plan. I hope it becomes part of the format because I'm sure it is a special memory for this year's participants."[25] The innovation stuck, and to this day, the most memorable part of the annual Michener Awards ceremony is when the finalists stand and talk about their work and the impact their stories have had on the public good.

Tremors: The Industry and the Foundation

Gail Scott was three years into her tenure as president when she resigned in the spring of 1993, to take an appointment to the Canadian Radio-television and Telecommunications Commission (CRTC). In her short tenure Scott had brought energy and enthusiasm to renewed fundraising and publicity efforts. She also found herself asking for the resignation of a member of the board and executive after internal conflicts had affected the future of the Foundation.[26]

The board elected founding member Clark Davey as the third president of the Michener Awards Foundation. Davey was the dean of newspapers in Canada — a former managing editor of the *Globe and Mail* and former publisher of Southam News in Vancouver, Montréal and Ottawa. Among his peers he was respected as a "champion of the sort of investigative journalism that, in his words, have 'the kind of impact that moves peoples' hearts and their minds, that stirs their sense of justice, and changes the rules and laws, to make our society a better place."[27] Many young reporters owe their careers to Davey's mentorship, especially during his time at the *Globe and Mail*.

Davey's connection to Roland Michener went back a long way, to 1962. Roland Michener was the MP for St. Paul's in Toronto and Speaker of the House of Commons. Michener had come to ask Davey for "special attention to regain the support" in his riding because "as Speaker of the House of Commons, he was required to be non-partisan." As Dic Doyle noted in his biography *Hurley Burly*, it was a reasonable request, but Davey refused to make an exception. He told Michener, "If you make news, we'll report it."[28] Davey brought that astute sensibility as one of the new leaders shepherding the Michener Awards Foundation through what would be a tumultuous era.

Davey saw the work of the Foundation as "celebrating the best of the best in our business" and stated that his mission as president would be to ensure that "by this time next year, we'll have won the kind of support that will give us confidence in the future."[29] By May 1994, the treasurer, Grant MacDonald, reported a balanced budget and noted that the Foundation had met the investment target of $150,000.[30] Davey and vice president Bryn Matthews successfully raised money from libel-law firms and private broadcasters. Even board members had increased their annual donations. There was more good news. Paul Deacon, described in the board minutes as "an old friend of Roland Michener," had given the Foundation a considerable gift. He had deposited $100,000 with the Ottawa Community Foundation with instructions to hold it until the Michener Awards Foundation could raise matching funds. "Paul Deacon was a lifesaver . . . having Deacon's $100,000 sitting out there, that made all the difference in the world," Clark Davey said in an interview years later.[31]

At that time, Davey thought this would be the end of the exhausting and somewhat frustrating cycle of fundraising. At the 1994 annual meeting, he gave the optimistic prediction that "in a year or two the Foundation would be fully funded and could stop further fundraising."[32] At the 1994 awards ceremony that night, Davey announced that the board unanimously elected Paul Deacon as president *emeritus*, praising his work as "instrumental in keeping the Michener Foundation vibrant and strong."[33] Successive boards would work to ensure that momentum continued.

Two media outlets tied for the 1993 Michener Award.[34] The *Ottawa Citizen* series had scuttled a multi-million-dollar secret deal to privatize Toronto's Pearson airport, while the *Globe and Mail* investigation blew open the tainted blood scandal, considered Canada's worst public health disaster. The *Globe and Mail* stories detailed how tainted blood transfusions in the 1980s were responsible for more than a thousand AIDS-related deaths. Reporters Rod Mickleburgh and André Picard followed with a series on "how the provinces conspired to deny compensation to victims of tainted blood and how many of them were dying destitute because federal support had run out. Federal and other reviews followed quickly. Within weeks the provinces had reversed their seven-year-old policy and provided $159 million."[35]

This was just the beginning of the fight for compensation. In the obituary for Janet Conners — the "crusading activist" from Nova Scotia who contracted HIV in 1989 from her husband Randy, a hemophiliac who had unknowingly been infected by tainted blood products — André Picard wrote that, after the couple went public in 1993: "The political dominoes began to tumble, with every province and territory following suit on compensation and the federal government ordering a commission of inquiry — the Krever Commission — that would eventually result in more than $5 billion in compensation, the bankruptcy of the iconic Canadian Red Cross blood program, and a complete revamping of how drugs are approved in this country."[36] The *Globe* held those in authority to account and, as a result, changed public policy and saved the lives of citizens.

Four years later an "extreme sense of loss" marked the Michener Awards ceremony. Foundation members mourned the deaths of two of the people in 1998 who were instrumental in its founding and growth: Bill MacPherson from cancer at the age of sixty-seven, and Paul Deacon from a heart attack at seventy-three. MacPherson, the founder, had shared a vision with Roland Michener in 1969, and for those first twelve years he was the driver in shaping and sustaining the award. "Bill was for the entire first 25 years and particularly in the early and somewhat chaotic years, the administrative glue which held together the various organizations which oversaw the award," said president Clark Davey.[37]

Without MacPherson it is unlikely that the Michener Award would have survived and become a charitable Foundation in 1983. He had protected it against poachers. He had protected the integrity and independence of the judging. He had protected it from financial insolvency. He remained active on the board, serving as executive secretary until 1994. The Michener Awards Foundation planted an Aspen tree just off the traffic circle in the Arboretum at the Experimental Farm in Ottawa to honour his service.[38]

If MacPherson germinated the idea and nurtured the Michener sapling, then Paul Deacon ensured that the tree grew deep roots to become strong and tall. At the May 1996 meeting, the Michener board honoured Deacon's urbane leadership, fundraising and personal generosity, noting that he was "directly responsible for the creation of the Michener fellowships and of the investment fund which guarantees both the award and the fellowships."[39] The following year the board honoured his dedicated service by re-naming the fellowships the Michener-Deacon Fellowships.[40] Deacon's greatest legacy — the scholarships — also became the Foundation's greatest ongoing financial challenge. Providing them was a way to demonstrate a commitment to journalism that went beyond the annual night of wine and self-congratulations and affirmed to the Foundation and media organizations that "what we do" is important.

Days after Deacon's death in March 1996, Senator Richard (Dic) Doyle, former editor of the *Globe and Mail,* stood up in the Red Chamber and paid tribute to his former colleague and all Deacon had done "to improve the calibre of his craft," particularly through his contribution to the Michener Awards Foundation. "It was Deacon's perseverance that secured the financing of the Foundation' program of annual 'Micheners' awarded for public service in the media. The Micheners are the most coveted prizes in Canadian journalism."[41] Deacon, alongside MacPherson and Roland Michener, had seen the awards through the thick and thin of the first two decades. The next thirty years would see new leaders meet new challenges — prompted mainly by the crumbling media business model — head-on.

The world of Michener, MacPherson, Deacon, Doyle and Davey was changing quickly. By the late 1990s, the number of media companies closing and consolidating started to escalate. With the rise of the Internet, audiences and advertisers were drifting away, and legacy media found they had no budget for beneficence. "The glory days of record advertising, however, were coming to an abrupt halt as the recession of the early 90s set in, with our revenues plummeting by a staggering one-third," wrote *Toronto Star* publisher John Honderich.[42] Furthermore, the Foundation was in competition for donors with other media organizations like the Canadian Journalism Foundation.

By April 1996, the Michener Foundation was showing an operating deficit of almost $20,000 mainly because three publishers — Thomson, Hollinger and Maclean-Hunter — had "dropped out as donors."[43] There also was little support from private broadcasters for the Micheners. "They weren't adamantly opposed. They were just smiley and indifferent,"[44] said Bryn Matthews, Michener vice-president (1994-95) who spent most of his later career in private broadcasting with CJOH in Ottawa. Davey appealed to board members to identify donors with "a vested interest in supporting public service journalism."[45] With fewer donations, the board dipped into its investment fund, now down to almost $280,000, to cover the cost of the two fellowships. It was time to tighten the belt and the board cut back and awarded only one in 1997.[46]

Once again, Michener directors started looking for options to get out of the annual fundraising cycle because "the job of raising annual operating funds for the Foundation, notably to finance the fellowships, is becoming increasingly difficult."[47] Bell Enterprises, the parent company of CTV, had been through a round of layoffs. Conrad Black's Hollinger had bought the controlling interest in the Southam newspaper chain. By the end of May 1996, Hollinger was the controlling shareholder of Southam's twenty dailies and could boast of a stable of fifty-eight newspapers. One company had control of nearly "41 per cent of Canada's total daily newspaper circulation."[48] The media buying and selling spree in Canada would continue and accelerate over the next decade, further destabilizing the Micheners' fundraising abilities.

Clark Davey was discouraged. "Most of the rest of the board seems to exist in a vacuum 364 days of the year, 365 in a Leap Year," he wrote to board member Tim Kotcheff, who had been sending out appeals for donations to various media and other groups. Davey advised, "Don't waste time with major paper publishers. Southam is becoming more centralized."[49] The one bit of good news for the Micheners was that after four years, the Foundation had finally met Paul Deacon's challenge. It had raised $100,000 to match Deacon's donation held in trust with the Ottawa Community Foundation. The goal was met thanks to Michener director Cynthia Baxter, widow of Clive Baxter, the first Michener winner and a close family friend of the Deacon family.

Cynthia Baxter appealed to Deacon's former work associates and single-handedly raised the difference, including $5,000 from the Audrey and Donald Campbell Foundation. Ten years later, the Baxter family would add to the endowment with a $200,000 donation to help sustain the work of the Foundation.[50] The investment fund with the Ottawa Community Foundation had reached $358,000 — nowhere near enough to generate enough income to cover two $40,000 fellowships or the Foundation's annual operating budget of $50,000. It must have galled Michener directors to hear that CJF was swimming in money and had passed an annual operating budget of $270,000.

By the time Clark Davey stepped down as president in 1998, he had managed to nudge the investment fund to $441,000 and whittle the operating budget deficit down to $1,200. Interest from the investment fund barely covered one fellowship. The directors wanted a larger annual draw from the investment fund and considered moving their money out of the Ottawa Community Foundation. This time, Adelle Deacon, wife of the late Paul Deacon, stepped in. She pledged $10,000 a year for five years to help the Michener Foundation bridge the gap between the fund's 4.5 per cent capped payout and the Michener's budget requirements.

Deacon was a long-time supporter of the community foundations in Toronto and Ottawa, so the board agreed to Deacon's request that the Micheners keep their money invested in the Ottawa Community Foundation. Her generous offer came at the right moment. Newly elected president Norman Webster understood that the board had "no appetite for another major round of fundraising." After all, the Foundation had already promised its faithful donors that an earlier appeal was the "final request."[51] For the most part, the Foundation has kept that promise, limiting fundraising to corporate sponsorships for the two fellowships.

The Foundation's new leaders had seen it through yet another period of financial insecurity, and by the end of the 1990s, the annual cycle clicked along. Each autumn, bilingual brochures went out to newsrooms across the country, advertisements were placed in media magazines inviting submissions for the awards and fellowships, and nominations opened. In March, judging began, with the finalists announced in the spring. The Michener executive spent each winter in a dance with Rideau Hall to find a hole in the governor general's itinerary to set a date for the awards ceremony. When that was settled, the executive would scurry around. The auditor general — holder of the envelope with the Michener winner — had to be invited, a guest list drawn up, the trophy engraved, the citations of merit printed and the annual general meeting called for the day of the ceremony.

The annual general meeting was a perfunctory affair. Board members entrusted the day-to-day operations of the Foundation to the executive — the president, past president, chief judge, treasurer, and at least one board member. This governance structure and protocol would eventually be challenged in 2017.

In the 2000s, discussions at the annual meeting centred on familiar issues — finances, fundraising, the need to raise the profile of the award and fellowships and the lack of French entries. In more recent years, the website and social media made it onto the agenda. If the meeting went on too long, some board members would start to fidget and sneak a look at their watches or phones. Everyone was keen to get to their hotels or go home and prepare for the awards ceremony. The excitement of the awards ceremony lasted for a single day, but the Foundation's behind-the-scenes work was an ongoing endeavour for the board executive.

Bridging Two Solitudes

From its creation in 1983, the Michener Awards Foundation was a tight-knit group, mainly from the Toronto-Ottawa establishment — former newspaper editors and publishers with Southam News service and Canadian Press pedigrees. To outsiders it might have seemed as if Gail Scott stepped into an old boys' club when she became president in 1990. But in an interview, Scott shrugged off any suggestion that she had entered a closed shop. "It was their charity. This was their cause."[52] She respected them as guardians of the integrity of the award. However, board members from the regions were not always as generous and pushed back when coming face-to-face with the Ontario compact.

During one of the perpetual board discussions about increasing entries from French publications and the regions, J. Patrick O'Callaghan, the plain-speaking Alberta newspaper publisher, cut through all the Upper Canadian niceties. With his acid tongue, he observed that the core directors were all in Ottawa and suggested that had given rise to a perception that the awards are a "Central Canada concoction." O'Callaghan's accusation at the 1992 annual general meeting brought a sharp retort from fellow director Clark Davey, who would become president in 1993. "I don't sense any feeling that the Michener is anything but a national award."[53] The Michener Award was national, but what Davey side-stepped was the fact that the organization administering the award was rooted in Ottawa with tentacles that reached not much farther than Toronto and Montreal.

"I think there was always a bit of national alienation. Those on the outskirts, the west coast, and prairies and the Maritimes felt that it was all controlled from Toronto, which wasn't far from the truth," said Bryn Matthews, who joined the board in 1992 and spent a year as vice president. "It still is to some degree, but that's not unusual."[54] Toronto was the centre for media and Ottawa the centre for political journalism.

Regardless of who occupied the seats at the board table, the focus remained on journalism in the public interest. "Everybody had an important story to tell," said Tim Kotcheff, former Toronto board member. "This was the award (*snaps his fingers*) that gets public attention and changes policy, which is what it's designed to do. So everybody on the board really pushed hard."[55] Regardless of geography, board members swallowed their institutional dissatisfaction. They stood united on the purpose of the award and fellowships — to encourage the Michener values among the scribbling class and to build a culture of public service journalism among media organizations.

Le Devoir's Michener Award win for the twentieth anniversary signalled a breakthrough with the French media for the Michener Awards Foundation. Since the founding of the award, almost every report of the judging panel included a note to the administrators about how much they "deeply regret the lack of entries from French-language newspapers and broadcasters."[56] In the early years, the judging panel did not keep data about the number and categories of entries. However, in the twenty years before *Le Devoir*'s 1989 Michener Award, sixty-one finalists received honourable mentions and citations of merit. Of those, only two were for a French-language medium. *La Presse* received an honourable mention in 1972 and a citation of merit in 1981.

The big question for the Michener board year upon year, as they tried to create some buzz in Québec and French-speaking communities in other provinces, was, why so few entries? Alienation from English Canada, nationalistic sentiment, the Anglo make-up of the Foundation, its association with Rideau Hall and by inference, the Queen? Or was it that the effort just wasn't worth it? Lindsay Crysler, executive editor of the *Montreal Gazette* (1972-1977) and founding director of Concordia University's journalism program, understood the French media's lacklustre involvement in the Michener Award as a "chez nous" attitude. French media organizations placed more value on provincial awards because the perception was that the Michener Award was "an English Canada thing."[57]

In late 1987, the Michener Foundation hired Margaret Pearcy of National Public Relations to develop a communication plan to increase awareness and participation in the Michener Awards and fellowships, with a focus on Francophone journalists and media from the regions.[58] Pearcy delivered an ambitious, albeit pricey, $40,000 communication plan that included national advertising and bilingual pamphlets, and a suggestion that the Michener Awards Foundation work with *La Fédération des Journalistes du Québec* and other Francophone organizations.[59] The action resulted in a rush of applications for the 1990 study fellowships — nine of nineteen came from Québec that year — but it did little to move the dial on French-language submissions to the award. Bridging the two solitudes would remain a struggle for the Foundation.

The election of Norman Webster, managing editor of the *Montreal Gazette*, as president of the Michener Foundation in 1998 was a nod to Québec. Though he came from an English background, his roots were in the Eastern Townships of Québec.[60] As one of the Michener Awards Foundation's new leaders, the bilingual Webster would work hard to build ties with his French-speaking peers. His privilege was offset by the fact that he rose through the journalism ranks the old-fashioned way, with hard work and talent. Webster's first job was as a summer student at the *Globe and Mail*, at the time owned by his uncle, R. Howard Webster.

It was soon clear to then-managing editor Richard Doyle that Norman Webster was not one to trade on his family ties or that he was an Oxford Rhodes Scholar. "He is a personable youngster who is genuinely interested in newspaper work for which he has demonstrated — so far — considerable aptitude," wrote Doyle in a 1959 memo. "Norman knows all about type lice and rubber lead."[61] Webster started at the *Globe*'s magazine *Weekly* for a princely sum of $45 a week and the privilege of working for another reporter on the youth page as a "leg man" doing research and other behind-the-scenes work.

By the time Webster became president of the Michener Foundation, he had distinguished himself as the *Globe*'s bureau chief in China and London. He succeeded his mentor, Richard Doyle, as editor-in-chief at the *Globe*, a position he held from 1983 to 1989. "Webster was part of the new generation who saw themselves as members of a profession," wrote David Hayes in *Power and Influence*. "He brought a social conscience rooted in *noblesse oblige*."[62] At the virtual book launch of Webster's book, *Newspapering: 50 Years of Reporting from Canada and Around the World,* in 2020, retired senator and journalist Joan Fraser aptly put it this way: "However faithful he was to journalistic codes, he was even more faithful to his sense of duty to the public," all of which aligned with the Michener values.[63]

Even though Webster spent most of his career in big media, he always retained his Eastern township Québec roots. During stints as a young reporter at John Bassett's *Sherbrooke Record* and later as "publisher-in-training" at the *Winnipeg Free Press* with Brigadier Richard Malone, he saw first-hand how smaller publishers had to work with few resources.[64] In his two years as president of the Michener Awards Foundation, Webster enlisted board members from Québec — André Préfontaine, who would later become the president of

Transcontinental Media, and Pierre Bergeron of *Le Droit* — to help make inroads with the francophone media publishers and those smaller newspapers with fewer resources.[65] It was clear that it would take more than bilingual pamphlets and advertising to attract French-language entries.

When work obligations forced Webster to step down in 2000, his vice president, Pierre Bergeron, took over. As the Foundation's first francophone president, Bergeron made it his mission to continue Webster's work by tapping into his contacts in the Québec media. As publisher of *Le Droit*, the French daily in the Ottawa area, Bergeron had a "can do" reputation. When he arrived, *Le Droit* was starting to break even. Under his leadership, the paper started to make money and, at the same time, invest in quality journalism. He put all its news and editorial resources into a community fight to save Montfort Hospital, the only francophone hospital in urban Ontario, from being closed by the province.

Directing the energies of the Ottawa-based French-language daily newspaper to be an advocate was something that Bergeron had never thought possible. In a 2019 interview, he recalled, "Going on stage at the stadium as the publisher speaking to 10,000 people and in front of everybody saying that we would continue the fight, but we did it."[66] The coverage included 371 news stories, thirty-one editorials and 177 letters to the editor. The sustained and noisy protests convinced the government to keep the hospital open and enhance services. It earned a Michener honourable mention.

As Michener president, Bergeron embarked on a different type of advocacy — to get more French-language media to participate in the awards. The challenges in breaking down language barriers soon became apparent. "Unlike major English language media, the French language organizations do not have senior editors designated to identify award-potential stories and prepare their entries," he explained.[67] Bergeron enlisted the help of board members René Roseberry, a former news editor with *Le Nouvelliste* in Trois Rivières and president of the *Grands Prix des Hebdos du Québec*, and Alain Guilbert, a distinguished senior editor and former manager of various Québec newspapers. Together the trio mined their deep connections and good relations with the French media. They systematically contacted every media manager to urge them to identify and submit their best public service journalism. "Keep the pressure on" was Bergeron's mantra. Five entries for 2002 were good, he said, but not good enough. Bergeron set a goal of eight. This push for greater Francophone representation met with the frequently expressed desire of Rideau Hall for more outreach to and involvement of French language media, which was emphasized yet again by then Governor General Adrienne Clarkson.

The one-on-one contact paid off. By the time Bergeron stepped down in 2005, the number of French-language entries had increased dramatically, from zero to an all-time high of eleven. Bergeron's leadership had helped to chip away some of the *ennui* Québec media had towards the award. Perhaps other media were encouraged when the 2003 Michener Award went to *La Presse* for its reports on the inhumane treatment of older people living in long-term care homes. The judges' citation praised the coverage: "The first series of stories by *La Presse* drew a shocking portrait of care provided to the elderly in residential and long-term care centres (CHLSDs) that made readers shudder and resulted in public protest. The second series of articles raised awareness about the wrongful treatment of patients at Saint-Charles-Borromée Hospital in Montreal."[68] The family of a patient at Saint-Charles-Borromée suspected that their fifty-one-year-old sister, a long-time resident with head injuries suffered in a car accident, was being sexually abused at the home. They installed a recording device that caught two staff making mocking, scornful, violent and sexual comments. The reports by investigative journalist André Noël resulted in quick action. The Saint-Charles-Borromée Hospital was placed in trusteeship. Québec established a task force to review the complaint system and started surprise inspections at residential and long-term care centres. The Human Rights Commission investigated 125 cases of suspected assault and financial exploitation of older adults and people with disabilities.[69] The *La Presse* stories provided heft for a 1999 class action suit by 600 victims against the institution, which was settled out of court ten years later for $7 million.[70]

The robust number of French entries received in 2005 did not hold, and over the next twenty years, French entries fluctuated between one and eight entries. Among the French-language media, the Michener Award had neither the recognition nor the star appeal of a home-grown award from *La Fédération professionnelle des journalistes du Québec*. Before becoming governor general in 2005, former CBC Montreal journalist, presenter and news anchor Michaëlle Jean regarded the Michener Awards ceremony as a venue "for Francophone and Anglophone journalists to get together and to have a good discussion and to speak about the world, their work, their concerns, the challenges."[71] But too often the ceremony would be a reminder of the Anglo nature of the Michener Awards Foundation.

Many a French publisher, producer and reporter have squirmed uncomfortably in past years as a Michener official stood on stage and stumbled through the French-language citations. "It's a very Anglo group and you have to sometimes take for granted that you are the token Francophone, and it's not pleasant," recalled Pierre Bergeron.[72] "The elephant in the corridor is the problem of quality journalism in regional newspapers."[73] The issue was reflected in the paucity of Michener Award nominations.

Nominations among French-language media tend to go to the usual suspects: *La Presse* and Société Radio-Canada, occasionally *Le Devoir, Le Droit* and the magazine *L'actualité*. Submissions from smaller outlets such as *Le Courrier de Sainte-Hyacinthe*, a finalist in 2008, are rare. "If you remove *La Presse* and *SRC* participation looks even worse," said former president David Humphreys. "With this in mind we needed to try harder, and in reality, we have tried less." In his analysis, individual Québec colleagues worked hard and attracted interest through their personal contacts. But when they stepped down, there were no sustained efforts. "Outreach has been limited to one advertisement in the *Fédération professionnelle des journalistes du Québec* journal, no social media," Humphreys wrote in an email in 2019.[74] The problem, he said, was that the Foundation was patronage-rich and resource-poor. "We have perhaps ridden on all the patronage side of things too much [the Office of the Governor General and Rideau Hall] and neglected the resource side of things," he said in another interview.[75]

Experience has prepared French-language finalists to head to Ottawa with the expectation that they will be bridesmaids at the awards ceremony to an English-language winner and go home with the bride's bouquet, a citation of merit. "Those French entries have to be on the same level as the others and at some point, one of those French entries will win," Bergeron said."[76] Over fifty years from 1970 to 2020, French-language media have brought home just less than 10 per cent of Michener Awards (five of 57). They have received a little more than 10 per cent of citations of merit (23 of 221). The lower rate of French entries is the result of a combination of factors — attitude, newsroom mergers and cutbacks resulting in fewer reporters producing impactful stories, and the Michener Awards Foundation's inconsistent and under-resourced promotion of the awards among French media.

The lack of French entries is an issue that does not sit well with the Michener board. In 2019, when Pierre-Paul Noreau took over as Foundation president, he revived the focus of past presidents Norman Webster and Pierre

Bergeron. Noreau was a well-respected journalist and media executive in the francophone press. He started in the 1970s at *La Tuque*, reported in Ottawa and Québec for *Le Soleil*, and was publisher of *Le Droit* before retiring and taking on the role of president of *Le Conseil de presse du Québec* (CPQ). During his three-year tenure, Noreau made a concerted effort to speak with every Francophone publisher and broadcast outlet in Québec and as past president remains a huge promoter of the Michener Awards in Québec.

Small Towns, Big Stories

When it comes to winning a Michener Award, the perception is that the big media organizations with a lot more resources have a better chance of winning.[77] But data for 1970-2020 show smaller media have done well: 25 per cent (14/57) won Michener Awards, and about 27 per cent (60/221) received citations. Even so, publishers and reporters from French-language and smaller media organizations often say that when they receive a nomination, they temper their expectations. They welcome the trip to Rideau Hall, the ceremony and the chance to mingle and nosh, but most expect to go home with just a citation, and many do.

For example, in 1987, the *Eastern Graphic*, a small weekly on Prince Edward Island, led the debate over building the Confederation Bridge to connect PEI to New Brunswick. Publisher Jim MacNeill jumped in the ring with both fists up and the newspaper punched above its weight. The paper printed secret reports that provided Islanders with the necessary information to make an informed decision for an upcoming plebiscite.[78] In Québec, *Le Courrier de Saint-Hyacinthe* was recognized in 2008 for exposing financial mismanagement at the local college.

In 2010, *Eastern Door* was honoured with a citation for its courageous stand against the Mohawk Council of Kahnawake in Québec and its plans to actively evict thirty-five non-Indigenous people from the community. For Steven Bonspiel, publisher/reporter, it was a human rights story. In retaliation against the coverage, the Mohawk Council slashed advertising, called for a boycott of the paper and tried to enact a media blackout. With support from the community, Bonspiel held his ground. Council did not proceed. Bonspiel called the decision a victory for compassion and inclusion against "racial tyranny."[79]

The *Prince George Citizen*, a small daily (now a weekly), was nominated in 2006 for its in-depth coverage of trucker fatalities on logging roads. Reporter

Gordon Hoekstra had written stories about how dozens of truckers had died in the past decade. His stories identified the problem, suggested solutions and asked why the province had not acted. As a result of his in-depth coverage the province appointed a coroner to look at forestry-related deaths and announced a $20 million upgrade to logging roads.

Hoekstra considered the Michener nomination to be a "token" to recognize the work of small media. When Michener Foundation president David Humphrey declared the *Prince George Citizen* a winner, Hoekstra's surprise was written all over his face; his jaw dropped, his eyes popped wide open and his hands shot up to cup his cheeks. Others seated in the row, who thought they were a shoo-in for the award, smiled tightly and tried to mask their shock and disappointment. It is natural for journalists from larger, better-resourced media organizations to expect a win, and those from smaller organizations, who run on a shoestring, to gauge their chances of winning the main prize to be slim. So, when smaller media outlets win a Michener Award, it is because their coverage demonstrated public service impact despite limited resources.

It is gratifying when a smaller media outlet breaks the glass ceiling. For example, the 1990 Michener Award went to the feisty and often controversial *Elmira Independent*, a small Ontario newspaper with 7,400 subscribers, for its "blanket coverage of a prolonged legal battle over contamination of the municipal water supply."[80] For president Gail Scott, Elmira's Michener was a demonstration that "meritorious public service in journalism can be attained without the benefit of a large operating budget."[81] It was only the second weekly newspaper to win a Michener.[82] There would be fewer submissions from smaller outlets in subsequent years, as media outlets continued to consolidate, close and cut staff to cope with reduced advertising and subscriber numbers and the arrival of the Internet. But that night, the owner-editor of the *Elmira Independent*, Bob Verdun, had the swagger that harkens back to the shepherd David of biblical fame after he slew the giant Goliath.

Uniroyal Chemical was the biggest employer in Elmira. Verdun had been covering the multinational since 1970 when he began as a reporter for the weekly *Elmira Signet*. Fired by the *Signet* in 1974, Verdun started the *Elmira Independent*. He took the newspaper's watchdog role seriously. Uniroyal's "waste disposal practices historically were outrageous," Verdun said.[83] Dangerous levels of the cancer-causing chemical, dimethylnitrosamine (DMNA) — a byproduct from the production of rubber products — had seeped from Uniroyal's lagoons into the aquifer and poisoned the groundwater. "It's an unintentional pollutant that they didn't really even know that much about it until it started to show up," said Verdun. The Ontario Ministry of the Environment ordered Uniroyal Chemical Ltd. to stop dumping its wastewater. In an attempt to quash the order, the company went to the Environmental Appeals Board, knowing full well the appeal hearings would clog up the system. Hearings dragged on for most of 1990 and into 1991.

The *Elmira Independent* was the only media outlet that showed up to every session of the appeals process and stayed to the end, even when the meetings ran until 3:30 in the morning. Each week, details of the hearing filled the paper — not what the business establishment wanted to read because they felt "it was giving the community a bad name," said Verdun. [84] He said they blamed the *Independent*'s coverage saying, "Elmira was never going to be known as anything but the pollution capital of Canada." On top of that, Uniroyal was also the largest employer in the region with 200 to 250 employees.

The *Independent* lost readers, but Verdun was chuffed when the three-member appeal board bought subscriptions. "They said it was extremely valuable for them for two reasons. First of all we were summarizing for them. And we were reporting from the point of view of the community." In the end, Uniroyal was forced to change its disposal practices. The environment ministry gave the company thirty years to clean up the contaminated aquifer and soil.[85] Uniroyal Chemicals Ltd. has changed hands and names several times, each company taking over the cleanup. Since 2017, a German company, LANXESS, has been manufacturing "synthetic lubricants and additives for lubricants, plastics and rubber" at the site.[86] Its website states that, by the 2028 deadline, 99 per cent of the pollution will be cleaned. But, "we are at a point in the remediation where there is no known scientifically available methodology to remove that last bit of contaminant from such a massive aquifer."[87]

Bob Verdun sold the weekly in 1999 to Metroland, who shuttered it in 2015. Verdun remains proud because out of the *Elmira Independent*'s news coverage grew a "permanent and influential environmental committee that has never given up monitoring Uniroyal."[88] The grassroots community action group, APT Environment, still watches for new infractions and monitors the cleanup[89] — a lasting legacy of the Michener values of public service.

As with the 1982 Michener winner, the *Manitoulin Expositor*, Verdun didn't expect to win, so he had no speech prepared. "I tried not to be too long, be brief and be off," he said with a laugh. He still remembers the way the bigger outlets reacted to his win. "There's a kind of touchiness about it, a weekly newspaper should not be winning their award." He was not far off. There may be a latent attitude among the bigger media with all their resources that they have earned the top prize, and it is an act of benevolence for smaller media outlets to get a nomination. So, when smaller media outlets win the Michener Award, they may encounter some indignation after the ceremony.

Verdun recalled that the best part of the awards ceremony in 1990 had been spending time with Roland Michener. "I was so privileged because it was his last presentation in his lifetime. And he attached himself to me and I spent most of the evening with him." Verdun found Michener "so down to earth for somebody who has been so important in Canadian history."[90] Michener died four months later, in August.

For twenty-one years Roland Michener was deeply committed to the values of public service in journalism. In his mind "meritorious and disinterested" journalism in the public interest were integral to Canada's democracy and worthy of being recognized and encouraged by the state. It was something that all media regardless of size or language — including the *Elmira Independent*, *La Presse*, the *Le Devoir* and the Kingston *Whig-Standard* — could aspire to. The Michener Award provided validation to media outlets — both big and small — that what they were doing mattered.

As the Foundation approached the end of its third decade, it grappled with the persistent challenge of how best to share excellence in public service journalism with a wider audience — to amplify the impact of the award. One avenue to be explored was the emerging technology, the Internet, a new medium of communication. Ironically, it would be the very medium that would soon drive the news industry into a more profound crisis. Tuned-in members of the Michener Foundation board regarded the arrival of the World Wide Web as an ideal platform to house stories of award-winning nominees and the work of fellowship recipients.

At the 1999 board meeting, director Tim Kotcheff made what was at the time considered a radical suggestion. He said that if the Michener Awards Foundation wanted to be part of the twenty-first century, it needed a website to showcase journalism in the public interest to a national and even global audience. Kotcheff, a former vice president of news for both the CTV and CBC television networks, was an early adopter. In 1994, he was part of a team working on an online multimedia news service for Bell Canada. His proposal to create a website for the Michener Awards sparked a lively discussion. Some directors were sceptical and wondered out loud if the Internet might be a fad. But Kotcheff said more journalism was appearing online. Ida Entwistle, manager for CBC International Affairs, pointed to several international awards including the *Prix Italia* that had special digital categories.

Board member Ed O'Dacre, a writer and editor with the *Globe and Mail,* supported the idea of a Michener website which "by its very presence and example, might lead to better journalism on the Internet."[91] But there was a bigger question that no one that day knew how to address. Beyond providing a virtual gallery for inspiring impactful journalism, how would this trend to news on the Internet fit into the Michener Awards project?

The board gave Kotcheff tentative approval. Within six months, he returned with a mockup for a Michener website. At the 2000 annual meeting, the board gave Kotcheff a budget of $5,000 and free rein to produce "a quality, colorful (*sic*) website and to get it up and running."[92] Page by page, year after year, Kotcheff worked away. It was an obsession and a passion. At every opportunity he travelled from his home in Toronto and spent thousands of hours of his own time and money digging through files at Library and Archives Canada and Rideau Hall in Ottawa.

The bilingual website went live on December 22, 2000.[93] Kotcheff worked closely with his francophone colleague, the genial René Roseberry. In 2002, Alain Guilbert joined the board and signed on for "the onerous task" of translating the news releases, speeches and fellowship reports back to 1970. Guilbert was a warm man with an easy smile, always ready with an encouraging word. His breadth and depth of experience as a distinguished senior editor and manager in several Québec newspapers and marketing and communications "resulted in faithful and free adaptation, the expression of what is called 'the genius of the language'."[94]

If you build it, they will come, or so the saying goes. At the annual meeting in 2003, Kotcheff reported that the site had 9,000 visits and 34,000 hits in the past year. These numbers would only grow. Kotcheff and Guilbert had created a living bilingual archival history of the journalism of media organizations recognized by the Michener Award, the mid-career fellowships and the Foundation. It honoured public service journalism going back to its beginnings in the late 1960s. Much of the information in this book has been informed by the material on the archival website that Kotcheff lovingly created and maintained until he left the board in 2014.[95] (The website was discontinued in 2021 when the Michener Awards Foundation redesigned its website.) Kotcheff and Guilbert had taken the Foundation off the printed page and into the twenty-first century of the Internet.

Back in 1999, it was hard to imagine how online journalism would compete with established newspapers, magazines and broadcasters. Board member Pierre Bergeron was not far off base when he worried that "the awards deck would be stacked against that kind of [online] journalism."[96] It has taken time for small, independent online news organizations to mature and produce journalism that is both substantial and has an impact. The first entry from an online media outlet came in 2007, but the first online news organization to be a Michener finalist was the *National Observer* in 2016. The *Observer*'s hard-hitting investigation derailed the Energy East pipeline hearings after revelations that the panel members had met with former Québec premier-turned-lobbyist Jean Charest. "As the media landscape changes, I think it's important for us to demonstrate that responsible journalism matters and that it's critical for strengthening public trust in our democracy," said Ottawa bureau chief Mike de Souza at the awards ceremony. The Michener Award by its very mission would play a role in this debate, and the website helped to expose the award-winning stories from large and small media to a growing virtual audience.

New Media, Old Media Under the Microscope

As the twentieth century came to an end, miles of column inches and hours of airtime had been spent speculating and mostly predicting doom and gloom about what would happen when the clocks rolled over to 2000. Computer technology would fail, and in a flip of a switch, our wired world would shut down — Y2K. Canadians woke up on January 1, 2000, perhaps a bit tired, maybe hungover, but their coffee makers still worked, their cars started, and emails were still popping into the inboxes on their desktops. The Y2K threat never materialized, but over the following decade, the Internet would drastically change the media landscape and disrupt everything they had long taken for granted.

Indeed, the 2000s produced a constellation of challenges for Canadian media, especially newspaper outlets. The creation of the *National Post* in 1998 sparked a newspaper war, the introduction of free dailies produced further stiff competition, and — the most significant change of all — the growth of the Internet created virtual competition for news and information and siphoned off critical revenue streams for broadcasters and classified advertising for newspapers. As a whole, this loosely regulated landscape caused unprecedented closures and concentration — thus fulfilling the worst fears of the Davey and Kent reports. Media managers reacted to the massive disruption by putting business and profits to shareholders ahead of public service journalism. Of course, the Michener Awards Foundation — through its awards and fellowships — did its part to encourage media organizations to dedicate their limited time and resources to journalism that focused on system and policy issues. But given the industry's challenges, investigative journalists were forced to find innovative ways to continue producing public service journalism.

The Michener Foundation also had to find new ways to provide leadership and validation for this work. It recognized journalistic collaborations among organizations, as they became an increasingly common way to conduct in-depth projects. It invited journalism students and educators to the awards ceremony to spark interest in public service journalism. And it expanded the fellowship program to encourage best practices and reflect on the state of the industry and its workers.

The new century had ushered in mean times for editors and reporters trying to make a difference through their journalism. If ever the flagging profession needed encouragement to remember its purpose, it was now. Media organizations and journalists turned to the Michener Awards for validation, and the Foundation looked to Rideau Hall for support.

Contest, Collapse, Converge

In the late 1990s and 2000s, media organizations, particularly newspapers, fought to keep audiences and advertisers. The twenty-four-hour news channels — CNN, CTV and CBC's Newsworld — were luring people away from newspapers with instant news updates and 24/7 opinion. Readers were more computer savvy and went online for fast, free news. In the newspaper world, 1998 brought the first of several waves of intense competition, starting with the launch of a new daily, the *National Post*.

Newspaper baron Conrad Black's saucy conservative-leaning national broadsheet unleashed a two-year bare-knuckle sidewalk fight among Toronto's top newspapers for circulation numbers, readership and advertisers. The *National Post* was designed to be "more intelligent, more fun, and racier than the *Globe* could ever be."[1] It offered a new reading experience. "We came out with a lot more visually appealing product and a lot more noisier product in terms of the number of voices we had," said Kenneth Whyte, the founding editor-in-chief.[2]

When it came to news coverage, Whyte, a western come-from-away, had been well-schooled by his former boss, Ted Byfield of the *Alberta Report*, whose journalistic approach was "pitting different points of view against one another" as a way to work things out. "Ted was all about debate, rather than the resolution of the debate," Whyte said. This confrontational style of journalism in the *National Post* was encouraged by Whyte's deputy editor-in-chief Martin Newland, imported from Black's UK paper, *The Daily Telegraph*. "The *Post* was a lot more in your face and aggressive. We decided what our stories were, and we chased them relentlessly and didn't give up on them when the news cycle changed," Whyte recalled. The *Post* had "a handful of issues that we were determined to own," such as fiscal policy and government debt, Unite the Right and personalities.[3]

Instead of foreign bureaus, the *Post* had a huge travel budget, and editors used it liberally. "When the Concorde flew its last fight from Paris to New York, it was the end of an era," said Whyte. "We paid $14,000 and got Christie Blatchford on. I remember that flight and that we got a week's worth of journalism out of it. It was a big expenditure, but again everyone was reading it." Audiences were getting sizzle along with their journalism of substance. "It was our belief that most of the really good investigative opportunities came out of diligent reporting on particular stories or following beats." Whyte pointed to Andrew McIntosh's complicated investigation that became known as Shawinigate.[4] It exposed the dealings of Prime Minister Jean Chrétien involving "taxpayers' dollars and how millions of dollars found their way to ethically challenged businessmen in the prime minister's home riding."[5]

The competition — *Globe and Mail, Toronto Star* and the *Toronto Sun* — responded to the upstart *Post* with redesigns, colour pages, newspaper giveaways and bargain basement bulk sales to hotels and airlines. It was a golden moment for readers "The look and sound of the newspapers changed quite substantially in a fairly short period of time," said Whyte. So did the editorial content of the main competitors — the *Globe and Mail* and the *Toronto Star.* "The *Post*'s stable of writers, its capacity for dramatic display, its access to superb foreign stories, and its eclectic story selection all combined to forge a formidable competitor. We knew we were in for a real battle," wrote John Honderich in his memoir, *Above the Fold.*[6] The *Star*'s editorial strategy to keep subscribers and advertisers and win the newspaper war was to continue "to provide groundbreaking investigative journalism."[7] Honderich wanted *Star* reporters to tell stories that "revealed malfeasance, neglect or wrongdoing" and resulted in positive changes. "I felt all our investigations should aspire to this level," he said, referring to Michener Award-winning stories.[8]

It wouldn't be long before the fierce competition with the *National Post* would ebb. The writing was on the wall in late 2000. In three years, the paper lost an estimated $190 million.[9] In a shrewd move, Black put his wallet ahead of his heart and sold 50 per cent of his beloved *National Post,* along with thirteen metro dailies, 126 community papers and the website for $3.2B to Canwest Global Communications, owned by the Asper family of Winnipeg.

Nine months later, in August 2001, he sold the rest of the *Post* to Canwest. "The management and directors of Hollinger find this a painful, but a sensible decision. The *National Post* has been successfully launched and established, but now requires an intimate association with an indigenous Canadian media company to take it through the next competitive phase of its development to profitability," Hollinger said.[10] With that, the newspaper war ended, but it had lasting effects. It "was a confrontation that, by some estimates, would cost the three papers combined more than $1 billion — a crippling burden for all three," wrote Chris Cobb in *Ego and Ink*.[11] The *National Post* newspaper war would be the first blow to hit print in the 2000s.

The second blow came in 2000 when *Metro*, a Swedish company, announced it was entering the Canadian market. Its first free commuter daily would be launched in Toronto that July. *Metro* had plans to expand to other Canadian cities. While the free paper posed no threat to the *Globe and Mail*, Canada's national newspaper, the announcement sent off alarm bells at the *Toronto Sun* and *Toronto Star*. GTA was their turf, and no newcomer was going to siphon off their audience and advertisers. Thus began the second newspaper war.

In Toronto, reaction to the impending competition came quickly. Within weeks of the announcement, the tabloid Toronto *Sun* was on the streets handing out its new free daily *FYI Toronto*. "It's a quick read of top news you have to know on your way to work," said Lou Clancy of the *Sun* in an interview with CBC's *The National*. "It's information on what to do today and how to do it [and] where to go."[12] Three days later, *Toronto Star* carriers were handing out its free daily *GTA Today* at GO train and bus stations. That didn't deter *Metro*, which launched in July 2000 and expanded to eight other cities. Over the next twenty years, the free newspaper craze would see other commuter handouts such as *Dose*, *t.o.night* and *24 Hours* arise and disappear. There were mergers and renames in the fight for circulation and advertisers in the commuter market.

It all added up to yet another financial hit to the struggling newspaper industry. For the *Toronto Star*, "We knew that on an annual basis we would lose close to $4 million, but we figured *Metro*'s deficit would top $7.5 million."[13] John Honderich was prepared to go to the mat with *Metro*, but in March 2001, he had to settle for a draw. Against his advice, the parent company, Torstar, announced a merger between *Metro* and *GTA Today*. Three months later, the *Sun*'s owner, Québecor, pulled the plug on *FYI Toronto*, only to revive it in 2003 under the new name, *24 Hours*. In November 2017, Torstar acquired *24 Hours* in a newspaper swap with Postmedia and shuttered the Toronto and Vancouver editions. It would be another two years before Torstar ceased publishing its free newspapers, now *Star Metro*, in Halifax, Ottawa, Toronto, Edmonton, Calgary and Vancouver. The free newspaper frenzy in English Canada ended, and when everyone looked around, the media world had changed.

While the newspapers had been fighting over dead trees, the Internet had become the marketplace of the twenty-first century with free news, classified ads, videos, music, games, weather, sports and a steady stream of opinion. The newspaper wars that began in the late 1990s had served as a distraction to the industry's growing problem — how to adapt their business models to the digital age. From the industry's point of view, the Internet was stealing their audiences, advertisers and profits, and it seemed no one knew how to monetize this new platform.

In the 2000s, it seemed as if everything was in play. Mainstream media were unprepared for the multimedia, interactive and social online universe of bloggers and citizen journalists. Newspaper publishers were stunned when the cash cow — classified advertising — all but disappeared, in what seemed like an instant, from the back pages and flooded onto web services such as Craigslist and eBay. While traditional media panicked, communication companies such as Bell Canada Enterprises, Québecor, Canwest, Rogers and Astral Media saw opportunities to grow and cash in on the so-called Information Highway. They moved quickly to gobble up radio and television networks like CTV, TVA, City TV, Global and Standard Broadcasting, along with long-established newspaper groups like Sun Media, Osprey and the *Globe and Mail*. The convergence frenzy led to unprecedented buying and selling, mergers and consolidations, and closures and failures.[14] Between 1994 and 2017, communications and media companies spent about $45.43 billion buying and selling properties to leverage companies "in an ill-conceived attempt at communications and media convergence," wrote Dwayne Winseck of the Global Media and Internet Concentration Project.[15] This was about business, profits and shareholders, not about providing journalism in the public interest.

If they were lucky, journalists like those at the *National Post* found themselves working under new management in slimmed down newsrooms with fewer resources. Those less fortunate found themselves hunting for new jobs in an ever-constricting and changing media world. In 2000, journalists had come face-to-face with the ghosts of Senator Keith Davey and political mandarin Tom Kent, who, in 1970 and 1980, had predicted an increasingly concentrated and converged media that would collide with public interest. Volume 1 of Davey's Special Committee on the Mass Media report, "The Uncertain Mirror," set out "a hypothetical extreme" where "one man or one corporation could own every media outlet in the country except the CBC."[16] There were those in the industry who believed that this prediction would soon be a reality.

Once again, the concern about the lack of diversity and media concentration would find its way back onto the federal agenda. On March 19, 2003, the Senate of Canada authorized an investigation into the state of Canadian media industries — the third federal study in thirty-five years. In the chair at the start of the inquiry was Senator Joan Fraser, a former reporter and editor with the *Montreal Gazette* and the *Financial Times of Canada*.

The assignment of the Standing Senate Committee on Transport and Communication was to examine "emerging trends and developments in these industries; the media's role, rights and responsibilities in Canadian society; and current and appropriate future policies . . . "[17] Even then, no one could predict the profound effect the Internet and social media would have on the functioning of Canada's legacy media and how the disruption would undermine their role in society. As Fraser would write in the introduction to the interim report, "No real democracy can function without healthy, diverse and independent news media to inform people about the way their society works, what is going well and, perhaps more important, what is not going well or needs to be improved. The news of the day is . . . often the only such guide that can plausibly claim not to be self-interested."[18] Fraser recognized the fragility of news within an unstable information environment.

Two years later, at the Ottawa news conference to release the *Final Report on the Canadian News Media,* deputy committee chair Senator David Tkachuk quipped, "The horse has left the barn. You can't change all that." To which Senator Jim Munson, a former CTV parliamentary reporter, added, "There's no going back."[19] The Senators had travelled to ten locations across the country and heard testimony from 304 individuals and groups. The two-year study painted a grim picture in which "concentration of ownership has reached levels that few other countries would consider acceptable."[20] Their forty recommendations were "guided by the conviction that the more owners, the better." The report called for policy changes to the *Broadcasting Act* and the *Competition Act* "to develop a mechanism that allows discussion of the public interest in media mergers." This was not a radical proposal. As the committee pointed out, "it is not uncommon for restrictions to exist with respect to concentration, cross-media ownership and foreign ownership"[21] and pointed to such policies in countries like France, the United Kingdom and Australia.

The response from the minister of Canadian Heritage, Bev Oda, was in keeping with the Conservative free-market party line. "It is important to re-iterate that Canada has a highly diverse, dynamic and economically viable news media sector," and that "the current legislative, regulator, and policy frameworks, supported by the various government programs, has served Canadians well." Furthermore, she emphasized it was the job of the media sector — not the government — "to provide independent and diverse news and information and also adapt their business models to today's new technologies and media environment."[22] The message was clear. The government of Stephen Harper would let the marketplace of news and information play out.

The result was that the roller coaster of mergers, closures and downsizing continued throughout the 2000s with dizzying speed. Media organizations bloated with debt from acquisitions took a crippling hit after the markets crashed in 2008. With an exodus of advertisers — the primary source of revenue — and inflated expectations of shareholders, media conglomerates pulled back. They laid off massive numbers of media workers, and, in some cases, that was not enough to stay solvent. In 2009, nine years after paying $3.5 billion for Hollinger Inc., Winnipeg-based Canwest Global Communications declared bankruptcy. The papers, now part of Postmedia, were sold for $1.1B; the majority owner is Chatham Asset Management, a New Jersey hedge fund.

Despite closures and mergers, journalists in newsrooms across the country persisted. They found innovative ways to tell stories that mattered to Canadians. It was a matter of professional pride. As media managers tightened the purse strings, news producers, editors and reporters from different media outlets started to put journalism in the public interest ahead of competition.

Putting a Glow on the Awards

The appointment of Adrienne Clarkson as the twenty-sixth Governor General of Canada in October 1999 came at an opportune time for the industry and for the work of the Michener Awards Foundation. A former journalist, Clarkson was a familiar face to CBC viewers. She had a thirty-year award-winning career, starting as a host of *Take Thirty,* a national public affairs afternoon television show, before moving to CBC's flagship current affairs show *the fifth estate.* After a term as Ontario's Agent-General in France, Clarkson returned to CBC to create and host the cultural program, *Adrienne Clarkson Presents.* She was the first person of Asian heritage to become Governor General of Canada. She stepped into the role of governor general as if she were born to do the job.

Her predecessor, Roméo LeBlanc, had stepped down a year before the end of his term due to ill health. His Michener ceremonies had been low-key celebrations with a stand-up reception with drinks and hot and cold canapés. That austere menu alone spoke volumes about the health of His Excellency, who normally enjoyed entertaining his former colleagues. When Clarkson took over, she saw an opportunity and took on the Michener Awards as a pet project. She was sensitive to the effects of the media crisis and set her mind to making the Michener Awards ceremony an evening to remember. "I said it should be celebrated because freedom of the press is one of the glories that they're providing society," she said. [23]

Clarkson, like LeBlanc, held fast to the tenet that journalism was one of the four pillars of Canada's democracy and should be elevated and celebrated, especially in these tough times. It was a matter of great pride to ensure the work of media in a time of great stress was valued. She did that by giving the annual ceremony *panache.* That meant evening gowns and black tie, a sit-down four-course dinner, dancing and special guests, authors and journalists "who helped to shape our country and helped to shape us into the kind of people we are."[24] The invitation list included like authors Doris Anderson, Farley Mowat, June Callwood, Margaret Atwood, Graeme Gibson, Trent Frayne and Pierre Berton, who was called upon to be guest speaker at the 2002 ceremony.

At her first awards ceremony — the thirtieth anniversary of the Michener Awards — Clarkson reminded the gathering at Rideau Hall why journalism is so important. "We Canadians are well educated. We have a high standard of living and a huge amount of space in which to live, yet injustices occur here as do abuses of our systems and structures. So we need the press in all its forms to alert us to our situation, to awaken our indignation and to keep us uncomfortable. The recounting of greed, negligence, indifference, corruption and callous carelessness renders us psychically itchy, and perhaps, although that is not the journalists' responsibility, we will have to scratch."[25] Her enthusiasm for journalism would be the boost that enterprising media organizations and the Michener Foundation needed to navigate the choppy waters of disruption and technological change in the industry.

The Michener Award winner at the April 2000 ceremony, CBC National Radio News Winnipeg, was a great example of what Clarkson meant in her speech. The public broadcaster had exposed an illegal vote-rigging scheme in Manitoba. Reporter Curt Petrovich spent three years chasing down rumours and gathering evidence. CBC's stories proved that senior Manitoba Progressive Conservative party members, including some of the Premier's top advisors, had spent thousands of dollars, including some from the PC party bank account, to bribe three Indigenous people to run as 'independents' in NDP ridings with high Indigenous populations. The goal was to split the vote in the 1995 provincial election to favour the Conservatives. Petrovich said his big break came when one of the three unsuccessful independent candidates, Darryl Sutherland, finally broke the silence. Because of the gravity of the allegations, Petrovich went on to contact or interview another half dozen people to judge and verify the reliability of the information.

Petrovich wrote that the potential consequences of the story weighed heavily on his conscience. "The allegations, once public, could devastate careers and likely affect the political balance in Manitoba, which had been governed by the Conservatives for a decade."[26] When the story broke on June 22, 1998, Petrovich said the political reaction was predictable. "Premier Gary Filmon at first denied anything about the story was credible. He suggested it was NDP sleazy-mongering (sic)." But after CBC released more details, the premier called a public inquiry. The report of Commissioner Alfred Monnin confirmed CBC's findings of corruption among PC Manitoba party officials. The retired judge did not mince words: "As a trial judge I conducted a number of trials. As an appellate court judge I read many thousands of pages of transcript in a variety of cases: criminal, civil, family, etc. In all my years on the Bench I have never encountered as many liars in one proceeding as I did during this inquiry."[27]

The journalism and subsequent inquiry had a huge and lasting impact on the policies and practices of political parties, the government and associated groups in Manitoba. Monnin's recommendations tightened loopholes in the Manitoba elections laws and gave the Chief Electoral Officer broad powers of search and seizure of election records. Candidates and parties were required to keep election financial records for five years. Auditors had to resign if their professional judgement or objectivity had been impaired. The three main parties voluntarily adopted codes of ethics "to prevent anyone from believing they have tacit approval to cheat at an election." Voters also had their say. "The dark stain on the previously scandal-free Conservative government had influence on voters when they went to the polls again in September 1999. The Conservatives, after eleven successful years in government, lost to the NDP," wrote Petrovich.[28]

The 1995 vote-splitting scandal was huge, gigantic, said Cecil Rosner, head of CBC's investigative unit. "They actually tried to rig an election. How often does that happen that you get the proof of it and trigger an inquiry and all the rest of it," he said. "It took the Conservative party more than a decade to recover from that."[29] This is the kind of watchdog journalism that was under threat from the churn in the industry.

Despite the industry difficulties, the Michener Award was an incentive for media outlets still investing in time-consuming investigative journalism. It validated their work and the crucial role of journalism as a pillar of democracy. For example, persistent reporting over four years by the *Globe and Mail* uncovered allegations of fraud within the federal Liberal party. Reporters Daniel LeBlanc and Campbell Clark used access to information requests, government documents and interviews to put facts to rumours of patronage and uncontrolled spending at senior levels of Jean Chrétien's Liberal government following the 1995 Québec referendum. Their ongoing coverage earned the paper a Michener citation of merit in 2002 and a Michener Award in 2004. The journalism resulted in a scathing report by Auditor General Sheila Fraser, the recall of Canada's Ambassador to Denmark, the firing of three heads of Crown corporations and the launch of the public inquiry headed by Mr. Justice John Gomery.

Gomery's report revealed that "$100 million of federal government funds were paid to a variety of communications agencies in a complex web of transactions, involving kickbacks and illegal contributions to the Liberal Party in Canada."[30] The story of political patronage that started under Prime Minister Jean Chrétien came to rest with the defeat of his successor, Prime Minister Paul Martin, in the 2006 federal election.

Twenty years later, the impact of the reporting about the sponsorship scandal is evident in the way Ottawa handles outside contracts. After leaving the *Globe and Mail*, Edward Greenspon became President and CEO of the Public Policy Forum, an independent Ottawa public policy research firm. In 2016, he was looking for sponsors to fund research into "The Shattered Mirror," a report examining news, democracy and trust in the digital age.[31] He approached two federal departments and was quickly mired in a complicated process. "The hoops you have to go through," Greenspon recalled. "One day I complained to somebody senior in the government and I said, you want to work with people outside, but we're a small organization and we don't have 500 lawyers on staff and you make it so difficult. And he looked at me and said, weren't you the editor of the *Globe and Mail* when you did the sponsorship scandal? And I said, c'mon. The idea was to root out the bad guys, not make it impossible to do anything in future. He said, well, that's how it turned out."[32] The lasting effect of the reporting of the sponsorship scandal is that the federal government is ultra-cautious in engaging outside groups. "It keeps people on their toes because there are journalists watching the system and making sure that the system operates as it purports that it will operate," Greenspon said.

These vital investigations show the value of the persistence of the work of journalists — and their "personal pride and general journalistic excellence," Michener Foundation president Russ Mills said.[33] Without the journalists and the support of their editors, producers and publishers, important stories of the day like the vote-splitting scheme and the federal sponsorship scandal would likely have remained hidden from the public.

These were not comfortable stories. Her Excellency Adrienne Clarkson drove home that point when she said at the 2000 awards ceremony that Michener stories challenge "self-interest and mediocrity . . . which as fallible human beings, content in our own lives, we would really not have asked to know about. In afflicting us with the truth, they make it impossible for us to turn away, and our lives, as citizens of Canada, are better for it."[34] The publisher and CEO of the Ottawa *Sun*, Judy Bullis, was so moved by Clarkson's words, that she wrote to thank Clarkson for her "poignant and important" presentation. "The award ceremony is a testament to the excellence for which the media should constantly strive. . . . In fact, your words taught me the significance of the writer's obligation to inform first without bias, then, and only then, with input."[35] At a time when media organizations found themselves undermined on all fronts, the awards were a touchstone, to remind journalists of their important role as watchdogs of public interest in a democracy.

The industry would look to the Michener Awards and Rideau Hall to validate the importance of investigative journalism through this time of innovation, disruption and profound uncertainty in the industry.

Competition versus Collaboration

The fierce competition from the *National Post*, *Metro* and, most importantly, the Internet left media organizations struggling to remain financially solvent. A direct result of smaller news budgets and fewer journalists was a move toward journalistic cooperation and collaboration, within news organizations and even among competitors.

Because of the buying and selling, many organizations owned more than one media outlet in different locations. Cooperation among sister newsrooms made sense. For example, Torstar, Postmedia, CTV or CBC could draw on the expertise and resources spread across their organization to produce an in-depth story. In 2006, the *Hamilton Spectator*, *Toronto Star* and the *Kitchener-Waterloo Record* — all Torstar newspapers — received a citation of merit for their joint series "Collision Course" that documented 800 incidents where planes got dangerously close, putting 80,000 passengers at risk.[36] The joint submission of the *Edmonton Journal* and *Calgary Herald* — both Postmedia newspapers — was a Michener finalist in 2013 after the shocking series "Fatal Care" found that over fourteen years, half of the 145 children who died in Alberta foster care were of Indigenous heritage. As a result of this investigation, the Alberta government restructured the system, opened death records, and updated legislation.[37] While company cooperation happened with increasing regularity, it was rare, even unthinkable, for competing media outlets to work jointly on a story.

Michener records show that before 2007, only two such entries had made it to Rideau Hall: the 1971 Michener Award winner, *Financial Post* and CBC-TV for the "Charter Revolution" and the 1990 finalist, *Le Droit* and *Sault Star*, for their joint coverage of bilingualism. Plummeting profits and new technology, the Internet and social media saw former rivals becoming collaborators. In 2007, the Michener judging panel started to receive joint entries on a regular basis. Print and broadcast newsrooms pooled journalistic expertise and limited resources to produce big cross-media investigations that would reach larger and more diverse audiences. Take, for example, the investigation involving the financial relationship between former Prime Minister Brian Mulroney and German-Canadian businessman Karlheinz Schreiber. For years, *the fifth estate* and the *Globe and Mail* had been independently chasing the story before deciding to pool resources. The combined print-broadcast effort earned them a Michener nomination in 2017.

At the awards ceremony, Linden MacIntyre reminded journalists why he and CBC's Harvey Cashore collaborated with Greg McArthur of the *Globe* to chase down the Mulroney story. "For me the over-arching significance of the story is its power to remind us of the crucial importance of transparency and accountability in high places — not just for elected officials, but also regarding the conduct of the many people drawn to them by the magnetism of power and the prospect of easy personal enrichment at public expense."[38] It was a partnership that worked well, said then editor-in-chief Ed Greenspon. "Journalistic organizations are going to have animal spirits, and that's great that they want to win, that they want to be the ones that get the story. But, particularly in a world of limited resources, throwing your lot in with each other and not giving up your freedom to report the story as you feel like it, but sharing the base of information so you could put more firepower into the story."[39] While collaboration broadens the source base for journalists, it also brings the stories to a wider audience and as a result they have a bigger impact. The Schreiber coverage resulted in a public inquiry and hearings by the House of Commons Ethics Committee.

In 2008 the Canadian Broadcasting Corporation, its French counterpart *Radio-Canada* and the national news agency The Canadian Press won the Michener Award for their multimedia analysis of Taser stun guns, and in particular, their use by police services following the death of Robert Dziekanski, who died at the Vancouver airport after the RCMP used a Taser to subdue him.[40] The impetus for the collaboration came from the journalists CBC's David McKie and CP's Jim Bronskill, who co-taught a reporting methods course at Carleton's School of Journalism. "We are competitors, but we are friends and colleagues, as well. Both of us were accessing the same information through access to information," explained McKie. "I said, Jim, wouldn't it be great just to get beyond your limited sample and do it for all of them."[41] With approval from their managers, Bronskill worked on the digital, and McKie did the data to analyze RCMP Taser reports.

They found that, from 2002 to 2005, more than two-thirds of the people police Tasered were not armed with a weapon, contrary to the police narrative. "At the time the RCMP were saying that this [Dziekanski] is a one-off, this never happens," McKie said. The RCMP resisted handing over the next tranche of 4,000 RCMP Taser reports through 2007. "It was a long battle under the federal information law. The public outcry eventually forced the RCMP to release more data about how and why they were using Tasers."[42]

In his acceptance speech at the 2009 Michener Awards ceremony, Bronskill said. "And we found the RCMP were firing their Tasers multiple times in almost half of the incidents — despite an internal policy that warned multiple jolts may be hazardous." Frédéric Zalac of Radio-Canada, who did a lot of the national broadcast stories, picked up the story from there. "The RCMP immediately removed from active service all of its M26 Tasers across the country — 1600 in total and about half of its entire Taser arsenal — to get them tested.[43] He said the tests found close to 200 faulty Tasers and have resulted in new independent testing standards for Tasers being developed. Several police services adopted mandatory and regular testing of Tasers. Such joint investigations are, in most cases, the only way in-depth, time-consuming investigative stories will get done these days.

Sometimes media organizations produce independent but complementary coverage of an important story. For example, in 2017, the judging panel recognized both *Globe and Mail* and *La Presse* with a Michener Award for their combined coverage of the complicit role Canadian armed forces played in the abuse and torture of prisoners in Afghanistan. Canadian soldiers in Kandahar were handing detainees over to the feared Afghan National Directorate of Security (NDS), where many reported extreme torture and abuse. In reflecting on the situation, reporter Graeme Smith wrote, "None of the abuse was inflicted by Canadians, and most Afghans captured — even those who clearly sympathized with the Taliban — praised the Canadian soldiers for their politeness, their gentle handling of captives and their comfortable detention facility."[44] While sympathetic, *Globe and Mail* reporters Smith and Paul Koring provided evidence that Canadian forces knew that once the detainees were in the hands of the local authorities, they faced torture in Afghan prisons, and Canadian soldiers could do nothing about it.

In his acceptance speech at the Michener Awards ceremony, Koring spoke about why this story was important. "It's about all of us and the dangers of turning a blind eye. Fodor Dostoyevsky [*sic*], famously said: 'The degree of civilization in a society can be judged by entering its prisons.' If our coverage of the abuse and torture of detainees deserves merit, if it has forced a recalcitrant government to make changes, if it has compelled Canadians to consider whether we are asking our soldiers to be accessories to war crimes, it is because the *Globe and Mail* deserves its reputation as a great news organization."[45] The *Globe*'s reports in March and April of 2007 led to a public inquiry, a new defence minister and an agreement with Afghan authorities that gave Canadian investigators access to detainees.

The 2007 Michener co-winner, *La Presse,* had followed up on the *Globe* story, only to find that the agreement was in word only. Canadian soldiers were still handing prisoners to local authorities for torture in the notorious Sarpoza prison in Kandahar. Three suspected Taliban members told foreign correspondent Michèle Ouimet that Canadian troops gave them a document to give to local prison authorities that stated torture is no longer used in Afghanistan. "The people from the secret service tore it (the document) up and threw it in my face. They tortured me for twenty hours. I protested and said the Canadians had promised that nothing would happen to me. They replied: 'We're not in Canada, we're at home. The Canadians are dogs!'" one detainee told Ouimet.[46]

Following the *La Presse* series, the Canadian government stopped transferring prisoners to Afghan authorities. "One of the important and enduring values of journalism is that people get due process, and it's not for us to judge if they're necessarily good or bad people. They still deserve due process," said the *Globe and Mail*'s Ed Greenspon. "The post 9-11 world has reinforced our sense of importance that we keep our eye on, that society doesn't fall down on its commitments to human rights and due process."[47] Combined, the two series took Canadians beyond the day-to-day conflict in Afghanistan to expose larger issues.

Collaborative stories these days are national, even international in their scope. In 2016 one of the Michener finalists was a collaboration involving the *Toronto Star,* Global TV and CBC. They pooled resources — dollars and staff — to produce the multi-faceted series, the "Panama Papers" that "put a Canadian face on a global story" about offshore tax haven in Panama.[48] Their in-depth stories identified Canadian lawyers, accountants and financial consultants involved in aggressively structuring offshore businesses to avoid taxes, with Canadian banks playing supporting roles," the citation of merit noted. Following the series, the Canada Revenue Agency received millions of dollars to hire more staff to investigate individuals identified in the papers. Two years later, the *Toronto Star* teamed up with CBC and Société Radio-Canada to expose "lax approval, regulation and oversight of Canada's medical device industry."[49] The Michener citation of merit noted the shocking revelations from "The Implant Files." "Since 2008, defective implants have killed 1,400 Canadians and sickened another 14,000. Health Canada has approved the marketing of breast implants that are now associated with auto-immune diseases and a rare form of cancer."

Toronto Star investigative reporter, Rob Cribb, who could be called Mr. Co-Pro, has been a lead on these series and most other major national and international co-productions over the last fifteen years. He speaks about this move towards collaboration with the conviction of the converted. "Nothing beats a lot of brain power in the same room, mobilized and focused precisely on that thing. You know, that, that changes the game," he said. "Not on every story, but on the big ones where you think there is true injustice or a lapse or an oversight or a legislative glitch that is doing true harm to a significant number of people."[50] Given the constraints that emerged out of the 2000s — reduced budgets and fewer journalists in the newsrooms — collaborations were one way that journalists found the time and money to produce major stories that exposed wrongdoing and effected change.

For the journalistic watchdogs in the newsroom, a Michener Award nomination was more than just validation of a job well done. A Michener was the ace up the sleeve for a journalist and their editor to get more funding from managers to do stories that strengthen the social safety net for vulnerable groups and change laws, policies and practices of our fundamental democratic institutions. The idea of journalism as a public good, once a fundamental value of most newsrooms, was becoming an ideal as media organizations put all their efforts into the survival of their businesses.

8

Big Media, Big Stories

The 2000s upended the traditional business model of media and journalism. The lavish spending of the late 1990s had given way to tightened budgets, thinner newspapers and sparsely populated newsrooms. The lifeboat called convergence was foundering. Big media companies were not saving money or earning the profits they anticipated. The 2008 recession was not the blip many media managers had hoped. Craigslist and eBay had siphoned off classified advertising, and it was not coming back. Facebook and Google hijacked broadcast and print advertisers with large online audiences. Younger readers were migrating to sites like VOX, Reddit and YouTube.

As the 2000s progressed, the financial pressures from shareholders, the markets and escalating digital disruption hit the budgets and staffing at community newspapers and local radio and television stations hard. Big media companies dominated the lists of annual finalists.

The threat to media independence to do stories in the public interest was on the mind of newly appointed Governor General Michaëlle Jean, a passionate defender of free speech. She had lived under a dictatorship in Haiti before escaping to Canada, where she worked as a journalist, presenter and news anchor on the French and English networks of the Canadian public broadcaster from 1998 until she was appointed governor general in 2005. Just forty-eight years old, Jean brought a youthful and less formal attitude to the position. Despite searing criticism in the media over her French citizenship — which she would later renounce — and suggestions that she was a separatist sympathizer, Jean remained a passionate supporter of the Michener Awards and what they stood for.

At that first ceremony in 2006, she urged journalists in the room to be vigilant. "This is why I am delighted that the Michener Award, which promotes not only excellence but also independence of thought, freedom of speech and the public interest, is awarded to a news organization. This award recognizes the commitment of an organization that endeavours not only to disseminate information, but also to arm the citizens with knowledge so that they might look more closely at reality."[1]

Her words resonated with the 2005 Michener finalists. Their journalism had made huge differences. The *Toronto Star* had helped to overturn a wrongful murder conviction, Radio-Canada exposed security issues at two major hydroelectric dams. *La Presse* found huge safety gaps in Montreal's metro, The *Canadian Medical Association Journal* revealed privacy breaches involving women seeking emergency contraception at pharmacies, and the *Victoria Times Colonist* and the *Vancouver Sun* uncovered fatal flaws in B.C.'s child protection system.

That year, the *Globe and Mail* won the Michener Award for its in-depth coverage of the scourge of breast cancer. The recognition was a testament to the value of beat reporting. The lead reporter in the series, Lisa Priest, had been on the national health beat since the early 1990s. Before being hired away from the *Toronto Star*, Priest had been to Rideau Hall twice. In 1993, the *Toronto Star* received a Citation of Merit for her two-part series that detailed long delays in radiation treatments for breast cancer patients in Ontario. Those stories resulted in the government adding twenty-six more radiation specialists and the promise of a long-term cancer treatment plan.[2] Five years later, the *Star* won the Michener Award for its series that exposed further deficiencies in Ontario's troubled healthcare system. Lisa Priest and Leslie Papp's six-month investigation in 1998 documented lengthy delays in mental health services and cancer radiation treatment that resulted in the province adding $16.6 million to the system. "It was powerfully written and powerfully done," said John Honderich. "I remember how that affected people and the reaction to it was very powerful. Very proud of it."[3]

At the *Globe and Mail*, Priest continued her focus on health care, winning the 2005 Michener Award for two series about breast cancer. The judging panel noted how the coverage resulted in improved diagnosis and treatment. Her stories pushed the Ontario government to fast-track the approval process for the drug Herceptin and expand its availability beyond women who were dying of breast cancer. A second *Globe* series about mammogram screening resulted in tighter regulations for clinics including a national quality test for screening machines.

Priest's then editor-in-chief Ed Greenspon said the 2005 Michener changed how the *Globe and Mail* approached and covered policy and social issues. "Changed it in terms of looking very carefully in various systematic ways at how policy affected people, how policy played on citizens. And you know, the Herceptin story was so outrageous. I mean, here you had this miracle drug so successful that they had to take it off, out of the trial because it would be considered unethical to keep trials and just not to move forward with that." As Priest told him, "The most rewarding part of journalism is the ability to make a difference. It's like oxygen to me. Journalists don't change things all the time, but every once in a while, we do. And there is no better feeling."[4]

The following year, the *Globe* was back at Rideau Hall, a Michener finalist for its "in-depth examination of the impact of cancer on the lives of Canadians." The paper profiled more than sixty Canadians affected by cancer and told stories of Canadians who were experiencing delays and running up large debts to pay for basic treatment. While the series was running, Prime Minister Stephen Harper announced a national cancer strategy. Ontario promised more than $190 million for colorectal cancer screening.[5] In 2011, the *Globe* received a Citation of Merit for Priest's reporting on government funding cancer drugs, especially Herceptin. As a result, the government changed its policy and directed Cancer Care Ontario to review its guidelines. It amounted to an overdue audit of the historic move in the 1960s to a national Medicare system.

This concentrated, continuing focus on the shortcomings of the healthcare system remains an outstanding example of the essential role of journalism in the public interest in Canada. Now a new generation of reporters, editors and producers had questions about how well the system served a growing diverse population. People, policy, process and priorities were all on the agenda. In this striving, a Michener Award was the ultimate badge of honour for the Fourth Estate. A Michener Award — or the prospect of one — helped to open up the purse strings of media executives and buy precious time to conduct investigations. This is especially true when it comes to difficult and sensitive stories that take time, commitment and money and can piss off people in authority.

The prospect of a Michener may be on the minds of journalists but not the primary motivation of reporters who set out to expose systemic institutional problems — illegal activity, corruption, cover-ups, sexualized violence and discrimination in local, provincial and national organizations. However, many a reporter considers the possibility when pitching these uncomfortable stories that would shake the foundation of pillars of democracy and Canada's self-narrative — for example, investigations into Canada's military and police services, institutions that, for years, were regarded as "above the law" because they were defenders of our democratic freedoms.

Questioning military and police services is fraught with problems, given the weight of institutional secrecy that persists to this day. For example, in 1995, the horrific revelations from the Michener Award-winning story involving Canada's military and a failed peacekeeping mission in Somalia were still very raw. CBC Radio's revelations of torture, racial slurs and a cover-up damaged the reputation of Canada's peacekeepers — once thought to be above reproach. Two years earlier, 900 Canadian peacekeepers had gone to Somalia on "Operation Deliverance" to restore order. Citizens were suffering from civil war and famine. The CBC investigation revealed "wrong-doing, a breakdown of discipline and a failure of leadership and accountability."[6] It was brutal. Peacekeepers had tortured and murdered a Somali teenager and killed another local man, and there were reports of other atrocities. The results were immediate: several courts martial, an inquiry and the disbanding of the Canadian Airborne Regiment.

In the aftermath, CBC's Michael McAuliffe discovered that senior officers had deliberately altered some documents given to CBC Radio and erased computer logs that contained information about what happened in Somalia. The subsequent Somalia inquiry was so damning that after sixteen months the Liberal government of Jean Chrétien shut it down in 1996 — before it had the chance to examine the details surrounding the torture and killing of Shidane Arone, a Somali teenager. Despite the premature end, the Inquiry produced a 2,000-page report that concluded the Canadian military system was "rotten to the core."[7] It made 157 recommendations to deal with institutional failures, including higher standards for overseas recruitment and training, and reforming of the military justice system. This kind of journalism required time, commitment and money from an organization. The results were profound, and a Michener nomination was a way to recognize and encourage enterprising journalists who uncovered problems with Canada's military and law enforcement agencies closer to home.

The top-down rigid culture of the military exposed its members to physical and mental abuse with few options for redress. In 2014, the magazine L'actualité received a Michener citation of merit for its eight-month investigation into sexual assault and harassment in the military. The series started just weeks after a review had pronounced the army's sexual harassment policies effective. *L'actualité* found that more than 15 per cent of the 6,700 females in the military had been sexually assaulted or had unwelcome sexual contact at least once a month. But only one in ten reported the incidents because of a culture of inhibition where their superiors pressed them to forgive and forget or face retaliation. *Crimes Sexuels dans l'armée* garnered a swift response from senior government and military officials. The military set up a response team, and an independent investigation recommended sweeping changes. That did not end the problem.

Ongoing media coverage of Canada's military continues to bring to light further scandals and allegations of sexual harassment. In 2021, the Department of National Defence commissioned former Supreme Court of Canada justice Louise Arbour to review the "policies, procedures, programs, practices, and culture" in Canada's armed forces and the Department of National Defence. Her Independent External Comprehensive Review (IECR) report, released in December 2022, made forty-eight recommendations. The then federal minister of defence, Anita Anand, committed to ensuring both institutions acted on all the recommendations.[8]

In 2011 Michener finalist CBC Vancouver exposed similar abusive behaviour in Canada's national police service when journalists cracked open the RCMP's culture of suffering in silence and exposed "a toxic and long-standing environment of systemic sexual harassment of women."[9] It took one courageous female RCMP officer to speak out. Catherine Galliford "shook as she told us about her agoraphobia and PTSD after years of working with bosses who made offensive comments, unwanted sexual advances and assaults," CBC reporter Natalie Clancy said in her speech at Rideau Hall. She said that after her story aired, more than four dozen officers contacted the CBC and described a chilling culture of fear and bullying. The female officers said they were more afraid of their bosses in the detachment than the criminals on the street. They told CBC their experiences of "constant sexual harassment, cover-up, and minimal punishment for offenders."[10]

Reaction came swiftly. The federal Public Safety minister promised an investigation and legislation to modernize the RCMP Act.[11] "Something I don't think would have happened had we not forced the government to deal with an organization where women tell us they do not feel safe," Clancy told fellow journalists. The amended *RCMP Act* received royal assent in June 2013. It strengthened the Review and Complaints Commission and modernized discipline, grievance and human resource management for RCMP officers.

Survivors launched a class-action lawsuit, supported by an independent investigation by former Supreme Court of Canada justice Michel Bastarache. His 2020 report, "Broken Dreams, Broken Lives," found evidence of "entrenched issues of misogyny, racism, and homophobia" at every level of the RCMP and called for a "wholesale change" to build an inclusive and respectful workplace for all employees.[12] In the settlement, more than 2,000 survivors received a total of $125.4 million. In tandem with the Bastarache investigation into policing and sexual assault, the House of Commons Standing Committee on Public Safety and National Security investigated "the pervasive nature of systemic racism" in policing. Its 2021 report "concluded that a transformative national effort is required to ensure that all Indigenous, Black and other racialized people in Canada are not subject to the discrimination and injustice that is inherent in the system as it exists today."[13] While the report focused on federal policing, there was recognition of a supplemental report by the Conservative provincial government that made the point that provincial and municipal policing also faced similar issues regarding racist attitudes and actions, especially in Canada's largest and most diverse city — Toronto.

In the fifteen years since the *Globe and Mail* and *Toronto Star* each won the 1985 Michener Award for their coverage of immigration and multiculturalism, Canada, and in particular, Toronto had been transformed by the continuous influx of newcomers from around the world. However, it was increasingly evident that Canadian institutions struggled to keep up and to reflect that diversity in their attitudes and practices. "The *Star*'s always been the unofficial police complaints bureau. So starting early in my career, I heard a lot of anecdotal stories about people of colour being treated differently — driving while black, those kinds of phenomena," said reporter Jim Rankin.[14] The *Toronto Star*'s groundbreaking investigation into race and crime started in 1999 when Rankin received a police report that used the colour yellow to describe a suspect of Asian descent. He discovered that Toronto police services used five colours to code racial features of suspects, and all this information was kept in a database.

The *Star*, through an access to information request, gained access to five years of data for police arrests and charges. The data provided evidence to support the anecdotal complaints of systemic racism in Toronto's police service. "No matter how many variables were considered, race always emerged as a factor in the harsher treatment of blacks by police," Rankin said.[15] The first of hundreds of stories, that drew on the data, appeared on the front page of the *Toronto Star* on October 19, 2002, with the headline, "Singled out, *Star* analysis of police crime data shows justice is different for blacks and whites":

> But Toronto's black community has long worried about being singled out by police — especially its young black men.
>
> "I don't think a day will come, in my lifetime, when I won't be profiled or identified for who I am, and what I am," said Jason Burke, 28.
>
> Employed as a buyer in the fashion industry, Burke is suing Toronto police after being accused of dealing drugs, pushed to the ground, pepper sprayed and forced to rinse his burning eyes in toilet water while in custody. He was held for three days.
>
> No drugs were found. All charges against him were dropped just before he was due for trial.
>
> "I was violated that night for no good reason," Burke said, adding that just being black puts young men at risk of undue attention from police.
>
> Nowhere in Canada has debate over keeping, and analyzing, race-based crime data been as angst-ridden as in Toronto — a city boasting of its multicultural identity with a motto declaring diversity its strength. Latest census figures show that blacks make up 8.1 per cent of the city's population. [16]

That year, the *Star*'s landmark investigation won the Michener Award and the ire of the Toronto police, its union and municipal politicians.

The win came with high costs — the paper invested money and time in the investigation by a team of top *Star* reporters. It also risked its financial sustainability to tell the story. Supporters of the Toronto Police Service cancelled their subscriptions and companies withdrew their advertising. The financial hit came at a time when the *Star* had just been through two newspaper wars. Classified advertisements and readers were moving online. The paper was also slapped with a $7.2 billion libel lawsuit from the police union. The *Star* successfully fought the lawsuit to the Supreme Court of Canada and won. A loss would have sunk the paper. Its publisher and editor, John Honderich, said public interest was too great to back down. "We, in effect, broke the back of those who said racial profiling does not exist in this country. I thought after that, no police force or no one anywhere could ever say there is no such thing as racial profiling because here you had the entire database and we showed exactly, with every practical information, what went on. We had to fight the police. We had to fight the city establishment, but we did, and we won, and it was an unbelievable victory."[17]

The story didn't end with Star's 2002 Michener Award or the Supreme Court ruling. For the next twenty years, Rankin and Star's investigative team has continued to hold Toronto police services accountable. They continued to question racism in the police services including carding — the random stopping and documenting of racialized people. They looked at other institutions. "It's not just a policing story. These differences are seen in all systems — school suspensions and child apprehensions and the patterns are almost identical to what we found in policing. So it's systemic racism." While racialized people are still being stopped; they're no longer documented. In June 2022, speaking on behalf of the Toronto police services, acting chief James Ramer said he was sorry and apologized for systemic disparities towards members of the Black and other racialized communities. It was vindication for Rankin. In the intervening twenty years, he has seen incremental changes in police practices and more open discussions in Toronto about racism.

Rankin admits winning awards, especially the Michener, "always helps with you with your bosses. It buys you time and resources."[18] Time and resources keep the microscope on important issues and hold those in authority accountable. In its limited way, the Michener Awards provided incentives and validation for a struggling industry to aim high.

As it approached its fiftieth anniversary, the Michener Awards Foundation found that like the industry, it, too, had to face brutal economic realities and faced both internal and external challenges to how it operated.

9

Disruption on All Fronts

The disruptive explosion of the Internet in the 2010s gave rise to social media and a host of new challenges including mis- and disinformation. The long-established media ecology with its checks and balances fractured. Media organizations lost their gatekeeping role as purveyors of news and information. Journalists found their work undermined on all sides. Technology-driven social media platforms became a marketplace for unfiltered news, opinion, commentary and lies. Echo chambers, communities of interest or like-minded people, gathered in chat rooms, some to learn to crochet and others to foment dissent. The guy next door with a computer and a point of view could become an influencer with audiences bigger than his local newspaper. Political leaders like Donald Trump saw opportunities to advance their careers by discrediting the message of mainstream journalists and normalizing the fake news loop.[1] With that came abusive behaviour toward journalists, making the workplace unsafe in the field and online.

This polarization of civil discourse became endemic, aggravated by online manipulation of information from bots and trolls. It led to allegations of attempted electoral interference by China, Russia and Iran in Canada's 2019 and 2021 federal elections and Russia's involvement in the 2016 U.S. presidential campaign.[2] It gave rise to fake news conspiracies such as Pizzagate hatched in chat rooms on the Deep Web.[3] Democratic practices and principles were under threat. So was independent fact-based journalism. "Without facts, you can't have truth. Without truth, you can't have trust. Without all three, we have no shared reality, and democracy as we know it — and all meaningful human endeavours — are dead," wrote Nobel Peace Prize-winner Maria Ressa of *Rappler* in the Philippines[4]

As an organization dedicated to journalism in the public interest, the Michener Awards Foundation had a role to play in supporting facts, truth and trust — if it was ready to step up. The organization has a role in supporting journalists and news organizations, but first, the Michener directors had to deal with two internal challenges: conflict around the board's governance structure and decision-making process, and the possible loss of the patronage of the governor general. These two issues had to be resolved to renew and strengthen the purpose and direction of the Foundation. Then, the board could align the fellowships to address current problems of press freedom and misinformation and deepen its commitment to public service journalism. But first, the Michener Awards Foundation had to clean up its own house.

Cleaning house

Post-2015, institutions everywhere were being forced into change. Media companies were upended by the Internet and social media. The same was true at the Michener Awards Foundation. For years a tight executive ran the organization. "Board members do not participate in the governance of the Michener Foundation, nor are they responsible to raise funds or to donate funds themselves," noted the executive minutes from April 7, 2017.[5] Since 2005, the executive — most from the Ottawa area — had run the Foundation. "It was very clubby. The Ottawa residents, they all got together and that small group, it was very much their organization," said Alan Allnutt, a relative newcomer who had joined the board in 2014.[6] Allnutt was a Victoria-based writer and consultant who had an esteemed career as publisher and editor of the *Montreal Gazette,* publisher of the Victoria *Times-Colonist,* regional publisher for Postmedia's Alberta and Saskatchewan newspapers, and senior vice-president with Postmedia. It was clear to Allnutt and other directors that the executive was cautious when it came to change. Much of that caution focused on protecting the patronage of the governor general and Rideau Hall.

The executive had taken a safe, steady-as-she-goes approach and coasted through the 2000s. The annual cycle ran like clockwork year-on-year — the call for entries for the awards and fellowships, judging and preparation for the annual spring awards ceremony at Rideau Hall. The 1970 model was tweaked in the 1980s by Paul Deacon, the Foundation's first president. The volunteer judging panels operated independently, while the executive focused on fundraising to pay for the fellowships and, throughout the 2000s, cultivating warm relations with governors general Adrienne Clarkson, Michaëlle Jean and David Johnston, and with the Rideau Hall staff. The better the relationship with Rideau Hall, the bigger the celebration.

Each spring, the directors — a mix of publishers and retired media executives — flew to Ottawa for the annual general meeting, where the executive presented the business to be discussed and approved. Limited engagement was required from the board members. Without fail, the meeting adjourned before one o'clock to give members time to get ready for the annual trip to Rideau Hall and the celebration of journalism in the public interest.

After a seven-year term, Russ Mills stepped aside as Michener Foundation president at the June 2017 annual meeting, and I was elected president. On the surface, the appointment was a signal of change to the journalism community: I was a journalism professor, international trainer, university administrator, former CBC radio reporter and editor from Nova Scotia and the second female to take the job in the institution's forty-seven-year history. My unstated mission was to reengage the directors and tackle pressing issues. So before the annual meeting ended, members agreed to serve on three new sub-committees — social media, governance and fellowship review — with a request to report back in the fall. The industry was changing so quickly, and the Foundation needed to up its game.

At that meeting, the board elected Chris Waddell — the most senior member of the awards judging panel — to fill the now-vacant chief judge position.[7] He had served nine years on the awards panel and was well qualified to take on the top job. Waddell was a respected journalism professor and former director of the School of Journalism at Carleton University, an author and seasoned award-winning journalist with CBC Television News and the *Globe and Mail*. Waddell had one condition. He would take the job of chief judge if the Michener Foundation contracted the Canadian Journalism Foundation (CJF) to handle the online application process and compile the entries for the judges.

As a judge for the CJF, Waddell observed that "a lot of the same entries go to the CJF excellence award as go to the Michener Award and at the same time news organizations were getting smaller and smaller. There were fewer people managing in the newsroom. So they can't pull someone aside to spend a month working on all these [award submissions] because it takes a while to get these entries together."[8] If the Micheners wanted to encourage new organizations to share their work, Waddell felt the Foundation needed to make the process easier. After all, this was a digital, multimedia world.

Processing Michener entries had become far more complex and time-consuming than in the 1970s when Bill MacPherson and Fraser MacDougall managed this work on their own time in a spare bedroom. The media silos of print, TV, radio and magazine were crumbling and merging. Gone were the days of media outlets sending a VCR, audio cassette, CD or tear sheets from the newspaper. Now the chief judge was sorting electronic entries that contained text, audio, video and graphics and responding to as many as sixty media managers. Waddell was in the midst of setting up a new degree program at Carleton and did not have time to spend days on tedious administrative work as previous chief judges had done. While some on the board questioned the need to contract out services, director John Honderich, the chair of Torstar, supported the move to "reduce the burden on the chief judge for collecting and collating the entries."[9]

Waddell's nomination as chief judge received approval from the board at the annual general meeting. So did his pitch for some backroom help, as the minutes noted. "Prof. Waddell would lead a plan to negotiate an arrangement with the Canadian Journalism Foundation to accept and collate all entries using a program developed by the CJF while protecting the integrity of the involvement of Rideau Hall in all aspects of the judging process for the Michener Award and the Michener-Deacon fellowships."[10] As Waddell later explained, "It was a condition designed to both make it easier for judges, to bring the whole process into more modern times and to try to make it easier for news organizations who might be entering."[11] Little did anyone realize the internal brouhaha that would erupt.

The discussion over contracting out would bring to the forefront internal governance dysfunction within the Michener Foundation and initiate huge changes within the organization. What became evident in the fall of 2017 was a lingering wariness among long-serving directors about the intentions of the CJF.[12] The unease had its roots in the mid-1980s and the CJF's then business-friendly slant. The Michener board had watched CJF grow and become an important advocate for journalism — a long way from its rocky beginnings. Waddell's proposal to bring in the CJF revealed simmering frustration among board members with the top-down and closed decision-making process of the Michener executive. That crisis would lead to internal governance improvements, but not without some blood on the floor.

Waddell spent the summer working on a detailed proposal with Natalie Turvey, the President and CEO of the CJF. It outlined tiers with a price tag for various services. The package was presented to the September meeting of the executive. It met with a wall of resistance. "As presented, they feel the agreement would compromise the independence of the award," the minutes noted.[13] For some, the proposal went far beyond what was contemplated or presented at the AGM. Past presidents Russ Mills and David Humphreys, who were members of the executive, identified a long list of problems, including the application process, promotion, reporting, tickets to the ceremony and the price tag. The top tier estimate for service had come in three times higher than the $2,000 estimated cost at the AGM.

In any case, Mills asserted Rideau Hall would not approve the plan. "We administer the award for Rideau Hall. It is not our award. We are not free to contract out administration of the award," he explained.[14] For Mills, Rideau Hall had the same sense of ownership of the Michener that it had for the Order of Canada and other decorations.[15] It cut to the core of how long-serving members saw the place of the Michener Award in Rideau Hall. This belief had been passed down and guided decisions and actions of the executive since the formation of the Michener Awards Foundation in 1983. The long-held belief of the Michener executive was not the reality.

For Rideau Hall, the Michener Award differed from the Governor General's Awards for the arts, sciences and humanities, and the Chancellery of Honour awards.[16] The Michener Award belonged in the group of awards created by previous governors general and was considered independent of Rideau Hall.[17] The Michener Award and fellowships were the responsibility of the Michener Foundation, a self-governing, registered charitable organization — not Rideau Hall. As board member James Baxter, then publisher of *iPolitics,* explained, "We are partners of Rideau Hall, not some subordinate appendage. That is also how the staff at Rideau Hall see us. This award would have been relegated to the scrap heap of history were it not for the funds built by this Foundation."[18]

However, an important aspect of the awards was viceregal patronage and the recognition by the State of independent journalism as being essential to the functioning of a healthy democracy. The message from the executive was clear. It was prepared to do what was necessary to protect that relationship with Rideau Hall. The executive meeting ended with an understanding that Edith Cody-Rice, the secretary to the board and former CBC media lawyer, would amend the draft agreement.

The internal crisis among the executive deepened after Chris Waddell and I met with Stephen Wallace, Secretary to the Governor General and others at Rideau Hall in late September 2017. Following the practices of past Michener presidents, an introduction meeting was arranged in advance of the new governor general, who was to be installed on October 2. As my notes recorded, Secretary Stephen Wallace affirmed Rideau Hall's continued support for the Michener Awards: "More than ever this award is needed. The Michener Award Foundation has complete autonomy from Rideau Hall. Our job is to support the Foundation as a self-governing entity."[19] In an email to the executive I wrote, Rideau Hall "thought this proposal by the Foundation to contract the CFJ is not a distraction to the autonomy and distinctiveness of the Michener Award, and joining forces with the joint entry, administration and promotion of our brand to a wider audience will 'only strengthen the award.' Given the volunteer nature of the Michener Award Foundation, it was a great idea to get this support."[20]

In effect, as Waddell recalled, Rideau Hall did not care how the whole thing ran. "They just cared that nothing happened that would reflect badly on the governor general. Little did they know what was coming in their future."[21] Within months, Wallace would retire from the public service to make way for Assunta Di Lorenzo, a Montreal lawyer with no experience in navigating the public service but was a personal friend of incoming Governor General Julie Payette. The landscape of Rideau Hall would change drastically. So would the landscape within the Michener Awards Foundation.

Reaction from other members of the executive after the Rideau Hall meeting was swift and censorious. Some members of the executive were unhappy that Waddell and I had attended a meeting, even though the executive knew about the request in advance. They were spitting mad because we raised the CJF issue. "It's important to ensure that board members feel that their role is respected and that nothing is going on behind their backs or over their heads," wrote Russ Mills.[22] The pushback was surprising and ironic since I was only following observed established practices of Mills, the past president, who met annually with officials from Rideau Hall and reported after the event. For director Alan Allnutt, "The whole question was, was this partially gender-based? Like, wait a minute, you weren't supposed to be changing things on us here or proposing things that we being former presidents, former executive people wouldn't have done or didn't want to do."[23] The culture and practices of the organization had been challenged.

The governance furor sparked by the CJF proposal and the Rideau Hall meeting would only unearth and amplify tensions between the board and the executive about how decisions were made. While the executive debated, the directors remained in the dark. As a way to dial back the tension within the executive, I proposed Mills and Cody-Rice take over negotiations with the CJF — a move that had huge consequences — and would further reveal the board's dissatisfaction with the Foundation's governance structure. Their first move was to suggest the idea to engage the CJF be deferred for a year.

On September 27, Waddell resigned as the chief judge and as a member of the judging panel, effective immediately. In an email, he wrote: "While I respect your attempt to find a consensus on this issue, I do not agree with the decision simply to defer it for another year."[24] As Waddell later reflected, "Some of the people who'd been there for a long time perceived this [association with the CJF] as a threat to the future of the Michener Foundation and the awards and perceived it as an attempt to try to take over by stealth the awards so that they would no longer have an influence on them."[25] Waddell said he was just looking for a way to make the process easier for the Michener judges and media outlets. "I resigned because I'd said that if we weren't going to make the change, I didn't think I wanted to do the chief judge job because I thought that we actually needed to modernize what was happening."[26]

The governance by the executive was so entrenched that the entire board of directors only found out a month later about the CJF negotiations and proposal, the Rideau Hall meeting and Waddell's resignation. Over the next few days, emails started to fly fast and furious. Board members had hard and legitimate questions about the executive's lack of transparency, and why they had been kept in the dark. Directors John Honderich and James Baxter led the charge. "As Mr. Honderich rightly noted, all of this raises some serious questions of a governance structure that puts the affairs of the Foundation in the hands of an executive committee for 364 days of the year."[27]

At a special board meeting on November 3, director Catherine Cano pointed out that this was the only board she sat on that meets just once a year. "We need to review the objective of the awards, to be able to make sure we know what we could and should do," she said. "We have a good opportunity to decide what we are going to be like in five years' or ten years' time." Mills conceded that "the Michener Foundation sometimes operates like an old boys' club. That's how it started. Perhaps we have reached a point where we need to become more orderly and write more things down."[28] Mills read the room correctly. The directors demanded transparency and changed how the Foundation was governed. The Michener Awards Foundation had matured. It was no longer the upstart two-person operation of 1970 or even the same charitable foundation it became in 1983 and as such could not be run in the same manner.

By this point, I felt I could no longer work with the incumbent executive, so in a president's report written before the special meeting, I resigned. At the November special meeting, Alan Allnutt was elected interim president and Catherine Cano, vice-president. I remained a director on the board and executive. Without a chief judge I oversaw the panel for the 2017 awards and 2018 fellowship entries.

Negotiations would continue with CJF in the winter and spring of 2018. In that period, it was *status quo* for the judging procedures. A suitable service agreement was reached with the CJF to compile Michener Awards entries electronically. It was up and running in time for the new chief judge Margo Goodhand and the panel in early 2019. The agreement lasted two years until the Foundation updated its website and developed its own electronic system in partnership with the Rideau Hall Foundation.

Reflecting on that time, Allnutt said that, at first, he thought it was a perfectly good idea to align with the CJF. But then, in subsequent discussions with the CJF, "There was this whole sense of *ugh*, they just want to swallow us. . . . And that's the paranoia that I got struck with, that somehow the Canadian Journalism Foundation awards would end up being the big ones and that the Michener Awards would be a secondary thing that they also gave out."[29] This realization propelled Allnutt into the presidency, and other directors to become more actively engaged in the work of the Foundation. As Allnutt said, the internal crisis gave the board an opportunity to take stock and, once again, ask the questions, "What are we, why are we?"[30]

The existential event awakened new possibilities in Allnutt and the other directors on the Michener board. As Waddell now sees it, "It actually forced people to confront issues that should have been confronted previously. I thought for a while we might be able to make change without disruption and that wasn't possible, but that's the history of a lot of organizations."[31]

The immediate impact was the governance committee set up in June 2017 went into high gear. Allnutt led the process of transforming the Foundation from the "club" model — that it had long outgrown — to a governance model that met modern standards and best practices. In June 2018, the board approved a bylaw concerning the affairs of the Foundation that included set terms for directors.[32] Gone were the forever appointments, and the board was to meet at least twice a year. At that same meeting, a new policy expanded on the by-law and spelled out the responsibilities of each member of the executive and board.[33] These changes led to new board members and a renewed engagement of directors in the foundation's day-to-day business. With this challenge in hand, the Michener Awards Foundation turned its attention to Rideau Hall and the Office of the Governor General.

Patronage

In 2017, after David Johnston's successful six-year term, the Trudeau government appointed Julie Payette as the twenty-ninth governor general. Payette was francophone, female, an engineer and scientist, and a single mom with a teenage son. She had worked as an astronaut and had flown two missions in space. She had won great acclaim for her work at NASA's Mission Control Centre in Houston and with the Canada Space Agency.[34]

Soon after Payette's appointment, surprising revelations of her personal life appearing in the media gave the Michener Awards Foundation cause for concern. Board members wondered with Payette under the media's microscope, what this might mean for an award that honours investigative journalism. After forty-seven years, the Michener Awards faced the unthinkable possibility: the loss of the patronage of the Office of the Governor General and the ceremony at Rideau Hall.

The support of the governor general and Rideau Hall elevated the Micheners above other industry awards.[35] The Foundation had been fortunate. Five of the nine previous governors general had been journalists and understood the connection between journalism in the public interest and viceregal recognition. And with each appointment, the Foundation had made a great effort to ensure that the incoming governor general understood the value of her or his patronage for public interest journalism and the Micheners.

Since the beginning of the awards, the Michener directors had operated under the assumption of viceregal support. The question was not *if*, but *how much* support the awards would get. That long-held assumption was called into question in 2017 with Payette's appointment.

It was all smiles and promises on that July day on Parliament Hill when Prime Minister Justin Trudeau made the announcement, a beaming Payette at his side. Congratulatory media coverage followed. Stories praised Payette's "impressive resumé" and listed all her accomplishments.[36] In a glowing editorial, the *Toronto Star* wrote that "Payette has all the attributes to make an excellent governor general. . . . Payette embodies a rare blend of qualities — determination, ambition and singular achievement."[37]

Four days later, the tone of the news and commentary sharpened after Ottawa-based *iPolitics* broke the story that, in 2011 when living in Maryland, Payette had been charged with second-degree assault during a domestic dispute. The assault charges had been dropped within weeks and expunged from the court records. The online publication also reported that Payette had her divorce records sealed just weeks before the July announcement of her appointment as governor general. In a statement to *iPolitics*, Payette wrote: "For family and personal reasons, I will not comment on these unfounded charges, of which I was immediately and completely cleared many years ago, and I hope that people will respect my private life."[38]

The publisher of *iPolitics*, James Baxter, was also a long-serving director with the Michener Awards Foundation. As he explained to columnist Susan Delacourt, "We think this is a story because it was such a random [background] check and we turned up an arrest," Baxter said. "From there, as we began to look, we saw the elements of a concerted effort to sanitize the record. There's nothing wrong with that, of course. But the GG is not just any position. People call it ceremonial, but it carries a lot of weight."[39]

The *iPolitics* stories served to intensify media focus on Payette's past. A group of media outlets, including *iPolitics*, went to court to get access to sealed divorce court records. "The *Star* is seeking access to the court documents to determine if there is something in them of public interest in regards to Canada's next governor general," said the editor of the *Toronto Star*, Michael Cooke.[40] He made it clear that the media had no interest in publishing the private details of the child in the case. The records showed not only details of Payette's divorce but also information about a car accident a couple of months before the 2011 assault. Payette had accidentally hit and killed a pedestrian while driving home from a trip.[41]

As the stories rolled out, letters to the editor and members of the scientific community criticized the media for persecuting the new governor general. But from the perspective of journalists, they were doing their job by giving citizens information about an important public figure, the head of state in Canada. The directors of the Michener Foundation sat back and waited to see how this media coverage would affect Payette's regard for the Michener Award celebrations at Rideau Hall.

After that opening salvo, Payette said journalists and columnists found fault with her at every opportunity. "It was relentless," she recalled in a 2023 interview. "At one point in time, I wrote down what was the trend. The first year: I wasn't really representing all Canadians, I had said the wrong word at one speech, which I learned my lesson from. After that I didn't like my job and I was not fit for the job. Then I didn't work hard . . . then I was influencing the honour system, and so on, which was completely the opposite. And then I was a bad person."[42] In contrast, she pointed to some of her initiatives that received scant news coverage: GG Interactive and Conversations with classrooms across the country, her visits to smaller communities, her community involvement as a chorister, her Ottawa choir's Juno and her work with Rideau Hall staff to make the honours and awards system more inclusive and diverse.

Previous governors general — like all public officials — faced media scrutiny. For example, Jeanne Sauvé's health, Adrienne Clarkson's travel and spending and Michaëlle Jean's French citizenship and the alleged separatist sympathies of her husband. Media scrutiny was just part of holding such a high public position. Payette's predecessor David Johnston, reflecting on his tenure, understood that clearly. "When I was governor general some of the finalists had done stories that were critical of the Office of the Governor General. So be it. That's democracy."[43] Former governors general kept a stiff upper lip and did their duty when it came to opening Rideau Hall for the Michener Awards ceremony. In 2018, however, the Michener Foundation was worried the awards could be caught in the fallout from the public dissection and ongoing media scrutiny of Payette's past. Indications were leaning that way.

In January 2018, Michener president Alan Allnutt and vice-president Catherine Cano began a long and complicated dance with the Office of the Governor General to get a date for the awards ceremony. It did not look promising, especially after a conversation Cano had with Rideau Hall. "The Governor General is reviewing all award ceremonies to decide which ones she will keep. We are on a long list and not at the top of the list," Cano reported to the board in February 2018.[44]

From the perspective of Payette, awards come and go. "It's not like the whole thing was set in concrete," she explained. "In the case of the Micheners, it was very clear where it came from and the importance of it. But there were other ones that needed concentration."[45] She pointed to the Natural Sciences and Engineering Research Council of Canada (NSERC) Herzberg Medal in Science and Engineering. It came with a $1M prize and, for the longest time, had been presented in a hotel in Ottawa. Choices were being made.

Everything was in flux, including the landscape at Rideau Hall. Since the Michener meeting in September 2017, when the then secretary had assured the Michener Foundation of the support of Her Excellency for the awards, staff had changed. Many long-serving administrators and senior staff had been replaced or left.

With Rideau Hall weighing competing demands for recognition, months passed with no commitment to host an awards ceremony. In an interview, Payette recalled that the Michener was not a high priority for Rideau Hall for several reasons. One consideration, Payette said, was that even though former governor general Roland Michener founded the Michener Award, it was not part of Rideau Hall's embedded awards and honours. The Michener Foundation was independent, with its own rules, regulations and administration and out of the control of Rideau Hall. With all the negative media coverage, reputational problems for the Office of the Governor General had to be considered. Payette gave the example of the Innovation Awards that are administered externally but had been given at Rideau Hall. "We gave the award. And one of these persons that got an award while I was still in the position was expelled from the country for spying from a microbiology lab in Winnipeg. Whose picture do you think was in the newspaper with that person? The Governor General giving the award."[46] Payette already had enough bad press. She was not keen for more.

By May, the situation had become critical for the Michener Foundation. The judging was complete, the finalists for the Michener Award were announced and still no movement at Rideau Hall. Worry was turning into a crisis. The Foundation turned to John Fraser for help. If anyone could persuade Payette of the value of pushing through with the Michener ceremony, it was Fraser, a former Master of Massey College at the University of Toronto and head of the Institute for the Study of the Crown. He was a mentor and advisor to Payette going back to her student days at the University of Toronto.

"I called her and she said, well, why should I do it? . . . I had to listen to all the stuff that she was so angry still about the reporting on her, and I said, well, that just goes with the territory, I'm afraid." Fraser tried to impress upon her that "the whole mystique of those Michener Awards is that they're recognized by the nominal head of state as an important thing in journalism, more than just the article. . . . You just couldn't say anything good about journalists at that point, and I just said, you don't want to make them angrier at you than they already are."[47] As Payette recalled, Fraser was just one of many people she consulted about the situation. "And if I know someone who has direct knowledge of a particular thing, yeah, then of course, I will pay even more attention."[48]

While Payette weighed the options, the lobbying and contingency planning for the awards ceremony absorbed much of the Michener board's energies for the first five months of 2018. No one wanted to face the question: what would the Michener Award represent without the governor general and Rideau Hall? The Foundation did not have to face that crisis because despite "the extremely negative coverage, unrelentless coverage," in the end Payette "would welcome them. And I would show them I thought that their work is important right now and they should have judgement on what they focus."[49] On May 9, two days after a crucial board planning meeting, Rideau Hall set the date for the forty-eighth Michener Award ceremony for June 12, 2018.

Her Excellency Julie Payette put her stamp on the ceremony. The room was rearranged so that the chairs faced the side of the room and there was no raised platform. "Even with a pedestal I felt uncomfortable because I never felt I was above anybody. On the contrary, I was beside, if not behind,"[50] Payette explained. As Rideau Hall had requested, the ceremony was tighter, shorter and bilingual.[51] Her Excellency surprised everyone by entering and taking a seat in a row among the guests. It was a signal that she would do things her own way.

Payette's speech addressed the current media ecology and the echo chamber of information and disinformation. "As journalists, you are among the guardians and defenders of our liberty and our democracy. I believe deeply in the importance of having experienced, independent media organizations and journalists that are capable of casting a critical eye on the daily flow of events and information. Their existence, along with the standards to which they adhere, form part of the checks and balances that define a healthy society."[52] If Payette had any hidden message for the media that evening, it might have been when she said, "Striking the right balance between fostering maximum access to information and deciding which relevant facts to divulge, given the possible consequences, is no easy task. Rigour and excellence in ensuring that balance are precisely what the Michener Awards were created to celebrate."

That night the 2017 Michener Award went to the *Globe and Mail*. Its twenty-month investigation "Unfounded" collected data from more than 870 police forces to tell the story of serious flaws in how police across the country handle allegations of sexual assault, and the devastating results.

Reporter Robyn Doolittle took readers to a student party in London, Ontario, in October 2010. A young woman, "Ava", tells her story of being drugged and waking to find a man on top of her who would not listen to her pleas to stop:

> Terror shot through Ava's body. In that moment, she realized the man hadn't simply misunderstood her. He wasn't playing around. He was raping her. No one could hear her call for help. She had no idea what to do. She wondered if he would kill her when it was over. She stopped fighting and went still.

> Suddenly, there was a flash. Ava looked over and saw four or five men pointing cellphone cameras in her direction. She became frantic. The man on top of her ran away. He left his wallet behind, police later told Ava. She was left naked and curled on the ground, her back and hair covered in dirt . . .

> In fact, the London Police Service detective concluded that what happened to Ava that night was not a crime.

> There are many ways to shut a case without laying a charge. Not enough evidence? There's a closure code for that. Complainant doesn't want to proceed with charges? There's a code for that, too.

> On Nov. 13, 2010, the detective closed Ava's file as "unfounded," another formal police classification that rendered her allegations baseless.

> It meant a crime was neither attempted, nor occurred. It did not immediately brand Ava a liar, necessarily. But it meant she was not raped.

> According to police records, the suspect was given a warning.

> Ava's case is not an outlier. Her complaint is among the more than 5,000 allegations of sexual assault closed as unfounded by Canadian law enforcement every year, according to a *Globe and Mail* investigation into the authorities' handling of sexual-assault cases. Rape, the most serious of those, is a crime so

injurious to victims that the judiciary considers it second only to murder in severity.[53]

The series revealed that 'unfounded' rates varied from jurisdiction to jurisdiction. It raised questions about equity of access to justice.[54] "What has emerged is a picture of a system that is clearly broken," wrote Doolittle.[55]

Within six weeks of publication, the federal government promised better police oversight, training and policies. The prime minister also committed $100 million to specialized training to assist police in dealing with gender-based violence. Statistics Canada promised to resume collecting and publishing 'unfounded' rates. The biggest surprise was when the *Globe and Mail* received a letter from the RCMP to thank them for "instructing them on where they had fallen short."[56] That night at the awards ceremony in June 2018, Doolittle emphasized, "The real way to fix the system is for more people to come forward, and that's only going to happen if there's trust in the system." Following the series, police services across the country reviewed some 37,000 sexual assault cases and re-opened more than 400 'unfounded' cases.

If there were any doubts about the ongoing impact of this Michener Award-winning series, Doolittle did a follow-up in December 2022. The data showed that the rate of sexual assault complaints rejected as unfounded had dropped to 8 per cent from 19 per cent in 2017. New Brunswick — the province with the highest number of unfounded cases in 2017, saw the most significant change — from 32 per cent to 12 per cent. "I think what we've seen since "Unfounded" is a pretty profound culture shift in policing. Overall, what we're seeing is a lot better, and they're more open to collaboration. There was a level of humility that came out after the report," Jenn Richard, the director of strategic development at Sexual Violence New Brunswick, told Doolittle.[57]

Doolittle and editor-in-chief David Walmsley would be the only representatives of a media organization invited to the front during the ceremony to get the trophy and photo with Her Excellency. The other finalists would have to wait until after to get their certificates of merit and a group photo opportunity with Payette in a separate room. The biggest surprise, however, was that Her Excellency had not signed any of the certificates for the finalists and award winner, something that still rankles Walmsley. Payette showed surprise when this was brought to her attention. "I will take responsibility for everything. So if I didn't sign a certificate, I'm really sorry. This is all I can say."[58]

Still, Payette set aside her *animus* and, as with other governors general, she did her duty, hosting a buffet dinner and drinks with music for the media. At the end of the evening, there was a sigh of relief among the directors of the Michener Foundation

In year two of Payette's tenure, Rideau Hall rolled out the red carpet. Taking a page from her predecessors, Michaëlle Jean's "Art Matters" interactive discussions and Adrienne Clarkson's cultural roundtable lunches, Payette hosted a panel discussion on journalism in Canada at Rideau Hall the afternoon of the ceremony. Carleton's Chris Waddell, Pierre-Paul Noreau, publisher of *Le Droit*, David Akin of *Global News* and Althia Raj of *HuffPost* held a wide-ranging conversation about the challenges of gathering, sharing and communicating facts in the age of "fake news" and misinformation.[59]

That night her speech focused on ceremonies in France and Halifax to mark the seventy-fifth anniversary of D-Day, and Her Excellency spoke of the horrors of conflict. Turning to media, she said, that if we can learn anything from the two world wars, it is that "when democracy begins to die you often see that first is the death of the freedom of the press, when propaganda, disinformation, fake news will be able to turn the population around and provide people with false impressions, and then things change."[60]

After her speech, the emcees read the citations for the finalists. One by one, the journalists went to the podium and talked about the difference their stories had made. In the Niagara Region, voters turfed councillors connected to shady hiring practices, evidence of "the power of local news," said Grant LaFleche of the *St. Catharines Standard*. In Kitchener, more than 300 rubber workers will have their health claims reviewed. In New Brunswick, revelations of a dysfunctional and dangerous ambulance service played a role in the defeat of a provincial government. CBC's *the fifth estate* unearthed hidden evidence supporting seatbelts on school buses. Stories about faulty medical implants led to a national ban on textured breast implants, with more reforms promised. In the North, the Aboriginal Peoples Television Network (APTN) exposed a link between child welfare and the high rate of suicides. In the Yukon, revelations of neglect and abuse in group homes for Aboriginal youth prompted a government apology, an investigation and policy changes. "This is what the Michener Award is all about, the betterment of the public,"[61] said Mervin Brass, CBC North's managing editor.

The announcement of the 2018 Michener Award winner, the *Telegraph-Journal* for "Sounding the Alarm," an investigation into ambulance service in New Brunswick, brought applause that was mixed with excitement, re-lief, disappointment and celebration. This was the first Michener for the *Telegraph-Journal*, and to some in the room, it came as a surprise. After all, Irving-owned Brunswick News Inc. did not have a reputation across Canada for its investigative journalism.

After editor Wendy Metcalfe and her team received the Michener trophy and the photos were taken, Metcalfe took the podium. "The work celebrated here tonight is a staunch reminder of just how much journalism matters. Without it, secrecy would be rampant. Truth, trust and transparency would be scant. Without journalism, systemic problems . . . would deepen. Wrongs would not be made right. . . . With journalism, in the darkness, there's light, there's change."[62] No one could imagine that this panel and ceremony on June 12, 2019, would be the last in-person gathering at Rideau Hall before the COVID-19 pandemic shut down the world.

The board of the Michener Foundation had spent the first year and a half of Payette's tenure in a state of high anxiety. Survival dominated the agenda. Persistence and a little help from friends allowed the Foundation to hang on to the vital connection to Rideau Hall and secure the endorsement of the governor general. Survival was paramount to the Micheners' public service mission. The award — a symbol of excellence — was needed more than ever to provide support and validation to an industry that was being battered on all sides — failing business models, digital disruption, harassment and a flood of mis- and disinformation.

New times, new ways, new threats

As Payette pointed out in her 2018 speech, the professional environment in which journalists did their work had profoundly changed. Truth-telling was being undermined and was under attack. The Michener Foundation saw an opportunity to revamp its flagging education fellowship to support journal-ists navigating difficult times. The board started to address the issue in 2017 but first had to work through governance changes and focus on building a relationship with Rideau Hall. It would take another four years and advice from a consortium of journalism schools for the Foundation to revamp its education fellowship.

A discussion paper presented in the spring of 2017 set out the problem. Digital disruption was the root cause of declining applications for the $40,000 four-month fellowship. "Although journalism schools initially expressed enthusiasm for the fellowship, it came at a time when the media industry and media education were facing enormous challenges due to the impact of digitalization. Because of cutbacks, media organizations were unable to release reporters for the length of time required and journalists themselves became reluctant to take time off, for fear of not being able to return to their places of employment. Journalism schools were facing similar cutbacks and lacked faculty and staff to administer the fellowships, while at the same time facing union and other regulations that made it difficult."[63] The report suggested a review of the education fellowship.

In the summer of 2017, a sub-committee turned its attention to the problem. Members included director James Deacon, son of the Foundation's first president, Paul Deacon, who had raised the money for the fellowships in the 1980s. In the interim report, committee chair Donna Logan, professor emerita of UBC's School of Journalism, outlined options, including the creation of a Visiting Journalist program. It would fund Michener finalists and award winners to travel to journalism schools to hold workshops and lectures. Logan's committee, in the politest way possible, "foresaw implementational challenges"[64] to the proposed program, namely, someone from the volunteer board would have to administer it. The idea, a great one, came at the wrong time. In 2017-18, the board was transitioning, and no one had the energy or time to champion the project. The Visiting Journalist program never got off the ground.

When applications for the education fellowship fell from a high of five in 2012 to one in 2018, the board made the tough decision to suspend it for a year. The Michener board asked journalism educators associated with J-Schools Canada/ÉcolesJ, a consortium of post-secondary journalism schools across the country, to recommend a model and criteria that would benefit students and the industry. The board looked to the consortium to provide a framework to meet current issues.

What emerged in 2020 was a newly funded fellowship that reflected emerging trends and challenges in journalism. The revised criteria allowed applications from journalistic teams of up to four — including journalism schools and media organizations — who had support from a journalism educator and an experienced journalist. The proposal had to focus on a project that would "expand the knowledge of newsroom products, processes and practices."[65]

The name was changed to the L. Richard O'Hagan Fellowship for Journalism Education· named after "Dick" O'Hagan. and funded by BMO

Financial Group with a $100,000 commitment over four years.[66] O'Hagan had been a senior executive with the bank and had started his career as a reporter with the *Toronto Telegram* before moving into public relations. Over the years, he had served as Special Advisor to Prime Ministers Lester B. Pearson and Pierre Trudeau before taking a vice-president position at BMO. The revised fellowship would open the door to innovative solutions-based projects to support journalists transitioning to an increasingly hostile digital world. It was a world where fact-based journalism competed with fabricated information. It had become a nasty world where journalists — especially female and racialized reporters — faced harassment, hate and threats in the field and online from citizens and those in positions of authority.

The first O'Hagan fellowship was awarded in 2020 to a consortium led by the national journalism portal, *J-Source* to create the "Canada Press Freedom Project," a database to track attacks against journalists and instances of online hate and threats against journalists.[67] The idea for the hub was inspired by the U.S. Press Freedom Tracker.[68] When the project was conceived, no one could have predicted the escalation of violations against press freedom in Canada or the daily intimidation, harassment and threats faced by journalists reporting in the field, especially online.

As the isolation and shifting public health directives during the COVID-19 pandemic intensified, so did the vitriol in Canada. People felt empowered to attack not only the actions of provincial and federal governments but also the message of journalists covering the story. Threats — in person and online — from protestors at the so-called "freedom convoy," especially in downtown Ottawa in the winter of 2022, were serious enough for some journalists to cover the protest with a security guard at their side. Journalists found themselves increasingly in unsafe workplaces. They faced insults, threats and intimidation. They found their vehicles damaged and had to keep a tight grip on their equipment to keep it from being knocked from their hands. This was a new world. It did not end there. When journalists went online, especially if they were female or racialized, they found themselves navigating tidal waves of hate, insults and even death threats in their email and social media accounts.

Journalists also faced resistance from those in authority. Police set up "exclusion zones" at protest sites in isolated areas under the pretense of court injunctions to keep journalists at a distance. In 2021, RCMP arrested journalists trying to cover protests against a gas pipeline in Wetsuwet'en territory in central British Columbia and at Fairy Creek on Vancouver Island, the site of an old-growth logging protest. This increasing resistance from police and other authorities added yet another challenge to the work of journalists, a factor which projects undertaken through the Michener fellowships sought to address.

The home page of the Canada Press Freedom Project's website documents more than a hundred instances since 2021 where Canadian media workers have faced arrests or criminal charges, been denied access, had their equipment seized or damaged, faced intimidation, harassment or attacked in person and online. Journalists with the Press Freedom Project verify each report before posting it on the website. The site's searchable database gives a public face to instances of hate, abuse, harassment and other assaults on freedom of the press. In addition, the website offers resources to help journalists cope with a changing work environment. The seed money of $40,000 from the Michener Awards Foundation was crucial to develop this website.

The escalating verbal and physical abuse that journalists navigate has its roots in growing divisiveness in society as 'alternative facts' are presented and defended as truth against fact-based journalism.[69] To help fight the erosion of trust in the media in a post-truth era, the 2021 Michener - L. Richard O'Hagan Fellowship for Journalism Education funded two journalists to create the Truth in Journalism Fact-Checking Guide, a timely online resource to help educators and students[70]

Allison Baker, the head of research at *Walrus* magazine, and Viviane Fairbank, a journalist and philosopher now based in Scotland, consulted widely with working journalists, editors, authors and educators "about the most pressing challenges — and possible solutions — regarding gathering and verifying journalistic facts."[71] In 2022, Baker and Fairbank launched the "new guidelines for editorial fact-checking that are rigorous, inclusive, and informed by interdisciplinary expertise."[72]

These Michener-funded projects are part of a larger effort in Canada to rebuild trust in media under the long-held belief that strong independent journalism is essential to the health of democratic institutions. Media companies such as the *Globe and Mail, Toronto Star*, CTV Edmonton and CBC Radio are taking the initiative to educate citizens. As members of the Trust Project, these media outlets have agreed to follow prescribed international standards and protocols such as "transparent ownership and mission statements, ethics and reporting policies, clear labelling of story types, and links to detailed author information."[73] Think tanks such as the Public Policy

Forum,[74] *Centre d'études sur les médias*[75] at Laval University and the Centre for Media, Technology and Democracy[76] at McGill University conduct research into policy and other alternatives. All these actions are ways to counter mis- and disinformation and strengthen the media environment.

The Michener fellowships are a small part of this mix. Between 1987 and 2023, the Michener Award Foundation has supported fifty-eight working journalists for study leaves, education initiatives with journalism schools and investigative journalism projects. Journalists like Robb Cribb and Matthew Pearson have taken the initial idea of a "sabbatical" or "study break" for mid-career journalists to new levels. "The Press Freedom Project and Truth in Journalism Fact-Checking Guide" have made education resources widely accessible to meet the changes in the industry. These Michener-funded projects, along with the investigative fellowship, helped to build a culture of public service in journalism in newsrooms, which has survived technological disruption, economic collapse, the crumbling of business models and the emergence of new media.

Conclusion: Partnership, A Way Forward

After two successful Awards ceremonies with Her Excellency Julie Payette, president Alan Allnutt was confident that, despite some hiccups, the Foundation and Office of the Governor General were building bridges. He was looking forward to a big celebration for the fiftieth anniversary in the spring of 2020, including the launch of the revamped education fellowship.

With new governance policies, an engaged board and cordial relations with the Office of the Governor General, Allnutt turned his attention to fundraising. This problem has dogged the Micheners since its founding in 1970. "There was really a point probably early 2019 where I was like, oh my God, what are we going to do? We need to raise money,"[1] Allnutt recalled. Donor prospects were slim. He remembered how board members questioned his proposal to hire a professional fundraiser. They didn't understand "why would we need it?" Allnutt, a corporate governance expert, understood the complexities behind successful fundraising. Gone were the days when a volunteer could knock on the door and leave with a multi-year pledge. Now, funders wanted accountability, measurable goals and an organization that had the support to follow through with new initiatives. The Michener Foundation did not have the people, the resources or the organizational heft.

Then, *Fortuna*, the goddess of fortune and luck, sailed onto the horizon. In the course of being interviewed for this book in June 2019, former governor general David Johnston raised the question of the organization's future. "What's your strategic plan for the next ten years?" he asked. "You have a precious institution that's done important things for the country over the last fifty years. . . . And those fifty years have been a prologue of important distinction, but now we are where we are, and it's a world that is vastly different from the one Roly [Michener] saw fifty years ago."[2] Johnston challenged the Michener Awards Foundation to set out their ambitions for the next ten years, "Then you need goodwill and good people to do it, and then you obviously need to think of some funding."

The conversation led Johnston to suggest a partnership between the Michener Awards Foundation (MAF) and the Rideau Hall Foundation (RHF). He founded the independent and non-political charitable organization in 2012, "to amplify the impact of the Office of the Governor General as a central institution of Canadian democracy, and to better serve Canadians through a range of initiatives linked to learning, leadership, giving and innovation."[3] Johnston could see the natural link between the two foundations and saw opportunities to build on the Michener Awards and fellowships. He also saw how a lack of funding and a volunteer board limited the Micheners. "I would love it if, with the help of the Rideau Hall Foundation and other Canadians, we could take the Michener Award and strengthen it."[4] It was an exciting prospect.

After I presented the idea to Alan Allnutt, "It just went click for me. It was like, wow, this is the way to go," he said. "It was just like manna from heaven."[5] There were questions but no pushback when Allnutt raised it with the board of directors in the fall of 2019. They gave him the green light to begin negotiations. Absent was the hesitancy or suspicion surrounding past overtures from and discussions about the Canadian Journalism Foundation.

By December 2019, Allnutt had a draft partnership agreement for review. "It was a good and reasonable proposal to sustain activities of the MAF and professionalize them,"[6] said director Ed Greenspon at the January 2020 board meeting. Director Paul MacNeill saw the partnership as an opportunity to elevate the Michener Award and get the recognition and profile it deserved as journalism's most prestigious award. "It's a win-win for both the Michener Award Foundation and the Rideau Hall Foundation," he said.[7] For Allnutt, who was stepping down as president at the January 2020 meeting, it "felt like, mission accomplished."[8] For others on the volunteer board, it was a burden lifted. This agreement would secure the future of the Awards and fellowships. Finally, there was a path developing that would allow the Foundation to contemplate growth.

Incoming president Pierre-Paul Noreau took over negotiations. Over the next ten months, with the help of a sub-committee, he worked out details with Teresa Marques, the president and CEO of the Rideau Hall Foundation. The Michener would keep its status as a charitable organization. Its board would continue to administer the Michener-Baxter special prize along with the independent adjudication of the awards and fellowships. The RHF would manage the Michener endowment and budget, and they would collaborate on fundraising, marketing, promotion and events.

On August 31, 2020, the Michener board approved a "two-year collaboration agreement" with the Rideau Hall Foundation. It was like getting engaged. The couple would commit, but the wedding would take place at a later date. Director Miller Ayre spoke for other directors when he said, "This is the best opportunity to grow into a solid foundation. Right now, the Michener Award Foundation has no institutionalized support and no day-to-day follow-through. This partnership with RHF is positive and what's needed to strengthen the foundation."[9]

It was only fitting that in its fiftieth year, the Michener Awards Foundation should, at long last, find a compatible partner. This agreement would transform the future of the Michener. It was no longer a group of former journalists, editors and publishers who ran things off the side of their desks in their spare time for free. The Rideau Hall Foundation had staff with expertise. The Micheners finally had the support it needed to tackle some of the issues raised back in 2017 — such as a remake of the website, presence on social media and new projects to expand the reach of journalism in the public interest.

The value of this nascent partnership was never more evident than when the pandemic hit in March 2020. COVID-19 scuttled the Michener Foundation's plans for a big in-person fifty anniversary bash. The world shut down, and media organizations could barely keep up with the changing science as the virus mutated. There was social distancing, masking, lockdowns and quarantines. People got sick. Millions died. The world stayed home and went online.

The Foundation's volunteer board was in no position to pivot and produce an online virtual awards ceremony. It was its budding association with the Rideau Hall Foundation that turned out to be a lifesaver. With the pandemic ranging, staff stepped in and started planning for a pre-recorded half-hour awards ceremony to be broadcast online in December.[10]

The big question for the Michener board was whether Her Excellency would participate. Julie Payette was once again in the media spotlight. In July 2020, CBC News started to roll out a series of news stories about an alleged toxic work environment at Rideau Hall. Former and current employees had told journalists Ashley Burke and Kristen Everson that they experienced persistent verbal abuse, bullying and workplace harassment, and some described

Rideau Hall as "a house of horrors."[11] Within two days of the first CBC news story, the Privy Council Office ordered an independent review and hired Ottawa-based Quintet Consulting Corporation. For its part, Payette's office issued a news release affirming a strong belief "in the importance of a healthy workplace" and that "We deeply regret this reporting, which is in stark contrast to the reality of working in the OSGG."[12] The harassment allegations appear to have come as a surprise to Payette, who claimed she received no complaints from the union during her tenure. "I cannot imagine that if there were some issues, that they wouldn't have been breathing down our necks. . . . But we never heard."[13] That autumn, ninety-two people brought their complaints and comments to Quintet.

Despite the cloud over Payette, she put her best face forward for the Michener Awards fiftieth anniversary in December. In a red holiday dress, she smiled into the camera and praised journalists for their frontline work during this pandemic and for telling stories and keeping pace with the changing science. "Misinformation is everywhere, and we the public rely on you and on your vigilance to distinguish between the real and the not-so-real, through fact-checking and accuracy in reporting. This is what we celebrate today, by honouring news stories that have made a difference. All of them resulted in change for the better."[14]

Payette concluded the virtual fiftieth anniversary broadcast by announcing the 2019 Michener Award winner — the *Globe and Mail* — for its investigation into the exploitation of newcomers. "False Promises," a national investigation led by reporter Kathy Tomlinson, delved into the systematic exploitation of temporary workers and foreign students by corrupt immigration consultants and employers:

> As his former assistant puts it, Kuldeep Bansal preyed upon the weak and "had them by the necks."
>
> Mr. Bansal is a Canadian immigration consultant and international recruiter known for speeding around suburban Vancouver in a Lamborghini. Over the past decade, his agency collected up to $5 million a year from thousands of people who wanted a permanent life in Canada.

Eager recruits would borrow and scrape together as much as $15,000 apiece for a chance at one of the "guaranteed" jobs Mr. Bansal advertised for his employer clients. In recent years, those clients included such major fast-food franchises as Subway and Fatburger, as well as Best Western hotels and Mac's convenience stores, among others.

Many recruits made initial payments to Mr. Bansal overseas in Dubai or India, in cash, which his former assistant said he brought back to Canada in suitcases. Some waited months for job offers that never materialized. Others got to Canada but found the position they'd been promised didn't exist.

Mr. Bansal kept their money anyway, and, in some cases, went after them for more. It has made him a wealthy man. Along with his family, he now has a golf course, a banquet hall and at least $15-million worth of real estate, according to public records.

"It makes you feel disgusted. Totally sick to the bottom of my belly what had happened and is still happening now," Mr. Bansal's former assistant, Arjun Chaudhary, said. "I was a part of it, to be honest."

Mr. Bansal is among the more notorious of the thousands of job recruiters and consultants operating both in Canada and abroad. A four-month *Globe and Mail* investigation probed 45 such agents, who together have amassed scores of complaints, lawsuits and charges against them in Ontario, British Columbia, Alberta and Québec. Along with employers and career colleges who paid them to help fill their job openings and classrooms, they collectively stand accused of exploiting at least 2,300 people in recent years, from countries such as India, the Philippines, Mexico and Guatemala, for their money, their labour or both."[15]

The series prompted the federal government to introduce new open work visas allowing foreign workers facing abuse to switch employers, and it passed more stringent regulations for immigration consultants."[16] In her acceptance speech, Tomlinson emphasized change is "ultimately is the role of public-service journalism. . . . At its best, it not only reveals the truth, no matter how challenging, flawed or complex it might be, it goes further to spark the ideas and the conversations to correct it."[17] The broadcast was not the bash that the Foundation had hoped for. Still, the virtual ceremony and new partnership with the Rideau Hall Foundation signalled exciting possibilities that awaited the Micheners.

A month after the ceremony, Julie Payette stepped down as Governor General on January 21, 2021, along with her secretary, Assunta Di Lorenzo. Their departure came just days before the release of the heavily redacted 132-page Quintet report that found "serious problems" that needed the PMO's attention, "especially regarding toxic workplace behaviours."[18]

Three months later, when the finalists for the 2020 Michener Award were announced, the CBC News series "Inside Rideau Hall" was on the list. The news release noted CBC's investigation revealed "a toxic work environment, evidence of questionable spending, and a flawed government vetting process. . . . The CBC's investigation was not just about being a public service, it was about basic workplace standards, transparency and accountability. In the end, it held to account those in the nation's highest constitutional office."[19] This was what the Michener Awards was set up to do and the judges adjudicated without fear or favour.

The partnership with the Rideau Hall Foundation now gave it access to new donors and opened up opportunities to share the best in Canada's journalism with more people. It also allowed the Micheners to revive another idea to expand its public service role that had been around since its formation in 1970 — the development of a visiting journalist's program. An attempt had been made in the 1980s when a panel of Michener finalists would meet with journalism students at Carleton University on the day of the awards, but it had not taken root. The idea was resurrected in 2017-18, but again, it went nowhere because there was no champion or administrative support to get it off the ground.

President Pierre-Paul Noreau — based in Québec City — was anxious to amplify the Michener values of public service in journalism in the rest of the country. His idea was to bring the stories and research of Michener laureates and fellows to journalism students in other locations. With Noreau as the champion, funding from the Power Corporation of Canada and the administrative and marketing know-how of the Rideau Hall Foundation, the

Micheners hit the road in November 2022 under the banner "Positive Change for Public Good."

The pilot project was at the School of Journalism at the University of King's College in Halifax, Nova Scotia, where I had taught for twenty-four years. The timing was excellent. There was a lull in the spread of the COVID-19 virus, and the variant Omicron had yet to surface and run rampant.

Michener Award winner (2020) Kenneth Jackson of APTN and nominees from the previous two years, Gabrielle Duchaine and Caroline Touzin of *La Presse*, and Tim Bousquet of the *Halifax Examiner*,[20] were joined by the 2021 fellowship recipient, Ethan Cox of *Ricochet Media*.[21] The day was devoted to panel discussions and workshops, schooling students in the role of journalism as a public service. It was an inspiring moment when Duchaine looked at the journalism students in the audience and said, "I see our jobs as walking around with a flashlight, looking for rocks in the darkest corner, lifting them and putting the light on them. I want to fight injustice." Waving her hand in a circle, she said, to get change, "you have to write again and again and again and again and again on this same story and the same subject relentlessly."[22] Jackson agreed, "Change is going to be slow in terms of impact."[23]

They spoke about "living with the trauma of others," and "scars, images" and their obsession to find the truth.[24] They left students with solid advice. "When you're starting out it's going to be very deadline driven, hard news, pyramid style. You're going to be required to turn it around quickly because that's how you learn. You learn how to develop sources, how to talk to people and how to write. You learn what the truth is. You find it, you see what is wrong," Jackson said. "You look at us. We're a bunch of unicorns who get to do investigative journalism. . . . You have to work your way there. It's work, a lot of work." Their presentation that day left an impact on the students.

For Michener president Pierre-Paul Noreau, that was just the beginning. Another panel discussion with Michener laureates was held at Laval University in November 2023. And the Foundation is looking at other ideas. "Dream, dream, dream. So that's the beginning,"[25] Noreau said.

The fiftieth anniversary of the Michener Awards Foundation was golden. Despite the pandemic, the Foundation had found its footing. Since the first ceremony in 1971, the world of journalism has changed radically. In 1970, Michener's world of journalism was slower, simpler and siloed. Had he been alive in 2023, Roly Michener would have marvelled at how media have become instantaneous, social and multi-platform to stay relevant in this new media ecology. He would have lamented the decline of in-depth journalism. He would be astounded to see the flood of information online with alternative facts presented as truth, journalists harassed and threatened, and information manipulated and suppressed. He'd be interested in how these organizations have responded. With so many demands and fewer resources, he might worry that the essential role of journalism in the public interest was threatened. And because of that, Michener would likely conclude that journalists need more support than ever before. The Michener Awards and the fellowships are his small but lasting contributions to the effort. They remain his legacy and stand the test of time.

Torstar's former chair, the late John Honderich, saw the Michener Awards as "a metaphor for getting top-level work that has a social impact. It has achieved that kind of currency."[26] And essential to that currency remains the impartial role of the governor general as expressed through the annual awards ceremony at Rideau Hall. "There is nothing more humbling than to be allowed into Rideau Hall to see the head of state who takes a personal interest and has a commitment to understand why journalism as a central part of democracy also represents the very best of what Canada represents," said *Globe and Mail* editor-in-chief David Walmsley. "It's a high watermark for us in the calendar. There's nothing more important to us than getting into Rideau Hall. It's so validating."[27]

Three factors have contributed to the stability of the Michener Award: the ongoing support of Rideau Hall and Her Excellency Mary Simon, the timely intervention of former governor general David Johnston and the subsequent partnership with the Rideau Hall Foundation. The Michener Award Foundation has found new opportunities to expand its mission and serve as a beacon for journalism in the public interest for the next fifty years. "The Michener Foundation before the association with the Rideau Hall Foundation, and the Michener Foundation today — they're two worlds," said Noreau. "We have a lot of possibilities in front of us, and it's a major change in the life of the Foundation. You know, before I wasn't sure at all, but now I am comfortable to say that we will have another fifty years."[28]

If only media organizations could be as confident of their own future. Between 2001 and June 1, 2023, 474 local news operations have closed in 335 Canadian communities, reported the Local New Research Project at Toronto Metropolitan University. And the bad news keeps coming. In August 2023 Météo Media closed twenty free and flyer publications in Québec, and in

Ontario, Metroland announced that it would close most of its seventy regional papers. They are victims of declining advertisements and readers. Blame free online news, blame social media, blame COVID-19, blame bad management.

The wasting away of professional media outlets should raise alarm bells about the health of our communities, many of which are now news deserts. Community needs journalism to speak for those who are marginalized, to uncover corruption and abuses by those in authority, to draw our attention to what is not working in our society and to give examples of what success might look like. Fact-based journalism in the public interest helps us understand issues, make decisions and push governments to make changes. Without independent journalism, democracy is open to abuse of power, corruption, manipulation, propaganda and mis- and disinformation. The Michener Awards stands in opposition to that. So long as journalists are poking around, asking questions and holding those in power to account, sharing what they find out, and effecting change, the Michener Award will be there to honour and celebrate journalism organizations — in whatever form they take.

Appendix 1

Michener Awards Winners and Finalists, 1970-2022

2022 - *The Globe and Mail*, "Hockey Canada's Secret Funds"
Citations of Merit: CBC Saskatchewan, *The Eastern Graphic*, *The Globe and Mail*, Radio-Canada, and *Toronto Star*

2021 - CBC Saskatoon and *The Globe and Mail*, "Residential Schools"
Citations of Merit: CBC News, CBC Saskatchewan, Global News, *Kamloops This Week*, and *The Globe and Mail*

2020 - APTN, "Death by Neglect"
Citations of Merit: CBC News, *Winnipeg Free Press*, *The Gazette* (Montreal), *La Presse*, and *The Globe and Mail*

2019 - *The Globe and Mail*, "False promises"
Citations of Merit: *The Halifax Examiner*, CBC News, *La Presse*, *The London Free Press*, and the Institute for Investigative Journalism

2018 - *The Telegraph-Journal*, "Seat belts on school buses"
Citations of Merit: APTN, CBC, *The Standard* (St. Catharines), *Waterloo Region Record*, and *Toronto Star*, CBC News and Radio-Canada (joint project)

2017 - *The Globe and Mail*, "Unfounded, police records of sexual assaults"
Citations of Merit: *Vancouver Sun*, *The Globe and Mail*, CBC Edmonton, Cogeco Media, Global TV, and *Toronto Star*

2016 - *The London Free Press*, "Indiscernible"
Citations of Merit: *The Globe and Mail, Canada's National Observer, La Presse, Toronto Star*, and CBC, Radio-Canada and *Toronto Star* (joint project)

2015 - *Enquête* (Radio-Canada) "Police abuse of Indigenous women, Val d'Or, Québec"
Citations of Merit: The Canadian Press, *The Globe and Mail, The Telegraph Journal, Toronto Star*, and the CBC, *The Globe and Mail* and *Toronto Star* (for their combined work)

2014 - *The Globe and Mail*, "Thalidomide"
Citations of Merit: *L'actualité*, CBC-TV News, CBC North, The Canadian Press, and *Vancouver Sun*

2013 - *Toronto Star*, "Toronto Mayor Rob Ford and Crack Cocaine"
Citations of Merit: Canadian Press, CTV News, *Edmonton Journal* and *Calgary Herald*, and *Windsor Star*

2014 - Postmedia and *Ottawa Citizen*, "Robocalls"
Citations of Merit: CBC and *Enquête* (Radio-Canada), *The Coast* (Halifax), *La Presse, Toronto Star*, and *Vancouver Sun*.

2011 - *Times Colonist* (Victoria), "Underfunding for People with Developmental Difficulties"
Citations of Merit: CBC (Vancouver), *The Globe and Mail, La Presse, Toronto Star* and *Windsor Star*

2010 - *the fifth estate* (CBC-TV), "Ashley Smith: out of control"
Citations of Merit: *Calgary Herald, The Eastern Door, The Hamilton Spectator*, and *Découverte* (Radio-Canada), and *Vancouver Sun*

2009 - *The Gazette* (Montréal), "City Mismanagement of Water Construction Project"
Citations of Merit: *W5* (CTV), *The Globe and Mail, National Post, Times Colonist* (Victoria), and *Enquête* (Radio-Canada)

2008 - CBC/Radio-Canada and The Canadian Press, "Taser stun guns"
Citations of Merit: *The Hamilton Spectator, Toronto Star, Winnipeg Free Press, Le Courrier de Saint-Hyacinthe*, and *The Globe and Mail*

2007 - *The Globe and Mail* and *La Presse*, "The Treatment of Afghan Detainees" (for their combined coverage)
Citations of Merit: *Le Devoir*, *The London Free Press*, *The Province* (Vancouver), *Toronto Star* and CBC and *The Globe and Mail* (joint project)

2006 - *Prince George Citizen*, "Truckers' Deaths on Logging Roads"
Citations of Merit: CBC, *The Globe and Mail*, *The Hamilton Spectator*, *Nunatsiaq News*, *La Presse*, and *Toronto Star* and *Kitchener-Waterloo Record* (joint project)

2005 - *The Globe and Mail*, "Breast cancer"
Citations of Merit: *The Canadian Medical Association Journal*, *La Presse*, Radio-Canada, *Toronto Star*, *Times Colonist* (Victoria), and *Vancouver Sun*

2004 - *The Globe and Mail*, "Federal sponsorship scandal"
Citations of Merit: *Calgary Herald*, CBC, *Canadian Medical Association Journal* and *Découverte* (Radio-Canada), *The Globe and Mail*, and *The Independent* (NL)

2003 - *La Presse*, "Elderly in long term-care"
Citations of Merit: CBC News (Saskatoon), *Winnipeg Free Press*, *Toronto Star*, *The Globe and Mail*, and *National Post*

2002 - *Toronto Star*, "Race and Crime"
Citations of Merit: *La Presse*, Ottawa Citizen, *The Globe and Mail*, *The London Free Press*, and *Edmonton Journal*

2001 - *Kitchener-Waterloo Record*, "Municipal misuse of public funds"
Honourable Mention: *Vancouver Sun*
Citations of Merit: CBC News, The Canadian Press, *Toronto Star*, and *Winnipeg Free Press*

2000 - *the fifth estate* (CBC TV), "Police and the justice system"
Honourable Mention: *The Globe and Mail*
Citations of Merit: Ottawa Citizen, *The Telegram*, (St. John's, NL), *Toronto Star*, and the *Winnipeg Free Press*

1999 - CBC National Radio News (Winnipeg), "Manitoba P.C. vote splitting scheme"
Honourable Mention: *The Globe and Mail*
Citations of Merit: *The Province* (Vancouver), *Kitchener-Waterloo Record*, *Toronto Star*, and *Windsor Star*

1998 - *Toronto Star*, "Ontario's troubled health care system"
Honourable Mention: *Maclean's*
Citations of Merit: The Canadian Press, Ottawa Bureau, *the fifth estate* (CBC-TV), *Ottawa Citizen*, and *Winnipeg Free Press*

1997 - *The Daily News* (Halifax), "Shelburne school for boys"
Honourable Mention: *Le Droit*
Citations of Merit: *Calgary Herald*, *The London Free Press*, *Marketplace* (CBC-TV), and *Toronto Star*

1996 - *Toronto Star*, "Spousal abuse"
Honourable Mention: *Le Devoir*
Citations of Merit: *the fifth estate* (CBC-TV), *The Times-Globe* (Saint John, NB), *Stoney Creek News* (ON), and *Toronto Star*

1995 - CBC Radio (Ottawa), "Somalia military coverup"
Honourable Mention: *Vancouver Sun*
Citations of Merit: The Canadian Press, (Ottawa), *The Province* (Vancouver), and *Toronto Star*

1994 - CKNW / 98 (New Westminster), "Kemano power project"
Honourable Mention: *Le Devoir*
Citations of Merit: *Edmonton Journal*, *Prince Albert Daily Herald*, *The Telegraph-Journal* (Saint John, NB), and *Toronto Star*

1993 - *Ottawa Citizen*, "Privatizing Pearson airport," and *The Globe and Mail*, "Tainted blood scandal" (tied)
Honourable Mention: *The Standard* (St. Catharines)
Citations of Merit: *the fifth estate* (CBC-TV), *Edmonton Journal*, and *Toronto Star*

1992 - *Edmonton Journal*, "Psychiatry on trial"
Honourable Mention: *Winnipeg Free Press*
Citations of Merit: *Toronto Star* and *The Globe and Mail*

1991 - CBC-TV (Toronto and Winnipeg), "Five investigative reports"
Honourable Mention: *The Globe and Mail*
Citations of Merit: CKSL-Q103 (London), *Winnipeg Free Press, Prince Alberta Daily Herald*, and *L'Actualité*

1990 - *Elmira Independent*, "Industrial contamination of water supply"
Honourable Mention: *Le Droit* and *The Sault Star* (jointly), *The Yarmouth Vanguard* (NS), and BCTV (Vancouver)
Citations of Merit: CKNW (Vancouver), *Edmonton Journal*, and *Winnipeg Free Press*

1989 - *Le Devoir*, "Inuit self-government in Québec"
Honourable Mention: *Sunday Express* (St. John's, NL)
Citations of Merit: *The Kingston Whig-Standard, Reader's Digest* (Montreal), Southam News (Ottawa), *The Journal* (CBC Toronto), and CKNW (New Westminster"

1988 - *The Globe and Mail*, "A package of investigations"
Honourable Mention: CJOH-TV (Ottawa)
Citation of Merit: *Calgary Herald*, Rock 103 (Moncton), *The World-Spectator* (Moosomin, Sask.), *Vancouver Sun*, and *Winnipeg Free Press*

1987 - CBC-TV, "24-hours on the street," and Southam News, "The Literacy Project" (tied)
Honourable Mention: *The Eastern Graphic* (Montague, PEI)
Citations of Merit: *The Kitchener-Waterloo Record*, CFPL-TV (London) and *Vancouver Sun*

1986 - *The Globe and Mail*, "Police search and seizure in criminal code"
Honourable Mention: *The Kingston Whig-Standard*
Citations of Merit: *The Kitchener-Waterloo Record, Regina Leader-Post*, and *The Standard* (St. Catharines)

1985 - *The Globe and Mail*, "Illegal Immigrants," and *Toronto Star*, "Multiculturalism" (tied)
Honourable Mention: *The Standard* (St. Catharines)
Citation of Merit: *Calgary Herald* and *The Kitchener-Waterloo Record*

1984 - *The Kingston Whig-Standard*, "Tax reform"
Honourable Mention: Radio-Canada (Montréal)
Citation of Merit: *Ottawa Citizen, The Globe and Mail,* and *Winnipeg Free Press*

1983 - *The Kitchener-Waterloo Record*, "Quality control in farm supply, shady stock sales, and Revenue Canada tax collecting methods"
Honourable Mention: *The Kingston Whig-Standard* and *Ottawa Citizen*
Citations of Merit: *Calgary Herald,* CBC (*The Journal*), and *Edmonton Journal*

1982 - *The Manitoulin Expositor* (Little Current, ON), "Suicide crisis"
Honourable Mention: *The Hamilton Spectator*
Citations of Merit: *Edmonton Journal,* CBOFT (Radio-Canada, Ottawa), *The Globe and Mail,* and CKTV (Regina)

1981 - CRTM-TV (Télé Métropole, Montréal), "Bank mismanagement," and *The Kitchener-Waterloo Record*, "Land swindles" (tied)
Citations of Merit: *La Presse, The Battleford News-Optimist* (SK), and *Regina Leader-Post*

1980 - *Edmonton Journal*, "Child welfare abuses"
Honourable Mention: CHUM-FM (Toronto)
Citations of Merit: *The Globe and Mail* and *Toronto Star*

1979 - *The Kingston Whig-Standard*, "Fluoride poisoning Cornwall Island"
Honourable Mention: *Edmonton Journal*
Citations of Merit: *The Calgary Albertan, Calgary Herald,* and *The Windsor Star*

1978 - *The Kitchener-Waterloo Record*, "Contaminated meat packing plants"
Honourable Mention: BCTV (Vancouver) and *Edmonton Journal*
Citations of Merit: CFRN-TV (Edmonton), *The Hamilton Spectator, The Kingston Whig-Standard*

1977 - *The Globe and Mail*, "Child protection reform"
Honourable Mention: CBC-TV

1976 - *The Vancouver Sun*, "RCMP wrongdoings"
Honourable Mention: *The London Free Press*

1975 - *The Montreal Gazette*, "Women's detention centres," and *The London Free Press*, "Mercury poisoning Grassy Narrows" (tied)

1974 - *The Montreal Gazette*, "Montréal at the crossroads, development" Honourable Mention: *The London Free Press* and *Cape Breton Post*

1973 - CTV, "Hear no evil, see no evil, speak no evil, surveillance" Honourable Mention: *Dartmouth Free Press*, CHRC-AM (Québec) and CFCW-79 (Camrose, AB)

1972 - *The Globe and Mail*, "Government conflicts of interest" and *The Scotian Journalist* (Halifax), "Coverdale interprovincial home for women" (tied)
Honourable Mention: *The Windsor Star* and *La Presse*

1971 - CBC-TV, "The tenth decade"
Honourable Mention: *The London Free Press, Ottawa Citizen*, and *The Windsor Star*

1970 - *The Financial Post* and CBC-TV, "The charter revolution"
Honourable Mention: CKLG (Vancouver) and *The Windsor Star*

Appendix 2

Michener Award Fellowship Recipients, 1984-2023

2023 - Molly Thomas; Sarah Trick and Alanna King

2022 - Stéphane Blais; Rob Csernyik

2021 - Ethan Cox and Erin Seatter; Allison Baker and Viviane Fairbank

2020 - Laura Eggertson; Marie Claude Lortie; J Source/Canada Press Freedom project

2019 - Corbett Hancey; Greg Mercer

2018 - Tamara Baluja; Annie Burns-Pieper

2017 - Matthew Pearson; Valérie Borde

2016 - Patti Sonntag; Paul Webster

2015 - Rob Cribb; Marie-France Bélanger

2014 - Francine Pelletier; Rita Celli

2013 - Roger LeMoyne; Julie Ireton

2012 - Laura Eggertson; Melanie Coulson

2011 - Jane Armstrong

2010 - Julie Ireton

2009 - Ed Struzik

2008 - Denise Davy

2007 - Chris Cobb

2006 - Julian Sher

2005 - Jenny Manzer

2004 - Cecil Rosner

2003 - Margaret Munro

2002 - Pierre Duchesne

2001 - Martine Turenne

2000 - Catherine Cano

1999 - Christopher Grabowski

1998 - Jean-Pierre Rogel

1997 - Michel Venne

1996 - Heather Abbott, Jamie Swift

1995 - Pierre Sormany, Sue Rideout

1994 - Bob Hepburn, François Brousseau

1993 - David Evans, Christian Rioux

1992 - John Nowlan, Ruth Teichroeb

1991 - Jock Ferguson

1990 - Gisèle Lalande, Ann Pappert

1989 - Kristina von Hlatky

1988 - Jim Romahn, George Tombs

1987 - Moira Farrow, Roger Bainbridge

Notes

NOTES TO INTRODUCTION

1   Lindsay Crysler (journalist, editor, educator), Interview, Montreal, January 28, 2019.

2   David Walmsley (journalist, editor), Interview, Toronto, October 10, 2019.

3   In 1985, there was an entry from an Italian publication. It was not one of the finalists.

4   John Fraser (journalist, editor, educator), Interview by phone, October 5, 2021.

5   James Baxter (journalist, editor, publisher), Interview by phone, May 10, 2022.

6   John Honderich (journalist, editor, publisher, author), Interview, Toronto, October 9. 2019.

7   Kellyanne Conway, interview by Chuck Todd, *Meet the Press,* NBC, Twitter 11:03AM, January 22, 2017, https://twitter.com/MeetThePress/status/823184384559878144

8   "Canada's Most Respected Occupations, 2022," Maru Public Opinion, May 18, 2023, https://static1.squarespace.com/static/6405fa1b78abf0232468c763/t/64dd789fd0726e1a7896c1f8/1692235935833/Canadas%2Bmost%2Brespected%2Boccupations%2B2022.pdf

9   Cullen Crozier, "The 2020 Michener Awards Ceremony," June 16, 2021, 8:05, https://vimeo.com/566610045

10 Mitch Diamantopoulos, *-30- Thirty Years of Journalism and Democracy in Canada: The Minifie Lectures, 1981-2010* (Canadian Plains Research Center Press, 2009), 30.

11 David Johnston (former governor general, statesman, educator, author), Interview by phone, June 29, 2019.

12 Clark Davey (journalist, editor, publisher), Interview, Ottawa, November 8, 2018.

13 Edward Greenspon (journalist, editor), Interview, Toronto, October 9, 2019.

14 George Hutchinson (journalist), Interview by phone, May 2, 2022.

15 David McKie (journalist, educator), Interview, Halifax, August 12, 2019.

16 Margo Goodhand, "The 2020 Michener Award Ceremony," June 16, 2021, 6:53, https://vimeo.com/566610045

17 This book covers the period 1970-2020, before the appointment of Her Excellency Mary Simon, the 30th Governor General of Canada.

18 "Michener Awards Foundation announces finalists for the 2020 Michener Award for meritorious public service journalism," The Michener Awards Foundation, April 20, 2021, https://www.michenerawards.ca/media-release/michener-awards-foundation-announces-finalists-for-the-2020-michener-award-for-meritorious-public-service-journalism/

19   Jamie Strashin, "2019 Michener Awards Ceremony," December 16, 2020, 15:45, https://vimeo.com/489538006

20   Rideau Hall Foundation. "About," webpage, https://rhf-frh.ca/about/

NOTES TO CHAPTER 1

1   Statistics Canada, Fifty years of family in Canada: 1961 - 2011, July 23, 2018, https://www12.statcan.gc.ca/census-recensement/2011/as-sa/98-312-x/98-312-x2011003_1-eng.cfm

2   Gordon Thiessen, Bank of Canada, Speech: Canadian economic performance at the end of the twentieth century, June 2, 1999, https://www.bankofcanada.ca/1999/06/canadian-economic-performance-end-twentieth-century/

3   Peter Stursberg, *Roland Michener: The Last Viceroy* (McGraw-Hill Ryerson, 1989), xvi.

4   David Hayes (journalist, author, educator), Interview, Toronto, October 10, 2019.

5   Cecil Rosner (journalist, author, educator), Interview by phone, July 3, 2019.

6   Rosner, Interview.

7   Statistics Canada, Literary and Journalistic Awards in Canada / Le prix de littérature et de journalisme au Canada: 1923-1973 (Information Canada, 1976), https://publications.gc.ca/collections/collection_2016/statcan/81-407/CS81-407-1973.pdf

8   Rosner, Interview.

9   Peter Herrndorf (journalist, CBC executive, cultural icon), Interview, Toronto, June 27, 2019.

10   "The Federation of Press Clubs of Canada/La Fédération des Cercles des Journalistes du Canada," Letter C.W.E. MacPherson to Guy Robillard, Press Secretary, Government House, September 29, 1969, with attached Prospectus (n.d.), 90-91/016, Awards and Honours - Governor General Awards fonds RG7, volume 73, file 620-2, MG32A 4, Library and Archives Canada. Accessed 01-10-2006.

11   The Federation of Press Clubs of Canada / La Fédération des Cercles des Journalistes du Canada Award prospectus, (n.d.), Michener Award Papers, Carleton School of Journalism and Communication, Ottawa. (Hereafter cited as the Michener Papers, Carleton).

12   Awards and Honours - Governor General Awards fonds. Library and Archives Canada. See note 10.

13   John Miller (journalist, educator, author), Interview, Toronto, May 8, 2019.

14   David Hayes, *Power and Influence: The Globe and Mail and the News Revolution* (Key Porter, 1992), 125, 115.

15   Hayes, *Power and Influence*, 125, 115.

16   Cecil Rosner, *Behind the Headlines: A History of Investigative Journalism in Canada* (Oxford University Press, 2008), 35, 37.

17   Eric Kosh, "CBC Management Versus CBC Delinquents: The Case of 'This Hour Has Seven Days'," May 8, 2015, https://erickoch.wordpress.com/2015/05/08/cbc-management-versus-cbc-delinquents-the-case-of-this-hour-has-seven-days/

18   Kosh, "CBC Management Versus CBC Delinquents," also Eric Kosh, *Inside Seven Days* (Prentice Hall/Newcastle, 1986), 26, 30.

19   Kosh, "CBC Management Versus CBC Delinquents."

20   Rosner, *Behind the Headlines*, 72.

21   Silver Donald Cameron (educator, journalist, author) as quoted in Rosner, *Behind the Headlines*, 72.

22   Joseph Jackson, "Newspaper Ownership in Canada: An overview of the Davey Committee and Kent Commission Studies," Government of Canada, Political and Social Affairs Division, December 17, 1999, https://publications.gc.ca/Pilot/LoPBdP/BP/prb9935-e.htm

23   Canada, Special Senate Committee on Mass Media, *The Uncertain Mirror: Report of the Special Committee on Mass Media* (The Davey Report), (Ottawa: Queen's Printer: 1970), 67.

24   *The Uncertain Mirror*, 85.

25   *The Uncertain Mirror*, 212.

26   Broadcasting Act, R.S.C. 1970, Chap. B-11 as cited by Simon Claus, "Canadian Broadcasting Policy at Issue: Marconi to Netflix," Canadian Radio-television Telecommunications Commission, November 14, 2017, https://crtc.gc.ca/eng/acrtc/prx/2017claus.htm

27   *The Uncertain Mirror*, 65-66.

28   *The Uncertain Mirror*, 6.

29   *The Uncertain Mirror*, 71.

30   Peter Debarats, *Guide to Canadian News Media* (Harcourt Brace Jovanovich, 1990), 160.

31   Rosner, Interview.

32   *The Uncertain Mirror*, 203.

33   Herrndorf, Interview.

34   Herrndorf, Interview.

35   Richard J. Doyle, *Hurly-Burly: A Time at the Globe* (MacMillan of Canada, 1990), 368; see also Hayes, *Power and Influence*, 115.

36   Doyle, *Hurly-Burly*, 244.

37   *Toronto Star*, "Atkinson Principles," https://www.thestar.com/about/atkinson.html#:~:text=The%20editorial%20principles%20Atkinson%20espoused,%2C%20political%2C%20legal%20or%20racial

38   Jamie Bradburn, "Joseph E. Atkinson," December 20, 2021, https://www.thecanadianencyclopedia.ca/en/article/joseph-e-atkinson

39   Ross Harkness, *J.E. Atkinson of the Star* (University of Toronto Press, 1963), 382.

40   Notes for remarks by the Rt. Hon. Roland Michener at a dinner in honour of Fraser MacDougall given by the Ontario Press Council, June 17, 1987, Michener Papers, Carleton.

41   Federation of Press Clubs of Canada, October 13, 1969, Michener Papers, Carleton.

42   Letter Bill MacPherson to Governor General Roland Michener, October 16, 1969. Michener Papers, Carleton.

43   Letter Bill MacPherson to Gen Louis-Frémont Trudeau to Bill MacPherson, 12 January 1970, Michener Papers, Carleton.

44   Letter Bill MacPherson to His Excellency Governor General Roland Michener, October 2, 1970, Michener Papers, Carleton.

45   "National Press Sessions Slate for Moncton," *Moncton Times*, October 3, 1970. Michener Papers, Carleton.

46   Minutes, Meeting Rideau Hall and Bill MacPherson, February 17, 1971, Michener Papers, Carleton.

47   Letter, Barry Matheson to Ken MacGray, October 25, 1971, Michener Papers, Carleton.

48   Herrndorf, Interview.

49   Letter Jean Danard to Keith Davey, April 19, 1971, "Media '72, Conference of Journalism," MG 28 I 232-21, 1971-72 21-45 fonds Media Club of Canada, Library and Archives Canada.

50   Diana Michener-Schatz, (daughter of Roland Michener), Interview, Toronto, October 27, 2019.

51   Information about the Michener is documented in great detail in Peter Stursberg, *Roland Michener: The Last Viceroy*, 1989.

52   Peter Stursberg, *Lester Pearson and the Dream of Unity* (Doubleday, 1978), 21.

53   Stursberg, *Lester Pearson*, 31-32.

54   Michener-Schatz, Interview.

55   "Roland Michener," Editorial, *Toronto Star*, August 8, 1991, A24. Author's collection.

56   Stursberg, *The Last Viceroy*, 160-161.

57   Walter Stewart (journalist) as quoted in Stursberg, *The Last Viceroy*, 213, 211.

58   Joan Michener Rohr, *Memories of a Governor General's Daughter* (Bedford House Publishing, 1990), 41.

59   Stursberg, *The Last Viceroy*, 171-72.

60   Roland Michener, speech to the Canadian Press Association, Michener Papers, Carleton.

61   Roland Michener to annual dinner of the Canadian Press Association, April 16, 1969, Office of the Governor General Fonds, 1984-85/054 GAD, RG7 G28 Vol 67, "Registry Files from the Office of Governor General Roland Michener," Library and Archives Canada.

62   Les Lawrence (husband of Wendy Michener), Interview, Toronto, June 28, 2019. After spending Christmas at Rideau Hall with the Michener family, Wendy, Les Lawrence and their two young daughters, Caitlin and Miranda, returned to their home in Toronto. On January 1, 1969, Wendy was taken suddenly ill and died that afternoon. While the obituary report said Wendy Michener died from heart failure, Lawrence said she died from an embolism (a blood clot) in her leg that went to her lungs caused by edema, a side-effect of the birth control pill. Also, Les Lawrence, *Ottawa Beatles*, https://beatles.ncf.ca/wendy_michener_biography_p1.html; Joan Michener-Rahr, *Memoirs of a Governor General's Daughter*, 98; and Wendy Roland Michener Obit,

The Ottawa Journal. January 3, 1969, p. 30, https://www.newspapers.com/clip/24869668/wendy-roland-mitchener-obit/

63   Michener-Schatz, Interview.

64   Roland Michener, "Speech by His Excellency the Right Honourable Roland Michener, on the occasion of the presentation of the 1972 Michener Awards for Journalism - Rideau Hall, May 9, 1973," Michener Awards Foundation, https://kotcheff.com/michenerhistory/english/michener/michener1973.htm (private website)

65   Tim, Kotcheff, "The Michener Award and the artist who designed it," Michener Awards Foundation, https://kotcheff.com/michenerhistory/english/matthews/matthews.htm (private website)

66   Michener Awards, Minutes of the Meeting of Monday, February 15, 1971, Michener Papers, Carleton.

67   Letter, C.W.E MacPherson to His Excellency the Rt. Hon. Roland Michener, March 10, 1971, Michener Papers, Carleton.

68   Letter, C.W.E MacPherson to His Excellency the Rt. Hon. Roland Michener, March 10, 1971, Michener Papers, Carleton.

69   Letter, C.W.E MacPherson to His Excellency the Rt. Hon. Roland Michener, March 10, 1971, Michener Papers, Carleton.

70   Rideau Hall invitation to November 8, 1971, Michener Award Ceremony. Contributed by Alan Elrich. Author's electronic files.

71   Ken MacGray, November 8, 1971, https://kotcheff.com/michenerhistory/english/speeches/macgray1971.htm (private website)

72   Roland Michener, November 8, 1971, https://kotcheff.com/michenerhistory/english/michener/michener1971.htm (private website)

73   "The Charter Revolution: The deals will be there for a while at least," The Financial Post, November 28, 1970, 15-18.

74   Miles Murchison (former broadcaster), Interview by phone, October 2 2018.

75   Stursberg, The Last Viceroy, 212.

76   "The 1970 Michener Award Co-Winners: The Financial Post and CBC-TV, November 8, 1971," https://kotcheff.com/michenerhistory/english/winAward/winaward1970.htm (private website); also "Confidential Report from A.D. Dunton, chair of judges to Mr. MacPherson," March 31, 1971, Awards and Honours G G-Awards fonds, General, 55, 620-2-700, Libraries and Archives Canada and Michener Papers, Carleton.

77   Letter A.D. Dunton to Bill MacPherson, March 31, 1971, Michener Papers, Carleton.

78   Email, Alan Elrich to Tim Kotcheff, June 1; 2006.

79   Elrich, Email.

80   Elrich, Email.

81   Cynthia Baxter served on the Michener Board from 1998-2010.

82   Cynthia Baxter (former Michener director, philanthropist), Interview, Ottawa, January 31, 2019.

83   Herrndorf, Interview.

84   Edward Schreyer (former governor general), Interview by phone, May 13, 2019.

1   Bill Boss, adjudication report of the Michener judges, April 30, 1974, Michener Papers, Carleton.

2   Judges were Davidson Dunton, chair; Yves Gagnon, director of the School of Communications, Université Laval; Norman Mcleod, former correspondent, United Press International; and Sam Ross, retired Vancouver radio journalist.

3   Cameron Graham (CBC news producer), Interview by phone, November 1, 2018.

4   Cameron Graham, Interview.

5   Peter Herrndorf, Interview.

6   Letter, G.W. Boss on behalf of the judging panel to C.W.E. MacPherson, chairman of the Roland Michener Award Committee, March 28, 1973, Michener Papers, Carleton.

7   "Halifax weekly win Michener Journalism Award," *The Globe and Mail,* April 6, 1973, Michener Papers, Carleton.

8   *Globe and Mail,* April 6, 1973.

9   Jonathan Manthorpe (journalist), Interview, Toronto, April 23, 2022.

10 Manthorpe, Interview.

11 Debates of the Senate [Hansard], Hon. Lowell Murray, "The Honourable William M. Kelly, Tributes on Retirement," 2nd Session, 36th Parliament, Volume 138, Issue 69, June 20, 2000, https://sencanada.ca/en/Content/Sen/chamber/362/debates/069db_2000-06-20-e#0.2.W54BJ2.R839RJ.OD0NPH.TX [accessed 29 April 2022]; also Jonathan Manthorpe, *The Power and the Tories* (Macmillan, 1974).

12 "The 1972 Michener Award - Co-Winners - The *Globe and Mail* & The *Scotian Journalist,* May 9, 1973," https://kotcheff.com/michenerhistory/english/winAward/winaward1972.htm (private website)

13 For a history of the Interprovincial Home for Women, Coverdale see: Inter-Provincial Homes for Young Women, Inc, Rev. Karl Drew, n.d., https://web.archive.org/web/20201026004841/http://riverviewhistoryproject.ca/clubs-lodges-societies/inter-provincial-homes-for-young-women-inc

14 Rev. Karl Drew, n.d., https://web.archive.org/web/20201031163653/http://riverviewhistoryproject.ca/clubs-lodges-societies/inter-provincial-homes-for-young-women-contd

15 "The report of the Chairman of the Special Planning Committee," April 24, 1968, Home Executive meeting, as cited in Women, Coverdale, Inter-Provincial Homes for Young Women, Rev. Karl Drew, n.d., https://web.archive.org/web/20201031163653/http://riverviewhistoryproject.ca/clubs-lodges-societies/inter-provincial-homes-for-young-women-contd

16 Glenn R. Thompson, "The Coverdale Report: A Consultation Committee Appraisal of Correctional Services for Women in New Brunswick, Nova Scotia and Prince Edward Island," December 1972, 21, 49, 55, https://www.publicsafety.gc.ca/lbrr/archives/hv%209506%20c39.1-eng.pdf

17 Frank Fillmore, Debbie Sprague, "The Coverdale Report," *Scotian Journalist,* Halifax, NS, August 3, 1972, 11, Author's collection.

18   Frank Fillmore, "Farewell to the People," *The 4th Estate,* Halifax,
      April 17, 1969, 7. Accessed https://archives.novascotia.ca/newspapers/
      archives/?ID=378&Page=200909211. Also, Lisa Corra, "News to Make a Difference:
      The Environment and the 4th Estate 1969-77," (master's thesis, Saint Mary's University,
      2008), ProQuest dissertations, https://library2.smu.ca/bitstream/handle/01/22435/
      corra_lisa_masters.PDF?sequence=1&isAllowed=y

19   Paul Willes (former reporter), Interview by phone, February 2, 2022.

20   Lyndon Watkins, "Press award is painful to rival," *The Globe and Mail,* April 7, 1973, 10,
      Michener Papers, Carleton.

21   Letter, Gerard McNeil to the Secretary of the Governor-General, April 9, 1973,
      Michener Papers, Carleton.

22   Gerard McNeil letter.

23   The judging panel was Fraser MacDougall, chair, former Canadian Press executive
      and now executive secretary of the Ontario Press Council; Yves Gagnon, director of
      communications at Laval University; Sam Ross, retired radio news correspondent,
      Vancouver; and Bill Boss, director of public relations at the University of Ottawa.

24   Minutes, Press Clubs of Canada AGM, October 6, 1973, Michener Papers, Carleton.

25   "Michener Awards Foundation, 1973 Michener Award - CTV Television Network,"
      http://kotcheff.com/michenerhistory/english/winAward/winaward1973.htm (private
      website)

26   Rosner, *Behind the Headlines,* 163-64.

27   Hugh Segal, "The media through a looking glass: Building the brand by getting it right,"
      Policy Options Politiques, February 2010, https://policyoptions.irpp.org/magazines/
      after-copenhagen/the-media-through-a-looking-glass-building-the-brand-by-getting-
      it-right/

28   Rosner, *Behind the Headlines,* 163-64.

29   David Lewis, House of Commons Debates, Hansard, 29th Parliament, 1st Session: Vol.
      7 6942-3, October 17, 1973.

30   "Hear no evil, see no evil, speak no evil - The Story behind the 'Inquiry' investigation,"
      https://kotcheff.com/michenerhistory/english/inquiry.htm (private website); and Victor
      Mackie, "Bugging reaches the Hill." *Winnipeg Free Press,* October 18, 1973, Final
      edition, 1, 4. Author's collection.

31   "Hear no evil, see no evil, speak no evil" - The Story behind the 'Inquiry' investigation."

32   David Lewis House of Commons Debates, and Mackie, *Winnipeg Free Press.*

33   Tim Kotcheff, "'Hear no evil, see no evil, speak no evil' - The Story behind the 'Inquiry'
      investigation."

34   Columnist Geoffrey Stevens as quoted in Rosner, *Behind the Headlines,* 164.

35   Rosner, *Behind the Headlines,* 164.

36   "The 1973 Michener Award - CTV Television Network," May 16, 1974, https://kotcheff.
      com/michenerhistory/english/winAward/winaward1973.htm (private website)

37   Bill Boss, "Report of the Judging Panel," April 30, 1974, Michener Papers, Carleton.

38   In May 1973 Otto Lang, Minister of Justice introduced Bill C-175, *An Act to Amend the
      Criminal Code, the Crown Liability Act and the Official Secrets Act* [Assented January

14, 1974], https://historyofrights.ca/wp-content/uploads/statutes/CN_Privacy.pdf.
Also, *Canada's Human Rights History*, "Most of the privacy bills introduced between
1971 and 1973 shared the same essential characteristics. They made it illegal to use
wiretaps and other electronic listening devices without the consent of the target . . . "
https://historyofrights.ca/encyclopaedia/main-events/privacy/#:~:text=The%201973%20
Protection%20of%20Privacy,restraints%20placed%20on%20the%20police

39   CBC-TV Host Warner Troyer's introduction to "Connections: An Investigation into
     Organized Crime in Canada," CBC Television, June 12, 1977, as cited in Rosner, *Behind
     the Headlines,* 96. A follow-up CBC-TV documentary series "Connections: a further
     investigation into organized crime in Canada" was broadcast on March 26, 27, and 28,
     1978.

40   Herrndorf, Interview.

41   See Rosner, *Behind the Headlines,* Chapter 11, "Investigative Journalism Matures," 143-
     52.

42   For details see Rosner, *Behind the Headlines,* Chapter 10, "Dirty Tricks," especially 132-
     35.

43   John Sawatsky, "Break-in trail leads to RCMP coverup," *Vancouver Sun,* December 7,
     1976, A1.

44   "The 1976 Michener Award Winner - The Vancouver Sun," October 7, 1977, https://
     kotcheff.com/michenerhistory/english/winAward/winaward1976.htm (private website)

45   Investigative journalist John Sawatsky as cited in *Rosner, Behind the Headlines,* 134.

46   For example, in 2000, CBC-TV's *the fifth estate* was the Michener winner from among
     forty-four entries for its six investigative reports on how police and justice officials
     do business. In the citation for the Michener Award, the judges wrote that the six
     stories broadcast in 2000 revealed the ugly underbelly of the police and justice system.
     The May 24, 2001 news release noted that one program showed how "an aggressive,
     politicized Toronto police union threatened to target political enemies and carried out
     the threats." Two other programs looked at errors of police and prosecutors in the case
     of Steven Truscott, a fourteen-year-old boy who had been wrongfully convicted and
     sentenced to death for the rape and murder of a female classmate. The other *fifth estate*
     programs described how police paid criminals to be secret informers and examined
     injustices in the Saskatchewan justice system that allowed "preposterous charges
     ranging from sexual abuse to murder to proceed, knowing they were false."

47   Statistics Canada, Literary and journalistic awards In Canada = Le prix de littérature et
     de journalisme au Canada: 1923-1973.

48   Minutes. Press Club Canada, sixth AGM, October 6, 1973, Michener Papers, Carleton.

49   Minutes, Press Club Canada, October 6, 1973.

50   Letter, Bill Boss to Bill MacPherson, May 27, 1976, Michener Papers, Carleton.

51   Letter, Boss to MacPherson.

52   Minutes, Tenth Annual Meeting of Press Club Canada/*La Federation Des Cercles Des
     Journalistes Du Canada*, October 8, 1977, 7, Michener Papers, Carleton.

53   Environment Canada, "St. Clair River: area of concern," updated March 16, 2023,
     https://www.canada.ca/en/environment-climate-change/services/great-lakes-
     protection/areas-concern/st-clair-river.html

54 Al Hayden, "Mercury in Lake St. Clair Walleye," n.d., *State of the Strait,* http://web2.uwindsor.ca/softs/keyindicators/old/hg-walleye.htm

55 George Hutchinson (journalist), Interview by phone, May 1, 2022.

56 Hutchinson, Interview.

57 George Hutchinson, "Cats' 'dance of death' tells story of reserve disaster," *London Free Press* as distributed by CP and republished in the *Calgary Herald,* July 23, 1975, 42.

58 Hutchinson, Interview.

59 For visual documentation see George Hutchinson, Dick Wallace, *Grassy Narrows* (Van Nostrand Reinhold, 1977).

60 Hutchinson, Interview.

61 George Hutchinson, "Poisonous post-mortem on a northern native tragedy," *Toronto Star,* April 9, 2010, https://www.thestar.com/opinion/2010/04/09/poisonous_postmortem_on_a_northern_native_tragedy.html

62 Supreme Court of Canada, "Case in Brief - Resolute FP Canada Inc. v. Ontario (Attorney General)," https://www.scc-csc.ca/case-dossier/cb/2019/37985-eng.aspx. This gives background to and overview of the 1977 lawsuit and the 1985 initial settlement with the First Nations Community; also, "Supreme Court says companies must pay for Grassy Narrows mill site maintenance," *Turtle Island News,* Ohsweken, ON, December 6, 2019, https://theturtleislandnews.com/index.php/2019/12/06/supreme-court-says-companies-must-pay-for-grassy-narrows-mill-site-maintenance/

63 Michael Butler, "Hunger Strike for Grassy Narrows after Report Hidden by Ontario Government Comes to Light," Council of Canadians, July 28, 2014, https://canadians.org/analysis/hunger-strike-grassy-narrows-after-report-hidden-ontario-government-comes-light/

64 Jim Bronskill, "Supreme Court says companies must pay for Grassy Narrows mill-site maintenance," The Canadian Press, December 6, 2019, https://www.cbc.ca/news/politics/grassy-narrows-supreme-court-1.5386602 also Annette Francis, "Grassy Narrows members demand compensation because of mercury poisoning," APTN, July 22, 2022, https://www.aptnnews.ca/national-news/grassy-narrows-members-demand-compensation-because-of-mercury-poisoning/

65 Jody Porter, "Ontario announces $85M to clean up mercury near Grassy Narrows, Wabaseemoong First Nations," CBC Online, June 27, 2017, https://www.cbc.ca/news/canada/thunder-bay/ontario-mercury-cleanup-1.4180631

66 Government of Canada, "Government of Canada and Asubpeeschoseewagong Netum Anishinabek (Grassy Narrows First Nation) sign revised Framework Agreement for Mercury Care Home," July 26, 2021, https://www.canada.ca/en/indigenous-services-canada/news/2021/07/government-of-canada-and-asubpeeschoseewagong-netum-anishinabek-grassy-narrows-first-nation-sign-revised-framework-agreement-for-mercury-care-home.html

67 George Hutchinson, Interview.

68 Gillian Cosgrove (journalist), Interview by phone, May 29, 2020.

69 Gillian Cosgrove, "Jail handcuffs girls and straps them to concrete bed," *The Gazette* (Montréal), January 2, 1975, 1, 3.

70 Cosgrove, Interview.

71 *Rapport du Comité d'étude sur la réadaptation des enfants et adolescents placés en centre[s] d'accueil: guide des centres d'accueil de transition et de réadaptation du Québec* (Canada, Ministère des affaires sociales, Direction des communications), 1976.

72 Cosgrove, Interview.

73 Cosgrove, Interview.

74 Cosgrove, Interview.

75 "The forgotten: the children of Marion Hall speak," *the fifth estate,* 26:20, October 6, 2019, YouTube, https://www.youtube.com/watch?v=cT310zw-0Jk&ab_channel=TheFifthEstate

76 Québec Superior Court, No: 500-06-001022-199, Eleanor Lindsay vs. Attorney General of Quebec et al., January 17, 2020, https://cbaapps.org/ClassAction/PDF.aspx?id=12545

77 "Laurent Commission report on Quebec youth protection to be released Monday," *The Canadian Press,* May 2, 2021, https://montreal.ctvnews.ca/laurent-commission-report-on-quebec-youth-protection-to-be-released-monday-1.5410989

78 Selena Ross, "Kids at risk of abuse need earlier intervention, with more help for their parents: youth protection commission," CTV News Montreal, May 3, 2021, https://montreal.ctvnews.ca/kids-at-risk-of-abuse-need-earlier-intervention-with-more-help-for-their-parents-youth-protection-commission-1.5411886; and *Instaurer Une Société Beinveillante Pour Nos Enfants Et Nos Jeunes,* Govuernement du Québec, avril 2021, https://www.csdepj.gouv.qc.ca/fileadmin/Fichiers_clients/Rapport_final_3_mai_2021/2021_CSDEPJ_Rapport_version_finale_numerique.pdf

79 "1979 Michener Award Winner - The Kingston Whig-Standard," November 8, 1980, https://kotcheff.com/michenerhistory/english/winAward/winaward1979.htm (private website)

80 "1979 Michener Award Winner - The Kingston Whig-Standard," November 8, 1980.

81 "The 1996 Michener Award Winner - Toronto Star," May 1, 1997, https://kotcheff.com/michenerhistory/english/winAward/winaward1996.htm (private website)

82 "Michener Award goes to the Telegraph Journal," The Michener Awards Foundation June 14, 2019, http://www.michenerawards.ca/michener-award-goes-to-the-telegraph-journal/

83 Kenneth Jackson, "The 2020 Michener Awards Ceremony," June 16, 2021, 5:30, https://vimeo.com/564770591

84 "APTN wins the Michener Award for searing investigation into a 12-year-old's death in care," The Michener Awards Foundation, June 21, 2021, https://www.michenerawards.ca/media-release/aptn-wins-the-michener-award-for-searing-investigation-into-a-12-year-olds-death-in-care/

85 Minutes, Press Club Canada Ninth Annual Meeting, October 9, 1976, Michener Papers, Carleton.

86 Chief Judge Fraser MacDougall, adjudication report to the Board, July 4, 1980, Michener Papers, Carleton.

87 Letter Bill MacPherson to W.R. Anderson, president of Press Clubs Canada, July 5, 1979, in Michener Papers, Carleton.

88 The Governor General of Canada, "The Duke of Argyll," https://www.gg.ca/en/governor-general/former-governors-general/duke-argyll

89 The Governor General of Canada, "Edward Richard Schreyer," https://www.gg.ca/en/governor-general/former-governors-general/edward-richard-schreyer

90 The Canadian Encyclopedia, "Ed Schreyer," https://www.thecanadianencyclopedia.ca/en/article/edward-richard-schreyer

91 Edward Schreyer (former Governor General), Interview by phone, May 13, 2019.

92 Schreyer, Interview.

93 Michener Awards Ceremony program, November 3, 1979. Michener Papers, Carleton.

94 Bill MacPherson, speech, November 3, 1979, Michener Papers, Carleton; and Library and Archives Canada, RG7 1990-91/016 55 620-2-78.

95 Jim Romahn (journalist), Interview by telephone, January 26, 2022.

96 Jim Romahn, "Much wrong with Canada's meat inspection system, U.S. says," *Kitchener-Waterloo Record,* April 13, 1978.

97 Jim Romahn presentation, Eastern Canada Farm Writers Association webinar, January 28, 2020, Author's notes.

98 Romahn, Interview.

99 Romahn, Interview.

100 The Canadian Press and Citizen staff, "Meat plant exposé brings media prize," *The Ottawa Citizen,* November 5, 1979, 33.

101 Access to Information Legislation came into force on July 1, 1983. See Dean Beeby's "Ged Baldwin's 50-year-old crusade for freedom of information legislation in Canada," January 9, 2024, https://deanbeeby.substack.com/p/ged-baldwins-50-year-old-crusade?utm_source=post-email-title&publication_id=1211583&post_id=140510269&utm_campaign=email-post-title&isFreemail=false&r=1gcdut&utm_medium=email

102 Fraser MacDougall, Report of the Judging Panel, June 28, 1979, Michener Papers, Carleton; and "The 1978 Michener Award Winner: The Kitchener-Waterloo Record," https://kotcheff.com/michenerhistory/english/winAward/winaward1978.htm (private website)

103 Romahn, Interview.

104 Romahn, Interview.

105 Keith Davey, "How the Media Withheld the Message in Kitchener: For Good Journalists, Boosterism is Fatal," *Maclean's* magazine, June 1972, 24. Author's collection.

106 Letter, K.A. ("Sandy") Baird to Fraser MacDougall, May 1985, Michener Papers, Carleton.

NOTES TO CHAPTER 3

1 John Honderich, Interview, October 9, 2019.

2 Report, Fraser MacDougall to Bill MacPherson, July 5, 1982, Michener Papers, Carleton.

3 Alan Fotheringham, "Rideau Rebellion," *Toronto Sun*, November 10, 1980. Michener Papers, Carleton.

4   Fotheringham, "Rideau Rebellion."

5   George Fetherling, *A Little Bit of Thunder* (Stoddart, 1993), 281.

6   Lennart Krook and George A. Maylin, "Industrial fluoride pollution. Chronic fluoride poisoning in Cornwall Island cattle," *Cornell Veterinarian,* 69 (Suppl. 8): 1-69, 1979, PMID: 467082, https://pubmed.ncbi.nlm.nih.gov/467082/

7   Penny Stuart, "'I think eventually it will affect people'," *The Whig Standard,* June 12, 1979, A1.

8   Report, Chief Judge Fraser MacDougall to Bill MacPherson, July 4, 1980, Michener Papers, Carleton.

9   The factories in Massena, New York, legally continued to emit and pump PCBs, aluminum, mercury and other toxic chemical waste into the St. Lawrence River until the last factory closed in 2014. As of 2022, work continues to remove the contaminated sediment. Officers with Akwesasne Conservation and Compliance patrol the waters and monitor the situation. As recently as April 2019, *Nation Valley News* published a report advising residents of Cornwall Island (Kawehno:ke) not to eat certain species of fish that still have high levels of PCBs and mercury. See: https://nationvalleynews.com/2019/04/13/new-york-department-of-health-expands-advisory-against-eating-fish-caught-around-cornwall-island/

10 Fetherling, *A Little Bit of Thunder,* 299.

11 Fetherling, *A Little Bit of Thunder,* 281.

12 In the 1980s the *Whig-Standard* received many nominations including a Michener Award in 1984 for its authoritative investigation into Canada's tax system. In 1983, it received an honourable mention for its "painstaking and detailed examination" of Bell Helicopter's decision to open Canada's first helicopter factory near Mirabel Airport in Quebec, which resulted in the loss of 3,800 jobs and $766 million in investment for the Kingston economy. In 1986, the *Whig-Standard* received another honourable mention for its story of five Soviet prisoners of war supposedly kept in Afghanistan after a failed Canadian rescue mission. The story caught the attention of the Sunday *Observer* in the U.K., which commented that the *Whig's* scoop "was causing considerable embarrassment in Ottowa *[sic],* where bungling and back-biting between bureaucracies of two Ministries are blamed for the Government's failure to rescue the men." Six months later Canada secured the release of the five men. Sources: "1983 Michener Award Winner - *Kitchener-Waterloo Record,*" November 10,1984, https://kotcheff.com/michenerhistory/english/winAward/winaward1983.htm (private website); also Fetherling, *A Little Bit of Thunder,* 300, 311-16, and The *Observer,* April 27, 1986, as cited in Fetherling, 314.

13 Senate of Canada, *Royal Commission on Newspapers* (hereafter referred to as the Kent Report) Ottawa, Minister of Supply and Services, 1981, 1.

14 Kent Report, 215-17.

15 Kent Report, 1.

16 David Hayes, *Power and Influence,* 64.

17 Kent Report. Also, Mary Vipond, *Mass Media in Canada,* 3rd ed. (Lorimer, 2000), 61.

18 Kent Report, 2, 9.

19 Kent Report, 215, 225.

20   In 2015, the English language press councils merged to form the National NewsMedia Council "to serve as a forum for complaints against its members and to promote ethical practices within the news media industry," https://www.mediacouncil.ca/about-us-ethics-journalism/

21   See: Desbarats, p. 56; John Miller, *Yesterday's News: Why Canada's Daily Newspapers are Failing Us* (Fernwood, 1998), chapter 3, "Black Inc.," 60-85; and Gordon Pitts, *Kings of Convergence: The Fight for Control of Canada's Media* (Doubleday Canada, 2002), 9, 316.

22   President's remarks Michener Awards Dinner, November 12, 1983, Michener Papers, Carleton.

23   Clark Davey, Interview, November 8, 2018.

24   Clark Davey, Interview.

25   Canadian Press, "F. MacDougall, an influential force in journalism," *Toronto Star*, January 26, 2000, A 20, author's collection.

26   National NewsMedia Council, *Fraser MacDougall Prize*, https://www.mediacouncil.ca/fraser-macdougall-award/

27   Ron Lowman, "Fraser MacDougall steps down after 15 years at press council," *Toronto Star*, June 18, 1987, A 8, Michener Papers, Carleton.

28   Clark Davey, Interview.

29   Letters Patent, September 17, 1982. Michener Awards Foundation documents. Lawyers at the founding were John P. Manley, R. John Kearns, Janice H. Vauthier, James R. Hendry, Anne L. MacTavish, and James R. Robertson, Michener Papers, Carleton.

30   Founding president Fraser MacDougall was joined by nine directors: Rennie MacKenzie, vice-president (correspondent with Thompson Newspapers, Ottawa); Gordon Williams, treasurer (manager, Bank of Montreal, Ottawa); William MacPherson, secretary (associate editor, *The Citizen*, Ottawa); George Bain, (director, School of Journalism, University of King's College, Halifax, and former national affairs correspondent *Globe and Mail*); Clark Davey (publisher, *Montreal Gazette,* former editor *Globe and Mail);* J. Patrick O'Callaghan, (publisher, *Calgary Herald*); Doris Anderson, (author, Toronto); Murray Chercover, (president, CTV Television Network, Toronto); and Davidson Dunton (Carleton Institute of Cultural Studies, former chair of CBC, Royal Commission on Bilingualism and Biculturalism, Carleton University president), Michener Papers, Carleton.

31   Senator Richard Doyle, "The Late Paul Septimus Deacon," Senators' Statements, March 26,1996 https://sencanada.ca/en/content/sen/chamber/352/debates/006db_1996-03-26-e

32   James Deacon, text correspondence with author, August 29, 2019.

33   Doyle, "The Late Paul Septimus Deacon."

34   Minutes, Michener Awards AGM, November 12, 1983, Michener Papers, Carleton.

35   Minutes, November 12, 1983.

36   "Manitoulin Expositor wins 1982 Michener Award," November 12, 1983, https://kotcheff.com/michenerhistory/english/winAward/winaward1982.htm (private website)

37   Rick McCutcheon (newspaper publisher), Interview by phone, January 20, 2022.

38   Rick McCutcheon, Interview.

39 Peter Carter (journalist), Interview by phone, January 22, 2022.

40 Peter Carter, Interview.

41 "Manitoulin Expositor wins 1982 Michener Award."

42 Rick McCutcheon, Interview.

43 Rudy Platiel, "Tragic honour: Editor risked exploitation charge to sound suicide alarm," *The Globe and Mail*, March 26, 1984, retrieved from https://ezproxy. torontopubliclibrary.ca/login?url=https://www.proquest.com/historical-newspapers/ tragic-honor/docview/1313823198/se-2?accountid=14369. This story was first of a three-part *Globe and Mail* series that looked at social and education issues in Wikwemikong First Nation.

44 Peter Carter, Interview.

45 Rick McCutcheon, Interview.

46 "Report on judging in the Michener Award for Meritorious and Disinterested Public Service Journalism in 1982," Michener Papers, Carleton.

47 Geoff Chapman, *Toronto Star* editor, "Letter of Submission to the Michener Awards Committee," n.d., Michener Papers, Carleton.

48 Frank Jones (journalist), Interview by phone, January 24, 2022.

49 Frank Jones, "Khristine's downhill run to tragedy," *Sunday Star*, April 29, 1979, A3, retrieved from https://ezproxy.torontopubliclibrary.ca/login?url=https://www.proquest. com/historical-newspapers/page-a3/docview/1395087518/se-2

50 Jones, "Khristine's downhill run to tragedy."

51 Frank Jones, "Indian's 'murder' verdict wiped out," November 21, 1980, A1, A18, retrieved from https://ezproxy.torontopubliclibrary.ca/login?url=https://www.proquest. com/historical-newspapers/page-a1/docview/1398214954/se-2

52 Jones, "Indian's 'murder' verdict wiped out."

53 Frank Jones, Interview.

54 Government of Canada, "150 years of immigration in Canada," *Statistics Canada,* June 29, 2016, https://www150.statcan.gc.ca/n1/pub/11-630-x/11-630-x2016006-eng.htm

55 Olivia Ward, "A Minority Report: Our multiculturalism isn't perfect, but it works," *The Toronto Star,* December 22, 1985.

56 John Honderich, Interview.

57 Victor Malarek (journalist, author), Interview in Toronto, November 20, 2023. Malarek has received four Michener Awards for his investigative work. In 1977, he was part of a team focused on strengthening protections for children. In 1995 and 1998, his stories documented injustices towards refugees and newcomers and detailed flagrant abuses in immigration policy. In 2000, he exposed the aggressive politicization of the Toronto Police Union, detailing how it carried out threats against its opponents.

58 Victor Malarek, "Security guards called 'ill trained' Refugee Centre breaks UN Rules: report," *The Globe and Mail,* February 15, 1985, A1.

59 Victor Malarek, "Promised investments fizzle as immigrant status granted," *The Globe and Mail,* September 30, 1988, A1.

60 For details see: Victor Malarek, "Chapter 9: Nightmare on Bay Street," *Gut Instinct: The Making of an Investigative Journalist* (Macmillan Canada, 1996), 178.

61 Paul Palango as cited in Malarek, *Gut Instinct*, 217.

62 Victor Malarek, Interview.

63 Cecil Rosner, Interview.

64 Government of Canada, "Excessive Demand: Calculation of the Cost Threshold," Immigration and Citizenship, May 4, 2023, https://www.canada.ca/en/immigration-refugees-citizenship/corporate/publications-manuals/excessive-demand.html

65 Jeanne Sauvé was a journalist between 1952-1972, "Jeanne Sauvé," *Canadian Encyclopedia*, February 26, 2018, https://www.thecanadianencyclopedia.ca/en/article/jeanne-mathilde-sauve

66 Margo Roston, "Margo's People," *The Ottawa Citizen*, November 15, 1984, Michener Papers, Carleton.

67 Michaëlle Jean, Interview by phone, July 2, 2019.

68 "Speech by Her Excellency the Right Honourable Jeanne Sauvé, on the occasion of the presentation of the 1984 Michener Awards for Journalism. Rideau Hall," November 16, 1985, http://kotcheff.com/michenerhistory/english/sauve/sauve1985.htm (private website)

69 Letter, Paul Deacon to Leopold Amyot, May 5, 1986. Library and Archives Canada, Sauvé RG7, G29, Vol 42; Sauv 802-9, Five Vol 1, Awards Ceremonies-Governors General Awards-Michener Award for Journalism.

70 David McKie, Interview.

71 Jason Moscovitz, "Jeanne Sauvé: Governor General ceremony delayed," CBC Archives, January 28, 1984, https://www.cbc.ca/player/play/1775385927

72 Shirley Wood, *Her Excellency Jeanne Sauvé* (Goodread Biographies, 1982), 201.

73 Wood, *Her Excellency Jeanne Sauvé*, 201-202.

74 Wood, *Her Excellency Jeanne Sauvé*, 228.

75 Esmond Butler as quoted in Wood, *Her Excellency Jeanne Sauvé*, 202.

76 "Speech by Her Excellency the Right Honourable Jeanne Sauvé, on the occasion of the presentation of the 1986 Michener Awards for Journalism. Rideau Hall, November 6, 1987," https://kotcheff.com/michenerhistory/english/sauve/sauve1987.htm (private website)

77 "Speech by Her Excellency the Right Honourable Jeanne Sauvé, . . . November 6, 1987."

78 Dean Jobb, *Media Law for Canadian Journalists,* 3rd ed. (Emond, 2018), 211.

79 Jobb, *Media Law for Canadian Journalists*, 211, 130.

80 Peter Moon, Interview, Toronto, May 3, 2022.

81 Peter Moon, Interview.

82 Peter Moon, Interview.

83 The Criminal Code change was introduced in 1984. Peter Moon, "Law amendment gags media, MPs," *The Globe and Mail*, February 14, 1986, A1, ProQuest Historical Newspapers. https://ezproxy.library.dal.ca/login?url=https://www.proquest.com/historical-newspapers/law-amendment-gags-media-mps-say/docview/1151428281/se-2

84 Peter Moon, "Challenge launched in Supreme Court: Law amendment gags media, MPs say," *The Globe and Mail*, February 14, 1986, A1.

85   Peter Moon, Interview.

86   Letter, Geoffrey Simpson to Her Excellency Jeanne Sauvé, November 7, 1987, Michener Papers, Carleton.

87   William Thorsell, "The rights of the innocent can be easily trampled," *The Globe and Mail*, March 27, 2006, A17.

NOTES TO CHAPTER 4

1   Clark Todd died Sept 4, 1983.

2   "President's remarks Michener Awards Dinner," November 12, 1983, Michener Papers, Carleton, 2-3.

3   Paul Deacon, President's remarks.

4   Tim Kotcheff (journalist, media executive), Interview, Toronto, February 19, 2019. Also see Craig Oliver, *Oliver's Twist: The Life and Times of an Unapologetic Newshound* (Penguin, 2011); and Anthony Collings, *Capturing the News: Three Decades of Reporting Crisis and Conflict*, Chapter 8, "Two Endings" (University of Missouri Press, 2010).

5   Tim Kotcheff, "The Michener Award and the artist who designed it – John Matthews," https://kotcheff.com/michenerhistory/english/matthews/matthews.htm (private website)

6   "Clark Davey is the recipient of the 2009 Michener Special Award," June 10, 2009, https://kotcheff.com/michenerhistory/english/davey/davey2009.htm (private website)

7   Other Special Award recipients have been Tim Kotcheff and Alain Guilbert, June 11, 2014, and David Humphreys, June 17, 2016.

8   James Baxter, Interview.

9   The Governor General of Canada, "The Michener Award for Journalism - Presentation of the Michener Award for Journalism," May 27, 2010, https://www.gg.ca/en/media/news/2010/michener-award-journalism

10   "Bryan Cantley: A True Canadian Newspaper Superhero," *Q Media*, August 6, 2013, http://qmediasolutions.com/bryan-cantley-a-true-canadian-newspaper-superhero/

11   "Bryan Cantley: A True Canadian Newspaper Superhero."

12   "Michener Foundation Honours John Fraser," Michener Awards Foundation, June 18, 2020, https://www.michenerawards.ca/media-release/michener-foundation-honours-john-fraser/

13   "The 2019 Michener Awards Ceremony | La cérémonie de remise du Prix Michener 2019," Michener Awards Foundation, December 10, 2020, https://vimeo.com/489538006

14   "Michener Foundation Honours John Fraser."

15   National NewsMedia Council, "About Us," mediacouncil.ca

16   "The 2019 Michener Award Ceremony," Michener Awards Foundation, December 10, 2020, https://vimeo.com/489538006

17   Facebook message, Ken Ingram to author, March 7, 2022. Author's collection.

18   Thalidomide Victims Association of Canada, "What is Thalidomide," https://thalidomide.ca/en/what-is-thalidomide/

19   David Walmsley, Interview.

20   Walmsley, Interview.

21   Facebook message, Ken Ingram to author.

22   James Deacon, email to author, August 29, 2019.

23   "Paul Deacon - First President, Michener Awards Foundation: His Remarks at the Michener Awards Dinner," November 12, 1983. https://kotcheff.com/michenerhistory/english/deacon/deaconremarks1983.htm (private website)

24   Minutes, Federation of Press Clubs AGM, October 6, 1973, and "Minutes of the Tenth Annual Meeting of Press Club Canada/ La Federation des Cercles des Journalistes du Canada," October 8, 1977, 11-12. Michener Papers, Carleton.

25   The Centre for Investigative Journalism changed its name to the Canadian Association of Journalists in 1990. It continues to offer journalists support through advocacy, training, and workshops online and at an annual conference and awards ceremony.

26   Joanne Chianello, "Financial journalist makes Ottawa his home," *Ottawa Citizen*, March 25, 1996. Author's collection.

27   Minutes, Michener Awards executive committee, September 18, 1984, Michener Papers, Carleton.

28   Minutes, Michener Awards Foundation membership AGM, November 10, 1984, Michener Awards Foundation documents.

29   Michener Fundraising prospectus, March 21, 1985, Michener Papers, Carleton.

30   Minutes, Michener Awards Foundation AGM, November 10, 1984, Michener Papers, Carleton.

31   Statistics Canada, "Table 7.1 - Interest rates and exchange rates," modified December 19, 2012, https://www150.statcan.gc.ca/n1/pub/11-210-x/2010000/t098-eng.htm; Statistics Canada, "Chart 3 -Unemployment rates in Canada and the United States, 1976 - 2016," modified July 7, 2017, https://www150.statcan.gc.ca/n1/daily-quotidien/170707/cg-a003-eng.htm, and "1983 CPI and Inflation rate for Canada," *Inflation Calculator*, n.d., https://inflationcalculator.ca/1983-cpi-inflation-canada/

32   Robert Seamans, Feng Zhu, "Responses to Entry in Multi-Sided Markets: The Impact of Craigslist on Local Newspapers," *Management Science* 60(2) (2013) 476-93, https://doi.org/10.1287/mnsc.2013.1785

33   Letter, Robert Wright to Paul Deacon, December 13, 1984, Michener Papers, Carleton.

34   Memo, Paul Deacon to the Board of Directors, January 8, 1986, Michener Papers, Carleton.

35   John Honderich, *Above the Fold: A Personal History of the Toronto Star,* (Penguin Random House Canada, 2022), 186. The first Atkinson, a year-long funded fellowship, went to Ann Pappert in 1988 to investigate reproductive technologies. In 1990, Pappert received a $20,000 Michener fellowship to advance her Atkinson research into the creation of test tube babies.

36   Michener Award prospectus, March 21, 1985, Michener Papers, Carleton.

37   Robert Wright, Draft and revised donor letters, August 1985, Michener Papers, Carleton.

38   Robert Wright, Draft and revised letters.

39   Minutes, Michener Awards Foundation AGM, November 16, 1985, Michener Papers, Carleton.

40 Memo, John Fisher to Paul Deacon, September 10, 1986, Michener Papers, Carleton.

41 Memo, Lisa Balfour Bowen (journalist) to John Fisher, n.d., Michener Papers, Carleton.

42 Memo, Paul Deacon to Board, June 14, 1985, Michener Papers, Carleton.

43 Nieman Foundation at Harvard, "About - History," https://nieman.harvard.edu/about/history/

44 The William Southam Journalism Fellowships were established in 1962. See https://www.masseycollege.ca/journalism-fellows/

45 "Jim (*sic*) Tombs Report - 1988 Michener Foundation Fellowship," March 1989, https://kotcheff.com/michenerhistory/english/repFellows/reptombs1988.htm (private website)

46 The *Kitchener-Waterloo Record* received the Michener Award in 1978 for Jim Romahn's series on violations in Canadian meat processing plants and in 1983 for his series on problems with quality control for animal feed and fertilizer. In 1985, the paper was a finalist for his exposé of the Canadian Dairy Commission and again in 1986 for his coverage of flaws in the scientific research tax credit. Romahn no longer works at the *Record* but is a self-described semi-retired freelance journalist publishing stories focusing on agribusiness. His blog, *Agri 007*, states: "It's my role to report. It's your role to press for reforms." http://agri007.blogspot.com/

47 "Jim Romahn Report - 1988 Michener Foundation Fellowship," February 1989, http://kotcheff.com/michenerhistory/english/repFellows/repromahn1988.htm (private website)

48 Christopher Grabowski (1999) photo exhibit "Land's End" documented B.C.'s threatened coastal fishery; Edward Struzik's (2009) articles on Arctic sovereignty were published in the *Edmonton Journal*, May 23-June 27, 2010, and his book *Future Arctic: Field Notes from a World on the Edge* in 2015; and Roger LeMoyne (2013) published images from Canadian mining ventures in Colombia, Guatemala and other locales in numerous publications including *Maclean's* magazine, "Mining for the truth in Guatemala," https://macleans.ca/news/world/mining-for-the-truth-in-guatemala/

49 "Catherine Cano 2000 Michener-Deacon Fellowship Report," http://kotcheff.com/michenerhistory/english/repFellows/repcano2000.htm (private website)

50 "Julie Ireton - 2010 Michener-Deacon Fellowship Recipient," report 2011, http://kotcheff.com/michenerhistory/english/repFellows/repireton2010.htm (private website). See Ireton's blog "Public Service Investigation," https://www.cbc.ca/ottawa/features/investigations/

51 Margaret Munro's (2003) series "Drugs, Money and Ethics" was published in CanWest newspapers February 23-28, 2004. Jenny Manzer (2005) study which delved into Health Canada's drug approval and monitoring system that was published in the *Ottawa Citizen*, December 19-23, 2006.

52 Jean-Pierre Rogel, *La Grand Saga des Genes* (1999); Pierre Duchesne, *Jacques Parizeau, vol 3: Le Régent, 1985-1995* (2004), the last of three volumes published between 2001-2004; Cecil Rosner *Behind the Headlines: A History of Investigative Journalism in Canada* (2008); Julian Sher, *One Child at a Time: The Global Fight to Rescue Children from Online Predators* (2007); Edward Struzik, *Future Arctic: Notes from a World on the Edge* (2015).

53 Denise Davy's series "One in Five," a look into children's mental health, was published in the *Hamilton Spectator* in 2009.

54 Jane Armstrong's series examining foreign aid in Afghanistan was published in the *National Post,* October 15-19, 2011.

55 Jean-Pierre Rogel, "1998 Michener-Deacon report into work done into explaining genetics," http://kotcheff.com/michenerhistory/english/repFellows/reprogel1998.htm (private website)

56 Melanie Coulson, "Report –2012 Michener-Deacon Fellowship for Journalism Education," April 2013, http://kotcheff.com/michenerhistory/english/repFellows/repCoulson2012.htm (private website)

57 Julie Ireton (2013), "Media Innovation and Entrepreneurial Journalism at Carleton University"; Francine Pelletier (2014), "Big Data Journalism"; Matthew Pearson (2017), "Trauma-informed journalism, Carleton"; and Tamara Baluja (2018), "Decoding Social Media, UBC."

58 Matthew Pearson, (journalist, educator), Interview by phone, November 24, 2021.

59 Canadian Journalism Forum on Violence and Trauma, "Taking Care Report," May 2022, https://www.journalismforum.ca/taking-care-report

60 It would take another five years of furious fundraising before Paul Deacon would realize his dream.

61 Rob Cribb, (journalist, educator), Interview, Toronto, December 2, 2020.

62 Rob Cribb, Interview.

63 Rob Cribb, "Cash for marks gets kids into university," *Toronto Star,* September 16, 2011, https://www.thestar.com/news/canada/2011/09/16/star_investigation_cash_for_marks_gets_kids_into_university.html

64 Robert Cribb, Patti Sonntag, P.W. Elliott and Elizabeth McSheffrey, "That rotten stench in the air? It's the smell of deadly gas and secrecy," *Toronto Star,* October 1, 2017, https://www.thestar.com/news/world/2017/10/01/that-rotten-stench-in-the-air-its-the-smell-of-deadly-gas-and-secrecy.html; Elizabeth McSheffrey, Mike De Souza, Robert Cribb, Patti Sonntag and Patricia W. Elliott, *"Screams from the Yard," National Observer,* October 1, 2017, https://www.nationalobserver.com/2017/10/01/inside-saskatchewans-failure-stop-silent-killer; and Global News, "Troubling Issues in Saskatchewan Oil Boom," October 1, 2017, https://globalnews.ca/video/3779475/troubling-issues-in-saskatchewan-oil-boom

65 Concordia University School of Journalism renamed the "Institute for Investigative Journalism" to "Institute for Inclusive, Investigative and Innovative Journalism," https://www.concordia.ca/artsci/journalism/research/investigative-journalism.html

66 Taylor Tower, "Concordia's Institute for Investigative Journalism facilitates the largest collaborative investigation in Canadian history," November 4, 2019, https://www.concordia.ca/news/stories/2019/11/04/concordias-institute-for-investigative-journalism-facilitates-largest-collaborative-investigation-in-canadian-history.html

67 "Michener Awards Foundation announces finalists for the 2019 Michener Award for meritorious public service journalism, May 5, 2020," https://www.michenerawards.ca/media-release/michener-awards-foundation-announces-finalists-for-the-2019-michener-award-for-meritorious-public-service-journalism/

68 Investigative Journalism Bureau, https://ijb.utoronto.ca/

69 Investigative Journalism Bureau, "Generation Distress," November 23, 2020, https://ijb.utoronto.ca/projects/generation-distress/

1   Michener Awards Foundation, Letters Patent, September 17, 1982, Michener Awards Foundation document.

2   Minutes, Michener Awards Foundation, AGM, November 16, 1989, Michener Papers, Carleton.

3   Gemma Files, "Dr. Jackman Wants you to Feel Good about Yourselves," *Ryerson Review of Journalism*, June 9, 1991, https://rrj.ca/dr-jackman-wants-you-to-feel-good-about-yourselves/

4   Fraser MacDougall, "A system for marking Michener Award entries," April 23, 1985. Michener Papers, Carleton.

5   Christopher Waddell (journalist author, educator), Interview, Toronto, May 12, 2022.

6   Minutes, Michener Awards Foundation's AGM, May 6, 1996. Michener Papers, Carleton.

7   Russell Mills (publisher, former Michener president), Interview, Ottawa, November 9, 2018.

8   Victor Malarek, Interview.

9   Letter, Paul Deacon to Roland Michener, February 3, 1986, Michener Papers, Carleton.

10   Letter, Paul Deacon to Roland Michener.

11   Confidential letter, Roland Michener to Paul Deacon, March 17, 1986, Michener Papers, Carleton.

12   J. Patrick O'Callaghan, *Maverick Publisher: J. Patrick O'Callaghan* (Carrick, 2015), 339-40.

13   O'Callaghan, *Maverick Publisher,* 339-40.

14   The Canadian Journalism Foundation's media advisory committee was a list of who's who: Eric Jackman; Bill Dimma; Trevor Eyton; Elly Alboim, CBC-TV's bureau chief on Parliament Hill; Mickey Cohen, a former federal deputy minister of finance and president and CEO of The Molson Companies; Hershell Ezrin, former chief aide to Ontario premier Peterson and an executive with the Molson Companies; John Honderich, editor of The *Toronto Star*; Neville Nankivell, publisher of *The Financial Post*; Robert Lewis, managing editor of *Maclean's*; Bruce Phillips, director of communications in the PMO; Peter White, former publisher of *Saturday Night* and Principal Secretary to the Prime Minister; Paddy Sherman, president of the Southam Newspaper Group; and Hugh Winsor, national political editor of *The Globe and Mail*; journalism professors Stuart Adam (Carleton), Peter Desbarats (Western) and Fred Fletcher (York); Stephen Bindman, Centre for Investigative Journalism; and William Morgan, CBC. See Anthony Westell, "Journalism Foundation in the Works," *Content,* May-June 1989, 6; and Westell, "Group wants to Improve Journalism," *Content,* July-August, 1989, 7.

15   O'Callaghan, *Maverick Publisher,* 342-43.

16   Memo, Paul Deacon to the Board of Directors, October 3, 1989. Michener Papers, Carleton.

17   Letter, Paul Deacon to Bill Dimma, October 3, 1989, Michener Papers, Carleton.

18   John Miller, Interview.

19   Letter, John Miller to Paul Deacon, October 12, 1989, Michener Papers, Carleton.

20   Letter, Paul Deacon to John Miller, November 1, 1989, Michener Papers, Carleton.

21   Paul Deacon, "President's remarks - Annual Meeting November 16, 1989," Michener Papers, Carleton.

22   O'Callaghan, *Maverick Publisher,* 339-40.

23   Minutes, Michener Awards Foundation AGM, November 16, 1989, Michener Papers, Carleton.

24   Memo, Paul Deacon to Board, December 1, 1989, Michener Papers, Carleton.

25   The closest the Michener Foundation and the Canadian Journalism Foundation would come to forging that relationship came in 2019 when the Michener Foundation contracted the CFJ to do the technical and administrative work of compiling Michener nominations through the CJF's online portal. That contract ended in the fall of 2021 when the Michener Awards Foundation took back the administrative duties after entering into a partnership with the Rideau Hall Foundation and upgrading its website.

26   Minutes, Michener Awards Foundation AGM, May 9, 1994, Michener Papers, Carleton.

27   Minutes, Michener Awards Foundation executive, November 5, 1997, Michener Papers, Carleton.

28   Letter, Clark Davey to Tim Kotcheff and other Board members, December 10, 1996, Michener Papers, Carleton.

29   Minutes, Michener Awards Foundation executive, November 5, 1997. Michener Papers, Carleton.

30   Minutes, Michener Awards Foundation AGM, May 6, 1996, Michener Papers, Carleton.

31   Letter, Clark Davey to Tim Kotcheff, May 28, 1996, Michener Papers, Carleton.

32   Memo, Clark Davey to Michener Awards Foundation Board, April 23, 1997, Michener Papers, Carleton.

33   Chris Waddell, Interview.

34   "Toronto Star wins 2013 Michener Award," June 11, 2014, https://kotcheff.com/michenerhistory/english/winAward/winaward2013.htm (private website)

35   John Honderich, Interview.

36   Chris Waddell, Interview.

37   "The 2000 Michener Award Winner," May 24, 2001, https://kotcheff.com/michenerhistory/english/winAward/winaward2000.htm (private website)

38   Jean Pelletier, Entry form for 2015 Michener Award, February 20, 2016, Personal collection. See *Enquête,* "Abus de la SQ: des femmes brisent le silence," November 12, 2015, https://www.youtube.com/watch?v=NqtxZf9rFCU&ab_channel=Radio-CanadaInfo

39   The broadcast resulted in an independent investigation into police activities at the detachment and the reinstatement of an inquiry into the disappearance of Sindy Ruperthouse, an Indigenous woman whose investigation had sparked the initial Radio Canada coverage. Furthermore, the Quebec government promised $6 million for programs to help Aboriginal women in the remote northern community.

40   Letter, John Honderich to Arch MacKenzie, May 11, 1994, Michener Papers, Carleton.

41   Letter, James Travers to Arch MacKenzie, May 20, 1994. Michener Papers, Carleton.

42 Confidential memo, Arch MacKenzie to Board, May 24,1994, Michener Papers, Carleton.

43 Draft news release, May 26, 1994. The Foundation sent out the final release on May 27, 1994, Michener Papers, Carleton but there is no copy of it.

44 "1994 Michener Award Winner, CKNW/98," May 12, 1995, https://kotcheff.com/michenerhistory/english/winAward/winaward1994.htm (private website)

45 Saskatchewan, Court of Queen's Bench, "Prince Albert (City) v. Zatlyn, 1995," https://www.canlii.org/en/sk/skqb/doc/1995/1995canlii5965/1995canlii5965.html?resultIndex=1&resultId=118a262636a54c009acadaa031cf6df7&searchId=897be9c8145a49d1a70ca4fcd51d8468

46 Rafe Mair, *Rafe: A Memoir* (Harbour Publishing, 2004), 83.

47 Mair, *Rafe: A Memoir*, 19.

48 Mair, *Rafe: A Memoir*, 126.

49 Letters: W.J. Rich, Vice president Alcan to Tom Plasteras, Program Director CKNW, June 20, 1994; Les Holroyd, Director of Corporate Information and Public Affairs to the Editor of the *Georgia Straight*, January 21, 1994; Les Holroyd to the Editor of *Equity*, June 8, 1994; Les Holroyd, Director of Corporate Information and Public Affairs to the Editor of *The Financial Post*, October 28, 1994, Michener Papers, Carleton.

50 Mair, *Rafe: A Memoir*, 126.

51 Letters: Len and Jo Mammerquist, to Alcan's Les Holryod, September 27, 1994; C.H. Whicher, March 31, 1995; David Dunsmuir, March 30, 1995; L.A. Broddie, March 31, 1995; and Trafford Hall, Municipal Manager, District of Kitimat, May 2, 1995, Michener Papers, Carleton.

52 Letter, Les Holroyd, Director of Corporate Information and Public Affairs to Arch MacKenzie, March 30, 1995, Michener Papers, Carleton.

53 Letter, Trafford Hall, Municipal Manager, District of Kitimat, May 2, 1995; and Motion by District of Kitimat, May 2, 1995, Michener Papers, Carleton.

54 Letter, C.H. Whicher to Clark Davey, May 9, 1995. Michener Papers, Carleton.

55 Minutes of Michener Awards Foundation AGM, May 12, 1995, Michener Papers, Carleton.

56 "His Excellency the Right Honourable Roméo LeBlanc - Speech on the Occasion of the Presentation of the 1994 Michener Awards for Journalism. Rideau Hall, Friday, May 12, 1995," https://kotcheff.com/michenerhistory/english/leblanc/leblanc1995.htm (private website)

57 Roméo LeBlanc, May 12, 1995.

58 Bill MacPherson died a month later. See: Christopher Young, "Farewell to a Champion of Public Interest," *Ottawa Citizen*, June 23, 1995, A11, Author's collection.

59 "The 1994 Michener Award Winner - CKNW/98," May 12, 1995, https://kotcheff.com/michenerhistory/english/winAward/winaward1994.htm (private website)

60 Letters, Allen M. Wakita, Kitimat Community Coalition to Arch MacKenzie, May 27, 1995; Bruce Strachan to Clark Davey, n.d., Michener Papers, Carleton. Michener Papers, Carleton.

61 Mair, *Rafe, A Memoir*, 127.

62 "950204 Supreme Court of British Columbia between Thomas Siddon (Plaintiff) and Rafe Mair Westcom Radio Group Ltd. (Defendants), Statement of Claim," January 13, 1985, 2-3 and Schedule "A" 10 -11, 17. Michener Papers, Carleton; Mair, *Rafe: A Memoir*, 232.

63 Letter, Eric Rice to Arch MacKenzie, August 3, 1995, Michener Papers, Carleton.

64 Letter, Clark Davey to Anthony P. McGlynn, October 3, 1995. Michener Papers, Carleton.

65 Letter, Clark Davey to Eric Rice, October 18, 1995. Michener Papers, Carleton.

66 Letter, Anthony P. McGlynn, Perley-Robertson, Panet, Hill & McDougall to Eric Rice, QC, Campbell Froh May & Rice, Richmond B.C., October 26, 1995, Michener Papers, Carleton.

67 Memo, Clark Davey to the Board, April 23, 1997, Michener Papers, Carleton.

68 Fax, R.J. ("Rod") Gunn, president and general manager of CKNW to Clark Davey, April 3, 1997, Michener Papers, Carleton.

69 Ross Howard, "Leading B.C. radio station lands in warm water," *Globe and Mail*, April 3, 1997, A3, Michener Papers, Carleton.

70 Minutes, Michener Awards Foundation AGM, May 1, 1997, Michener Papers, Carleton.

71 Minutes, May 1, 1997.

72 Letter, Michael Flatters, Burnet, Duckworth & Palmer LLB to Kim Kierans, May 24, 2018. Michener Awards Foundation documents.

73 Letter, Grant Stapon to Kim Kierans, May 29, 2018. Michener Awards Foundation documents.

74 Letter, Grant Stapon to Kim Kierans, June 1, Michener Awards Foundation documents.

75 Charles Rusnell and Jennie Russel, "Private Health, Public Risk: How the Alberta government allowed a private foundation to offer an unproven 'experimental' health program to its citizens," CBC News, July 14, 2017, https://www.cbc.ca/news/canada/edmonton/topic/Tag/Private%20Health%20Public%20Risk

76 Letter, Grant Stapon, June 1, 2018.

77 Letter, Michael Flatters to Kim Kierans, June 8, 2018.

78 Charles Rusnell and Jennie Russel, update to "Private Health, Public Risk?" CBC News, May 25, 2022, https://www.cbc.ca/news2/interactives/unproven/

79 Email, Charles Rusnell to Kim Kierans, May 12, 2020, Author's collection.

80 Email, Charles Rusnell to Kim Kierans, June 19, 2022, Author's collection.

81 "Daily News wins national award," *Halifax Daily News,* April 28, 1998, A3. Author's collection.

82 Letter, Cameron S. McKinnon to Editor *Daily News*, April 29,1998, Michener Papers, Carleton.

83 Letter, Arch MacKenzie fax to Cameron S. MacKinnon, April 30,1998, Michener Papers, Carleton.

84 Letter, Dale Dunlop to Michener Awards Foundation, August 2005, Michener Papers Carleton.

85   "The 1997 Michener Award Winter - *The Halifax Daily News*," April 28, 1998, https://kotcheff.com/michenerhistory/english/winAward/winaward1997.htm (private website)

86   Letter, Dale Dunlop to Michener Awards Foundation, August 2005, Michener Papers, Carleton.

87   "The 1997 Michener Award Winter - The Halifax Daily News."

88   Stephen Kimber (journalist, author, educator), Interview, Halifax, September 23, 2019.

89   Stephen Kimber, Interview.

90   John Miller, Interview.

91   David Walmsley, Interview.

92   Walmsley, Interview.

93   Margo Goodhand (author, editor, publisher), Interview by phone, March 31, 2023.

94   Goodhand, Interview.

NOTES TO CHAPTER 6

1   Library and Archives Canada, RG7G30 Vol 49 HNAT 802-9V1.

2   Fraser MacDougall, interview by Bill MacNeill, *Voice of the Pioneer*, CBC-TV, May 10 and 23 1990.

3   Minutes, Michener Awards Foundation AGM, November 16, 1989, Michener Papers, Carleton.

4   Minutes, Michener Awards Foundation AGM, June 19, 1990, Michener Papers, Carleton.

5   Minutes, Michener Awards Foundation AGM , May 1, 1997, Michener Papers, Carleton.

6   "*Le Devoir* wins1989 Michener Award," June 19 1990, https://kotcheff.com/michenerhistory/english/winAward/winaward1989.htm (private website). *La Presse* won two more Michener Awards, one in 2003 for its coverage of seniors' health care, and the second, in 2007, for an exposé of the treatment of Afghan detainees.

7   "*The Globe and Mail* wins the 2005 Michener Award for series on Breast Cancer," April 11, 2006, http://kotcheff.com/michenerhistory/english/winAward/winaward2005.htm (private website)

8   Michener Awards Foundation judging panel, Citation of Merit, 1989. Michener Papers, Carleton. Also see, Anne Kershaw., *Rock A Bye Baby: A Death Behind Bar* (McLelland & Stewart, 1991).

9   "The Story behind the Story: Host/Reporter Hana Gartner - *the fifth estate*," June 14, 2011, http://kotcheff.com/michenerhistory/english/reporters2010/gartner.htm (private website)

10   Supreme Court of Canada, "Backgrounder: 'A Preventable Death'," Office of Correctional Investigator, April 28, 2014, https://www.falconers.ca/wp-content/uploads/2015/07/Smith-A-Preventable-Death.pdf

11   "The Story behind the story: Host/Reporter Hana Gartner - *the fifth estate*."

12   "Ashley Smith: Out of Control (2010) - *the fifth estate*," *the fifth estate*, CBC, posted August 5, 2015, https://youtu.be/yryXNq00c0

13　"Behind the Wall," *the fifth estate*, CBC, November 12, 2020, https://www.cbc.ca/player/play/2675576109

14　Falconer's LLB, "Ashley Smith Inquest," documents, December 19, 2013, https://falconers.ca/casestudy/ashley-smith/; and Government of Canada, "Response to the coroner's inquest touching the death of Ashley Smith," December 2014, https://www.canada.ca/en/correctional-service/corporate/library/response-coroners-inquest-death-ashley-smith.html

15　"Hana Gartner on Ashley Smith," *the fifth estate*, April 9, 2015, https://youtu.be/sDyBYxD1ouk

16　Randy Richmond, "Indiscernible," *London Free Press,* October 11, 2016, https://medium.com/@London.Free.Press/by-randy-richmond-the-london-free-press-507bd5a1d462

17　Judges' citation, 2016, Michener Papers, Carleton.

18　Emily Colye and Jackie Olmstead, "The use of solitary confinement continues in Canada," *Policy Options Politiques*, January 18, 2022, https://policyoptions.irpp.org/magazines/january-2022/the-use-of-solitary-confinement-continues-in-canada/. Also see Patrick White, "Despite new laws, inmates still face time in solitary confinement," *Globe and Mail*, October 31, 2022, https://www.theglobeandmail.com/canada/article-despite-new-laws-too-many-inmates-in-isolation-are-indigenous-panel/

19　"His Excellency the Right Honourable Ray Hnatyshyn - Speech on the Occasion of the Presentation of the 1989 Michener Awards for Journalism. Rideau Hall, Tuesday, June 19th, 1990," https://kotcheff.com/michenerhistory/english/hnatyshyn/hnaytshyn1990.htm (private website)

20　Memo Judith Larocque to His Excellency Raymon Hnatyshyn, Library and Archives Canada, Awards Ceremonies – Governor General Awards – Michener Award 5/02/90 – 10/04/91, RG7-G30 Vol 49, HNAT 802-9 Vol 1.

21　"His Excellency the Right Honourable Ray Hnatyshyn - Speech on the Occasion of the Presentation of the 1991 Michener Awards for Journalism. Rideau Hall, Tuesday, May 5, 1992," https://kotcheff.com/michenerhistory/english/hnatyshyn/hnaytshyn1992.htm (private website)

22　"His Excellency the Right Honourable Ray Hnatyshyn - Speech on the Occasion of the Presentation of the 1991 Michener Awards for Journalism." Rideau Hall, Tuesday, May 5, 1992.

23　Cecil Rosner, Interview.

24　"1991 Michener Award Winner - CBC-TV," May 5, 1992, https://kotcheff.com/michenerhistory/english/hnatyshyn/hnaytshyn1992.htm (private website)

25　Library and Archives Canada, HNAT 802-9 Vol 3 22-04-92 3-05-93.

26　Letter, Gail Scott to Don Hoskins October 4, 1991, Michener Papers, Carleton.

27　Bruce Deachman, "Clark Davey, 1928-2019: 'The true journalist of journalists'," *Ottawa Citizen*, February 26, 2019, https://ottawacitizen.com/news/local-news/clark-davey-1928-2019-the-true-journalist-of-journalists

28　Richard J. Doyle, *Hurly-Burly: A Time at the Globe*, 97.

29　Minutes, Michener Awards Foundation AGM, May 4, 1993, Michener Papers, Carleton.

30　Minutes, Michener Awards Foundation AGM, May 9, 1994. Michener Papers, Carleton.

31   Clark Davey, Interview.

32   Minutes, Michener Awards Foundation AGM, May 9, 1994.

33   "Clark Davey - President of the Michener Awards Foundation - His Remarks at the Michener Awards ceremony, May 9, 1994," https://kotcheff.com/michenerhistory/english/davey/davey1994.htm (private website)

34   In fifty years, media outlets have tied for the Michener Award six times, 1972, 1975, 1981, 1985, 1987 and 1993.

35   "The *Ottawa Citizen* & *The Globe and Mail* - Co-winners of 1993 Michener Award, May 9, 1994," https://kotcheff.com/michenerhistory/english/winAward/winaward1993.htm (private website)

36   "André Picard, "Tenacious activist lobbied for the victims of Canada's tainted blood tragedy," *The Globe and Mail,* August 26, 2022, https://www.theglobeandmail.com/canada/article-tenacious-activist-lobbied-for-the-victims-of-canadas-tainted-blood/; also see André Picard, *The Gift of Death: Confronting Canada's Tainted Blood Tragedy* (HarperCollins Canada, 1995 and 1998).

37   Minutes, Michener Awards Foundation AGM, May 6, 1996, Michener Papers, Carleton.

38   In 2022, the Aspen tree was no longer standing. The Experimental Farm has no record of what happened to it.

39   Minutes, Michener Awards Foundation AGM, May 6, 1996, Michener Papers, Carleton.

40   Minutes, Michener Awards Foundation AGM, May 1, 1997, Michener Papers, Carleton.

41   Richard Doyle, "Senators' Statements," Canada, Senate, March 26, 1996, https://sencanada.ca/en/content/sen/chamber/352/debates/006db_1996-03-26-e

42   John Honderich, *Above the Fold: A Personal History of the Toronto Star,* 199.

43   Minutes, Michener Awards Foundation AGM, May 6, 1996.

44   Bryn Matthews, Interview by phone, February 15, 2022.

45   Minutes, Michener Awards Foundation AGM, May 12, 1995, Michener Papers, Carleton.

46   Minutes, Michener Awards Foundation Executive, April 4, 1996, Michener Papers, Carleton.

47   Minutes, Michener Awards Foundation Executive, December 5, 1996, Michener Papers, Carleton.

48   Joseph Jackson, "Newspapers ownership in Canada: An Overview of the Davey Committee and the Kent Commission Studies."

49   Letter, Clark Davey to Tim Kotcheff, December 19, 1995, Michener Papers, Carleton.

50   Letter, Clark Davey letter, June 15, 2006. Michener Papers, Carleton.

51   Minutes, Michener Awards Foundation Executive November 6, 1998, Michener Papers, Carleton.

52   Gail Scott (broadcast journalist, educator), Interview, Toronto, March 13, 2019.

53   Minutes, Michener Awards Foundation AGM, May 5, 1992. Michener Papers, Carleton.

54   Bryn Matthews, Interview.

55   Tim Kotcheff, Interview.

56   Michener Awards Foundation, Report of the Judges, November 4, 1988, Michener Papers, Carleton.

57   Lindsay Crysler, Interview.

58   Letter, Margaret Pearcy to Paul Deacon March 7, 1988; and Memo, Paul Deacon, December 1, 1989, Michener Papers, Carleton.

59   Margaret Pearcy, "National Public Relations N.P.R. Inc, Communications Planning Phase I for The Michener Awards Foundation 1990-1991," October 24, 1990, Michener Papers, Carleton.

60   Hayes, *Power and Influence*, 242.

61   Richard Doyle, *Hurly-Burly*, 120.

62   Hayes, *Power and Influence*, 188, 242.

63   Virtual book launch for Webster's book was held November 25, 2020 at Massey College, University of Toronto, https://www.youtube.com/watch?v=EIkNnOSeb9Y&ab_channel=MasseyCollege

64   Hayes, *Power and Influence*, 188.

65   Norman Webster (journalist, author, editor, publisher) Interview by phone, June 7, 2021.

66   Pierre Bergeron (journalist, publisher), Interview, Gatineau, PQ, November 9, 2018.

67   Minutes, Michener Awards Foundation AGM, April 10, 2003, Michener Papers, Carleton.

68   "*La Presse* wins 2003 Michener Award for reporting on social issues," April 15, 2004, https://kotcheff.com/michenerhistory/english/winAward/winaward2003.htm (private website); and Radio Canada, Léon Lafleur savait que les médias savaient, November 28, 2003, https://ici.radio-canada.ca/nouvelle/137280/lettre-lafleur

69   The *Gazette* revisited the issue in 2020 with its focus on horrific conditions inside a nursing home in the Montréal suburb of Dorval. It was early in the pandemic. Reporter Aaron Derfel found residents "dehydrated, malnourished, soiled in their own feces and abandoned by staff after COVID-19 began spreading through the home." Families and the health authority swooped in, and the premier ordered a police investigation for "gross negligence" inspections of forty privately run operations, https://www.michenerawards.ca/organization/montreal-gazette/

70   Tommy Chouinard, "Saint-Charles-Borromée: des patients maltraités bientôt dédommagés," *La Presse,* April 18, 2013, https://www.lapresse.ca/actualites/sante/201304/18/01-4642073-saint-charles-borromee-des-patients-maltraites-bientot-dedommages.php

71   Michaëlle Jean (former governor general, broadcast journalist, diplomat), Interview by phone, July 2, 2019.

72   Bergeron, Interview.

73   Email, Pierre Bergeron, January 26, 2019, Author's collection.

74   Email, David Humphreys, March 24, 2019, Author's collection.

75   David Humphreys (journalist, communications consultant), Interview, Ottawa, November 12, 2018.

76   Bergeron, Interview.

77 Data between 1970 and 2020 show French language media have won about 9 per cent (or 5/57) of the Michener Awards, and received 1 per cent (23/221) of the honourable mentions or citations of merits. This may reflect the fact that fewer French media enter the Michener Awards. Smaller media are better represented. Twenty-five per cent (14/57) have won Michener Awards, and 27 per cent (60/221) have received honourable mentions or citations of merit.

78 "CBC-TV and Southam News tie for the 1987 Michener Award," December 8, 1988, https://kotcheff.com/michenerhistory/english/winAward/winaward1987.htm (private website)

79 Author's notes, 2016.

80 "1990 Michener Award Winner — *The Elmira Independent*," April 25, 1991, https://kotcheff.com/michenerhistory/english/winAward/winaward1990.htm (private website)

81 "1990 Michener Award Winner — *The Elmira Independent*."

82 As of 2022 the *Elmira Independent* (1990) and the *Manitoulin Expositor* (1982) are the only two weeklies to win a Michener Award. In 1973 the *Scotian Journalist*, a bi-weekly, won the Michener.

83 Bob Verdun (journalist, publisher), Interview by phone, January 21, 2022.

84 Bob Verdun, Interview.

85 "Uniroyal Groundwater Clean-up and Treatment, Elmira," *Canadian Consulting Engineer*, October 1, 1999, https://www.canadianconsultingengineer.com/features/uniroyal-groundwater-clean-up-and-treatment-elmira/

86 "Manufacturing Facility," LANXESS, n.d., https://lanxess.ca/sites/elmira/manufacturing-facility/

87 "Frequently Asked Questions," LANXESS, n.d., https://lanxess.ca/sites/elmira/environmental-remediation/faqs/

88 Bob Verdun, Interview.

89 Robert A. Case (2017) "Environmental oversight and the citizen activist: Lessons from an oral history of activism surrounding Elmira, Ontario's 1989 water crisis," *Community Development, 48*(1), (2017), 86-104, https://www.tandfonline.com/doi/full/10.1080/15575330.2016.1249491?needAccess=true; Jeff Outhit, "Clean up launched after Elmira chemical factory taints farm next door," *The Waterloo Region Record,* January 3, 2019, https://www.therecord.com/news/waterloo-region/2019/01/03/cleanup-launched-after-elmira-chemical-factory-taints-farm-next-door.html; and, Leah Gerber, "Why you still can't drink the local water in Elmira," *The Observer,* November 2, 2020, https://observerxtra.com/2020/11/02/why-you-still-cant-drink-the-local-water-in-elmira/

90 Verdun, Interview.

91 Minutes, Michener Awards Foundation AGM, April 19, 1999, Michener Papers, Carleton.

92 Minutes, Michener Awards Foundation AGM, April 10, 2000, Michener Papers, Carleton.

93 By 2000, Statistics Canada, "The Daily" reported that 41.8 per cent of households had at least one regular user logging on to the Internet though only 28.7 per cent reported having access at home. "The Daily - Household Internet Use," Statistics Canada, May 19 2000, https://www150.statcan.gc.ca/n1/daily-quotidien/000519/dq000519b-eng.htm

94   "Tim Kotcheff and Alain Guilbert – Recipients of the 2014 Michener-Baxter Special Award," June 11, 2014, https://kotcheff.com/michenerhistory/english/reporters2013/kotcheffGuilbert.htm (private website)

95   The Michener Awards Foundation archival website created by Tim Kotcheff was discontinued in 2021 and the Foundation has stored all the archival information. The new website for the Michener Awards Foundation can be found at: https://www.michenerawards.ca/.

96   Minutes, Michener Awards Foundation AGM, April 19, 1999, Michener Papers, Carleton.

NOTES TO CHAPTER 7

1   Chris Cobb, Ego and Ink: The Inside Story of Canada's National Newspaper War (McClelland & Stewart, 2004), 138.

2   Kenneth Whyte (journalist, publisher), Interview, Toronto, March 24, 2022.

3   Whyte, Interview.

4   Staff, "The Shawinigate affair: a timeline," The National Post, May 7, 2010, https://nationalpost.com/news/canada/the-shawinigate-affair-a-timeline

5   Cobb, Ego and Ink, Chapter 19, "L'Affaire Grand-Mère," 250-63.

6   John Honderich, Above the Fold, 226.

7   Honderich, Above the Fold, 231.

8   Honderich, Above the Fold, 232.

9   Karen Howlett and Colin Freeze, "Black abandons his Post, sells out to Aspers," Globe and Mail, August 24, 2001, https://www.theglobeandmail.com/news/national/black-abandons-his-post-sells-out-to-aspers/article4152189/

10   "Black out: CanWest to buy 100% of National Post," CBC News, August 24, 2001, https://www.cbc.ca/news/business/black-out-canwest-to-buy-100-of-national-post-1.290327

11   Cobb, Ego and Ink, 265.

12   "When 'a flood of free newspapers' washed over Toronto," CBC Archives, June 27, 2019, 8:30 AM EDT | Last Updated: June 27, 2022, https://www.cbc.ca/archives/when-a-flood-of-free-newspapers-washed-over-toronto-1.5180505

13   Honderich, Above the Fold, 255.

14   Dwayne Winseck, 2021, "Figure 2: Major Communications and Media Ownership Changes in Canada 1994-2020, Media and Internet Concentration in Canada, 1984-2020," https:// doi.org/10.22215/gmicp/2021.2. Global Media and Internet Concentration Project, Carleton University, 22.

15   Dwayne Winseck, Media and Internet Concentration in Canada, 23.

16   Canada Parliament, The Uncertain Mirror: Report of the Special Senate Committee on Mass Media, Vol. 1, Senate of Canada (Information Canada, 1970), 6.

17   Canada, Parliament, "Proceedings of the Standing Senate Committee on Transport and Communications Issue 6 - Order of Reference," Senate of Canada, March 20, 2003, https://sencanada.ca/Content/SEN/Committee/372/tran/pdf/11issue.pdf; and

"Proceedings of the Standing Senate Committee on Transport and Communications, Issue 1 - Order of Reference," Senate of Canada, Special Committee on Mass Media, October 19, 2004, https://sencanada.ca/en/Content/SEN/Committee/381/tran/01or-e

18 Canada, Parliament, Interim Report on the Canadian News Media, The Senate of Canada, April 2004, 1, https://sencanada.ca/en/content/sen/committee/373/tran/rep/rep04apr04-e

19 Kim Kierans, "Media Concentration in Atlantic Canada: Media by Monopoly," Center for Journalism Ethics, University of Wisconsin at Madison, August 18, 2016, https://ethics.journalism.wisc.edu/2006/08/18/media-concentration-in-atlantic-canada-media-by-monopoly/

20 Senate of Canada, Final Report on the Canadian News Media, vol. 1, June 2006, 63, https://sencanada.ca/en/content/sen/committee/391/tran/rep/repfinjun06vol1-e

21 Final Report on the Canadian News Media, vol. 1, 65.

22 Bev Oda, "Response to the Report of the Standing Senate Committee on Transport and Communications: Final Report on the Canadian News Media," Canadian Heritage, 23 November 2006, https://publications.gc.ca/collections/collection_2007/ch-pc/CH44-80-2006E.pdf, 13-14. Minister of Public Works and Government Services Canada 2006, Catalogue No. CH 44-80/2006 ISBN 0-662-49675-2.

23 Adrienne Clarkson (former governor general, author, broadcast journalist), Interview, Toronto, May 21, 2019.

24 "Her Excellency the Right Honourable Adrienne Clarkson's speech on the occasion of the presentation of the 2002 Michener Awards for Journalism," April 10, 2003, http://kotcheff.com/michenerhistory/english/clarkson/clarkson2003.htm (private website)

25 "Her Excellency the Right Honourable Adrienne Clarkson's speech on the occasion of the presentation of the 1999 Michener Awards for Journalism," April 10, 2000.

26 "Background to Manitoba Vote Splitting Scheme - by Curt Petrovitch," April 10, 2000, https://kotcheff.com/michenerhistory/english/votesplitting.htm (private website)

27 "Background to Manitoba Vote Splitting Scheme."

28 "Background to Manitoba Vote Splitting Scheme."

29 Cecil Rosner, Interview; also Rosner, Behind the Headlines, 3-4.

30 Clinton Free and Vaughan Radcliffe, "Accountability in Crisis: The Sponsorship Scandal and the Office of the Comptroller General in Canada," Journal of Business Ethics, 84(2), (Jan. 2009), 189-208, https://www.jstor.org/stable/40294737

31 Public Policy Forum, "The Shattered Mirror: News, Democracy and Trust in the Digital Age," January 26, 2017, https://ppforum.ca/project/the-shattered-mirror/

32 Edward Greenspon, Interview.

33 Russell Mills, Interview.

34 "Her Excellency the Right Honourable Adrienne Clarkson's speech on the occasion of the presentation of the 1999 Michener Awards."

35 Letter, Judy Bullis to Adrienne Clarkson, received April 14, 2000, Library and Archives Canada, Clarkson fonds R178 1339 File CLAR 813-2 VOL1.

36 "The Prince George Citizen Wins 2006 Michener Award," June 8, 2007, http://kotcheff.com/michenerhistory/english/winAward/winaward2006.htm (private website)

37 "The Toronto Star Wins 2013 Michener Award," June 11, 2014, http://kotcheff.com/michenerhistory/english/winAward/winaward2013.htm (private website)

38 "The Story Behind the Story: Greg McArthur, The Globe & Mail & Linden MacIntyre, CBC-TV," June 13, 2008, http://kotcheff.com/michenerhistory/english/reporters2007/mcarthur_macintyre2007.htm (private website)

39 Greenspon, Interview.

40 "The CBC/Radio-Canada and The Canadian Press win 2008 Michener Award," June 10, 2009, http://kotcheff.com/michenerhistory/english/winAward/winaward2008.htm (private website)

41 David McKie, Interview.

42 "The Story Behind the Story: Jim Bronskill - The Canadian Press," June 10, 2009, https://kotcheff.com/michenerhistory/english/reporters2008/bronskill2008.htm (private website)

43 "The Story Behind the Story: Frédéric Zalac - Radio-Canada," June 10, 2009, https://kotcheff.com/michenerhistory/english/reporters2008/zalac2008.htm (private website)

44 Graeme Smith, "From Canadian custody to cruel hands," Globe and Mail, April 23, 2007, https://www.theglobeandmail.com/news/world/from-canadian-custody-into-cruel-hands/article585956/

45 "The Story Behind the Story: Paul Koring - The Globe and Mail," June 13, 2008, https://kotcheff.com/michenerhistory/english/reporters2007/koring2007.htm (private website)

46 David Ljunggren, "Canada brushes off allegations of Afghan torture," Reuters, October 29, 2007, https://www.reuters.com/article/us-afghan-canada-idUSN2949198720071029/ (link broken) and Author's collection.

47 Greenspon, Interview.

48 "News Release: Michener Awards Finalists Named," May 1, 2017, Michener Awards Foundation electronic files and Author's collection.

49 The Michener Awards Foundation / La Fondation Des Prix Michener, "Michener Award goes to the Telegraph-Journal," Cison, June 14, 2019, https://www.newswire.ca/news-releases/michener-award-goes-to-the-telegraph-journal-883276411.html

50 Rob Cribb, Interview.

NOTES TO CHAPTER 8

1 "Speech by Her Excellency the Right Honourable Michaëlle Jean, on the occasion of the presentation of the 2005 Michener Awards for Journalism," April 11, 2006, http://kotcheff.com/michenerhistory/english/jean/jean2006.htm (private website)

2 "The Ottawa Citizen & The Globe and Mail - Co-winners of 1993 Michener Award," May 9, 1994, http://kotcheff.com/michenerhistory/english/winAward/winaward1993.htm (private website)

3 John Honderich, Interview.

4 Ed Greenspon, "Reporting and friendship at its best," Globe and Mail, April 8, 2006, https://www.theglobeandmail.com/news/national/reporting-and-friendship-at-its-best/article794398/

5   "The Prince George Citizen Wins 2006 Michener Award," June 8, 2007, http://kotcheff.com/michenerhistory/english/winAward/winaward2006.htm (private website)

6   "The 1995 Michener Award Winner - CBC Radio," May 6, 1996, http://kotcheff.com/michenerhistory/english/winAward/winaward1995.htm (private website)

7   Anthony Wilson-Smith, John Demont and Luke Fisher. "Somalia Inquiry's Damning Report." *The Canadian Encyclopedia*. Historica Canada. Article published March 17, 2003; last Edited March 13, 2014, https://www.thecanadianencyclopedia.ca/en/article/somalia-inquirys-damning-report

8   Department of National Defence, "Update on Madame Arbour's Independent External Comprehensive Review Final Report and Culture Change Reforms in the Department of National Defence and Canadian Armed Forces to Address Sexual Harassment and Misconduct," December 13, 2022, https://www.canada.ca/en/department-national-defence/news/2022/12/update-on-madame-arbours-independent-external-comprehensive-review-final-report-and-culture-change-reforms-in-the-department-of-national-defence-an.html

9   "*Times Colonist* wins 2011 Michener Award," June 12, 2012, http://kotcheff.com/michenerhistory/english/winAward/winaward2011.htm (private website)

10 "*Times Colonist* wins 2011 Michener Award."

11 "Enhancing Royal Canadian Mounted Police Accountability Act, S.C. 2013, c. 18, Assented to 2013-06-19," Justice Laws website, https://laws-lois.justice.gc.ca/eng/annualstatutes/2013_18/FullText.html

12 Michel Basterache, *Broken Dreams Broken Promises: The Devastating Effects of Sexual Harassment on Women in the RCMP,* November 11, 2020, vii, https://www.rcmp-grc.gc.ca/wam/media/4773/original/8032a32ad5dd014db5b135ce3753934d.pdf

13 Hon. John McKay, Chair, "Systemic Racism in Policing in Canada: Report of the Standing Committee on Public Safety and National Security," June 2021, https://www.ourcommons.ca/Content/Committee/432/SECU/Reports/RP11434998/securp06/securp06-e.pdf

14 Jim Rankin (journalist) Interview, Toronto, May 17, 2022.

15 Jim Rankin, Michener Award acceptance speech, April 10, 2023, Author's papers.

16 Jim Rankin, Jennifer Quinn, Michelle Shepherd, John Duncanson, Scott Simmie, "Singled Out," *Toronto Star,* October 19, 2002, A1; and "Police target black drivers," *Sunday Star,* October 20, 2002, A1.

17 Honderich, Interview.

18 Rankin, Interview.

NOTES TO CHAPTER 9

1   Linda Monsees, "'A war against truth' - understanding the fake news controversy," *Critical Studies on Security, 8*(2), (May 2020), 116–29, https://www.tandfonline.com/doi/full/10.1080/21624887.2020.1763708?scroll=top&needAccess=true&role=tab

2   Hunt Allcott, and Matthew Gentzkow. "Social Media and Fake News in the 2016 Election," *Journal of Economic Perspectives, 31*(2), (2017), 211-36, https://www.researchgate.net/publication/316712634_Social_Media_and_Fake_News_in_the_2016_Election

3 Kayla, Keener, "Alternative Facts and Fake News: Digital Mediation and The Affective Spread of Hate in the Era of Trump." *Journal of Hate Studies, 14*(1), (2019): 137–51, https://www.researchgate.net/publication/333010056_Alternative_Facts_and_Fake_News_Digital_mediation_and_The_Affective_Spread_of_Hate_in_the_Era_of_Trump; Amanda Robb, "Pizzagate: Anatomy of a Fake News Scandal," *Rolling Stone,* November 16, 2017, https://www.rollingstone.com/feature/anatomy-of-a-fake-news-scandal-125877/; and Marc Tuters, Emilija Jokubauskaitė and Daniel Bach, "Post-Truth Protest: How 4chan Cooked Up the Pizzagate Bullshit," *M/C journal, 21*(3), (2018), https://journal.media-culture.org.au/index.php/mcjournal/article/view/1422

4 Maria Ressa, *How to Stand Up to a Dictator: The Fight for Our Future,* (HarperCollins, 2022), 4.

5 Minutes, Michener Awards Foundation executive meeting, April 7, 2017, Michener Awards Foundation (MAF) electronic files.

6 Alan Allnutt, (editor, publisher, columnist), Interview by phone, May 11, 2022.

7 Christopher Waddell, Carleton University, https://carleton.ca/sjc/profile/waddell-christopher/

8 Christopher Waddell, Interview.

9 Minutes, Michener Awards Foundation AGM, June 17, 2017, MAF electronic files.

10 Minutes, Michener Awards Foundation AGM, June 17, 2017.

11 Waddell, Interview.

12 Email, Edith Cody-Rice to Kim Kierans, September 27, 2017, 7:53 p.m.; Email, David Humphreys to Kim Kierans, September 27, 2017, 12:52 p.m. Author's collection.

13 Minutes, executive meeting, September 19, 2017. MAF electronic files.

14 Minutes, executive meeting, September 19, 2017. MAF electronic files.

15 Email, Russ Mills to Edith Cody-Rice and MAF executive, September 18, 2:45 p.m. Author's collection.

16 The Governor General of Canada, "Honours," https://www.gg.ca/en/honours

17 Office of the Secretary to the Governor General, conversation with the author, April 28, 2023.

18 Email, James Baxter to the Michener Board, October 21, 2017, 1:18 p.m., MAF electornic files.

19 Email, Kim Kierans to executive, September 27, 10:15 a.m., Author's collection.

20 Email, Kim Kierans to executive, September 27, 10:15 a.m.

21 Waddell, Interview.

22 Email, Russ Mills to Kim Kierans.

23 Alan Allnutt, Interview.

24 Email, Chris Waddell to Kim Kierans, September 28,2017, 9:59 p.m. Authors collection.

25 Waddell, Interview.

26 Waddell, Interview.

27 Email, James Baxter to the Board, October 21, 1:18 p.m., Author's collection.

28 Minutes, Michener Awards Foundation, Special Meeting of the Board of Directors, November 3, 2017, MAF electronic files.

29   Allnutt, Interview.

30   Allnutt, Interview.

31   Waddell, Interview.

32   The Board approved updated governance bylaws at its June 12, 2018 AGM to spell out procedures for election and terms of directors.

33   Policy, Board Roles and Responsibilities, June 12, 2018, Michener Award Foundaton electronic documents.

34   The Governor General of Canada, "Biography," https://www.gg.ca/en/governor-general/former-governors-general/julie-payette/biography

35   Other awards include the Canadian Association of Journalists (CAJ), National Newspaper Awards (NNA) and the Radio-Television News Directors Association (now called the Radio-Television Digital News Association (RTDNA).

36   Bruce Campion-Smith, "Julie Payette appears poised to launch into Governor General role," *Toronto Star,* July 12, 2017, https://www.thestar.com/news/canada/2017/07/12/canadas-next-governor-general-to-be-announced-thursday-by-trudeau.html; and, Jeff Lagerquist, "Julie Payette: Things to know about the woman chosen as the new governor general," CTVNews.ca, July 12, 2017, 11:02 p.m. EDT, https://www.ctvnews.ca/politics/julie-payette-things-to-know-about-the-woman-chosen-as-the-new-governor-general-1.3500650

37   Star Editorial Board, "Julie Payette as GG sends a powerful message: Editorial," *Toronto Star,* July 13, 2017, https://www.thestar.com/opinion/editorials/2017/07/13/julie-payette-as-gg-sends-a-powerful-message-editorial.html

38   B.J. Siekierski, "PMO has no comment on Julie Payette's expunged 2011 assault charge," *iPolitics,* https://www.ipolitics.ca/news/pmo-has-no-comment-on-julie-payettes-expunged-2011-assault-charge

39   Susan Delacourt, "Private lives, public scrutiny: Julie Payette and the media," *iPolitics,* June 18, 2017, https://www.ipolitics.ca/news/private-lives-public-scrutiny-julie-payette-and-the-media

40   Kevin Donovan, "Incoming governor general Julie Payette drops fight to keep divorce records sealed," *Toronto Star,* August 21, 2017, https://www.thestar.com/news/canada/2017/08/21/incoming-governor-general-julie-payette-drops-fight-to-keep-divorce-records-sealed.html

41   Kevin Donovan, "Incoming governor general Julie Payette drops fight to keep divorce records sealed," *Toronto Star.*

42   Julie Payette (scientist, astronaut, former Governor General), Interview, Toronto, April 18, 2023, 1:22.

43   David Johnston, Interview.

44   Minutes, Michener Awards Foundation Board, February 13, 2018, MAF electronic files.

45   Payette, Interview, 18:46.

46   Payette, Interview, 49:29.

47   John Fraser, Interview.

48   Payette, Interview, 1:59:56.

49   Payette, Interview, 22:00.

50 Payette, Interview, 25:00.

51 Email, Catherine Cano to Michener Board, May 14, 2018, 11:47 a.m., Author's collection.

52 Julie Payette speech, June 12, 2018, Author's collection.

53 Robyn Doolittle, "Unfounded: Why police dismiss 1 in 5 sexual assault claims as baseless," *Globe and Mail,* February 3, 2017, https://www.theglobeandmail.com/news/investigations/unfounded-sexual-assault-canada-main/article33891309/

54 Citation, *"Globe and Mail* - Unfounded," June 12, 2018, MAF electronic files.

55 Robyn Doolittle, "The Story behind Unfounded, *"The Globe and Mail,* February 3, 2017, https://www.theglobeandmail.com/news/investigations/unfounded-backstory-sexual-assault-claims/article33891825/

56 David Walmsley, Interview.

57 Robyn Doolittle, "Police dismissals of sexual-assault claims as 'unfounded' dropped by more than half since 2017," *The Globe and Mail,* December 26, 2022, https://www.theglobeandmail.com/canada/article-unfounded-sexual-assault-2022/

58 Payette, Interview.

59 Rideau Hall, "Panel Discussion on Journalism in Canada," June 14, 2019, Michener Awards Foundation electronic files.

60 Cable Public Affairs Channel (CPAC), "2018 Michener Award Ceremony," *Public Record,* June 14, 2019, https://www.cpac.ca/en/programs/public-record/episodes/66004982

61 CPAC, "2018 Michener Award Ceremony."

62 CPAC, "2018 Michener Award Ceremony."

63 "Michener-Deacon Education discussion paper," May 24, 2017, Michener Award Foundation electronic files.

64 "Progress Report: Board Committee on Michener-Deacon Fellowship," September 15, 2017, Michener Award Foundation electronic files.

65 The Michener Awards Foundation, "The Fellowships," https://www.michenerawards.ca/the-fellowships/info/

66 "Michener Awards Foundation announces the Michener-L. Richard O'Hagan Fellowship for Journalism Education," Michener Awards Foundation, December 11, 2019, https://www.michenerawards.ca/media-release/michener-awards-foundation-announces-the-michener-l-richard-ohagan-fellowship-for-journalism-education/

67 Canada Press Freedom Project, "Homepage", https://canadapressfreedom.ca/

68 U.S. Press Freedom Tracker, https://pressfreedomtracker.us/

69 White House advisor, Kellyanne Conway, Interview, NBC Meet the Press and excerpt rebroadcast on *Twitter,* January 22, 2017.

70 Vivian Fairbank and Allison Baker launched "Truth in Journalism Fact-Checking Guide," in October 2022, https://thetijproject.ca/guide/introduction/

71 Truth in Journalism Fact-Checking Guide.

72 Viviane Fairbank, https://vivianefairbank.ca/

73 The Trust Project, https://thetrustproject.org/.; and *The Globe and Mail,* "About Us," https://www.theglobeandmail.com/about/the-trust-project/. For more details see The Trust Project, thetrustproject.org

74 "The Shattered Mirror 5 years on," *Public Policy Forum,* March 3, 2022, https://ppforum.ca/publications/shattered-mirror-5-years-on/

75 Centre d'études sur les médias Centre d'études sur les médias, https://www.cem.ulaval.ca

76 Max Bell School of Public Policy, https://www.mcgill.ca/maxbellschool/research/centre-media-technology-and-democracyEducators

NOTES TO CONCLUSION

1 Alan Allnutt, Interview

2 David Johnston, Interview.

3 Rideau Hall Foundation, "About", https://rhf-frh.ca/about/

4 Johnston, Interview.

5 Allnutt, Interview.

6 Minutes, Michener Awards Foundation Board, January 9, 2020, Michener Award Foundation electronic documents.

7 Minutes, Michener Awards Foundation, January 9, 2020.

8 Allnutt, Interview.

9 Draft Minutes, Michener Awards Foundation Board, August 31, 2020, Michener Award Foundation electronic files.

10 "Michener Awards 2019," December 16, 2020, https://vimeo.com/489538006

11 Ashley Burke, Kristen Everson, "Gov. Gen. Payette has created a toxic climate of harassment and verbal abuse at Rideau Hall, sources allege," CBC News, July 21, 2020, 6:02 PM ADT | Last Updated: July 22, 2020, https://www.cbc.ca/news/politics/julie-payette-governor-general-harassment-allegations-1.5657397

12 Burke, Everson, "Gov. Gen. Payette has created a toxic climate."

13 Julie Payette, Interview.

14 Her Excellency the Right Honourable Julie Payette "Video Message – 2019 Michener Awards Virtual Presentation" (BILINGUAL TEXT 60/40). Delivery date: December 7, 2020, Author's collection.

15 Kathy Tomlinson, "False Promises: Foreign workers are falling prey to a sprawling web of labour trafficking in Canada," *The Globe and Mail,* April 5, 2019, updated April 6, 2019, https://www.theglobeandmail.com/canada/article-false-promises-how-foreign-workers-fall-prey-to-bait-and-switch/

16 Stefanie Marotta, "*The Globe and Mail*'s False Promises investigation wins Michener Award," *The Globe and Mail,* December 10, 2020, https://www.theglobeandmail.com/canada/article-the-globe-and-mails-false-promises-investigation-wins-michener-award/

17 Kathy Tomlinson, "The 2020 Michener Awards Ceremony," https://vimeo.com/489538006

18 "Protected B, Final Review Report, Privy Council Office, Ottawa, Ontario," Quintet Consulting Corporation, January 12, 2021, 2, 51, 53, https://www.theglobeandmail.com/files/editorial/News/GG/Report-into-workplace-conditions-at-Rideau-Hall.pdf

19 "Michener Awards Foundation announces finalists for the 2020 Michener Award for meritorious public service journalism," April 20, 2021, https://www.michenerawards.ca/media-release/michener-awards-foundation-announces-finalists-for-the-2020-michener-award-for-meritorious-public-service-journalism/

20 *The Halifax Examiner,* "The Wrongful Conviction of Glen Assoun," Michener Awards website, n.d., https://www.michenerawards.ca/organization/the-halifax-examiner/

21 "Investigating police misconduct: Ricochet wins 2021 Michener-Deacon Fellowship," April 14, 2021, https://ricochet.media/en/3600/investigating-police-misconduct-ricochet-wins-2021-michener-deacon-fellowship

22 Gabrielle Duchaine, "Positive Change for a Public Good: Michener Award Laureates Live," November 16, 2021; see also *La Presse,* "The Other Epidemic: sexual exploitation of kids on the Internet," n.d., Michener Awards website, https://www.michenerawards.ca/organization/la-presse-2/

23 Kenneth Jackson, "Positive Change for a Public Good: Michener Award Laureates Live," The Michener Awards Foundation, November 16, 2021, https://www.youtube.com/watch?v=XraiJRJW9YI&ab_channel=UniversityofKing%27sCollege

24 Jackson, "Positive Change for a Public Good"; "APTN wins the Michener Award for searing investigation in a 12-year-old's death in care," Michener Awards website, https://www.michenerawards.ca/media-release/aptn-wins-the-michener-award-for-searing-investigation-into-a-12-year-olds-death-in-care/; Caroline Touzin, "Positive Change for a Public Good: Michener Award Laureates Live," November 16, 2021, 1:38; *La Presse,* "The Other Epidemic."

25 Pierre-Paul Noreau (journalist, publisher president of Michener Awards Foundation), Interview by phone, March 28, 2023.

26 John Honderich, Interview.

27 David Walmsley, Interview.

28 Noreau, Interview.

Bibliography

"Abus de la SQ: des femmes brisent le silence." *Enquête*. Radio-Canada. Montreal. November 12, 2015. https://www.youtube.com/watch?v=NqtxZf9rFCU&ab_channel=Radio-CanadaInfo

Allcott, Hunt, and Matthew Gentzkow. "Social Media and Fake News in the 2016 Election." *Journal of Economic Perspectives* 31, No. 2 (2017): 211-36.

Bank of Canada. "Bank of Canada, Speech: Canadian economic performance at the end of the century." June 2, 1999. https://www.bankofcanada.ca/1999/06/canadian-economic-performance-end-twentieth-century/

Baker, Allison, and Viviane Fairbank. "Truth in Journalism Fact-Checking Guide." October 2022. https://thetijproject.ca/guide/introduction/

Bastarache, Michel. "Broken Dreams Broken Lives." November 11, 2020. https://www.rcmp-grc.gc.ca/wam/media/4773/original/8032a32ad5dd014db5b135ce3753934d.pdf

"Black out: CanWest to buy 100% of National Post." *CBC News*. August 24, 2001. https://www.cbc.ca/news/business/black-out-canwest-to-buy-100-of-national-post-1.290327

Bronskill, Jim. "Supreme Court says companies must pay for Grassy Narrows mill-site maintenance." *The Canadian Press*. December 6, 2019. https://www.cbc.ca/news/politics/grassy-narrows-supreme-court-1.5386602

"Bryan Cantley: A True Canadian Newspaper Superhero." *Q Media*. August 6, 2013. http://qmediasolutions.com/bryan-cantley-a-true-canadian-newspaper-superhero/

Burke, Ashley, and Kristen Everson. "Gov. Gen. Payette has created a toxic climate of harassment and verbal abuse at Rideau Hall, sources allege." *CBC News*. July 22, 2020. https://www.cbc.ca/news/politics/julie-payette-governor-general-harassment-allegations-1.5657397

Butler, Michael. "Hunger Strike for Grassy Narrows after Report Hidden by Ontario Government Comes to Light." *Council of Canadians*. July 28, 2014. https://canadians.org/analysis/hunger-strike-grassy-narrows-after-report-hidden-ontario-government-comes-light/

Campion-Smith, Bruce. "Julie Payette appears poised to launch into Governor General role." *Toronto Star*. July 12, 2017. https://www.thestar.com/news/

canada/2017/07/12/canadas-next-governor-general-to-be-announced-thursday-by-trudeau.html

Canada. Parliament. House of Commons Debates. Hansard, 29th Parliament, 1st Session: Vol. 7 6942-3, October 17, 1973.

Canada. Parliament. Senate. Special Senate Committee on Mass Media. *Report of the Special Committee on Mass Media, Vol 1: The Uncertain Mirror.* Ottawa: Queen's Printer, 1970.

Canada. Parliament. Senate of Canada. *Royal Commission on Newspapers.* Ottawa. Minister of Supply and Services, 1981.

Canada. Parliament. Senate of Canada. "Proceedings of the Standing Senate Committee on Transport and Communications Issue 6 - Order of Reference." March 20, 2003.

Canada. Parliament. Senate of Canada. "Proceedings of the Standing Senate Committee on Transport and Communications, Issue 1 - Order of Reference." October 19, 2004.

Canada. Parliament. Senate of Canada. *Interim Report on the Canadian News Media.* April 2004. YC19-0/373-4E-PDF. https://publications.gc.ca/site/eng/397476/publication.html

Canada. Parliament. Senate of Canada. *Final Report on the Canadian News Media.* Vol 1. June 2006. YC19-391/1-01-2E-PDF. https://publications.gc.ca/site/eng/9.562866/publication.html

Canada. Environment Canada. "St. Clair River: area of concern." Last modified March 16, 2023. https://www.canada.ca/en/environment-climate-change/services/great-lakes-protection/areas-concern/st-clair-river.html

Canada. Criminal Code of Canada Part VI. "Victim Privacy and Open Court Principle." https://www.justice.gc.ca/eng/rp-pr/cj-jp/victim/rr03_vic1/p8.html

Canada. "Government of Canada and Asubpeeschoseewagong Netum Anishinabek (Grassy Narrows First Nation) sign revised Framework Agreement for Mercury Care Home." July 26, 2021. https://www.canada.ca/en/indigenous-services-canada/news/2021/07/government-of-canada-and-asubpeeschoseewagong-netum-anishinabek-grassy-narrows-first-nation-sign-revised-framework-agreement-for-mercury-care-home.html

Canada. Immigration and Citizenship. "Excessive Demand: Calculation of the Cost Threshold." May 4, 2023. https://www.canada.ca/content/dam/ircc/migration/ircc/english/pdf/pub/excessive-demand-report-eng.pdf

Canada. Senate. "Senators' Statements." March 26,1996. https://sencanada.ca/en/content/sen/chamber/352/debates/006db_1996-03-26-e

Canada. The Governor General of Canada. "The Michener Award for Journalism - Presentation of the Michener Award for Journalism." May 27, 2010. https://www.gg.ca/en/media/news/2010/michener-award-journalism

Canada. The Governor General of Canada. "The Duke of Argyll." https://www.gg.ca/en/governor-general/former-governors-general/duke-argyll

Canada. The Governor General of Canada. "Edward Richard Schreyer." https://www.gg.ca/en/governor-general/former-governors-general/edward-richard-schreyer

Canada. The Governor General of Canada. "Honours." https://www.gg.ca/en/honours

Canada. The Governor General of Canada. "Biography: Julie Payette." https://www.gg.ca/en/governor-general/former-governors-general/julie-payette/biography

Canada. Department of National Defence. "Update on Madame Arbour's Independent External Comprehensive Review Final Report and Culture Change Reforms in the Department of National Defence and Canadian Armed Forces to Address Sexual Harassment and Misconduct," December 13, 2022. https://www.canada.ca/en/department-national-defence/news/2022/12/update-on-madame-arbours-independent-external-comprehensive-review-final-report-and-culture-change-reforms-in-the-department-of-national-defence-an.html

Canada Press Freedom Project. "Homepage." https://canadapressfreedom.ca/

Canadian Broadcasting Corporation. "Léon Lafleur savait que les médias savaient." Radio-Canada. November 28, 2003. https://ici.radio-canada.ca/nouvelle/137280/lettre-lafleur

Canadian Broadcasting Corporation. "The forgotten: The children of Marion Hall speak." The Fifth Estate. October 6, 2019. https://www.cbc.ca/player/play/1615490115975

Canadian Broadcasting Corporation. "Behind the Wall (2020)." The Fifth Estate. https://www.cbc.ca/player/play/2675576109

Canadian Broadcasting Corporation. "Ashley Smith: Out of Control (2010) - the fifth estate." The Fifth Estate. Posted August 5, 2015. https://youtu.be/yryXNq00_c0

Canadian Broadcasting Corporation. "Hana Gartner on Ashley Smith - the fifth estate." The Fifth Estate. April 9, 2015. YouTube. https://youtu.be/sDyBYxD1ouk

Canadian Broadcasting Corporation. "Voice of the Pioneer." Interview. Aired May 10 and 23, 1990.

Canadian Encyclopedia. "Ed Schreyer." https://www.thecanadianencyclopedia.ca/en/article/edward-richard-schreyer

Canadian Encyclopedia. "Jeanne Sauvé." February 26, 2018. https://www.thecanadianencyclopedia.ca/en/article/jeanne-mathilde-sauve

Canadian Journalism Forum on Violence and Trauma. "Taking Care Report." May 2022. https://www.journalismforum.ca/taking-care-report

Canadian Press. "Supreme Court says companies must pay for Grassy Narrows mill site maintenance." Turtle Island News. December 6, 2019. https://theturtleislandnews.com/index.php/2019/12/06/supreme-court-says-companies-must-pay-for-grassy-narrows-mill-site-maintenance/

Canadian Press. "F. MacDougall, an influential force in journalism." Toronto Star. January 26, 2000.

The Canadian Press and Citizen staff. "Meat plant exposé brings media prize." Ottawa Citizen, November 5, 1979.

Canadian Public Affairs Channel. "2018 Michener Award Ceremony." *Public Record*, June 14, 2019. https://www.cpac.ca/en/programs/public-record/episodes/66004982

Canadian Radio-television and Telecommunications Commission. Broadcasting Act, R.S.C. 1970,Chap. B-11. Cited by Simon Claus. "Canadian Broadcasting Policy at Issue: Marconi to Netflix." November 14, 2017. https://crtc.gc.ca/eng/acrtc/prx/2017claus.htm

Carleton University. "Waddell, Christopher." https://carleton.ca/sjc/profile/waddell-christopher/

Case, Robert A. "Environmental oversight and the citizen activist: Lessons from an oral history of activism surrounding Elmira, Ontario's 1989 water crisis." *Community Development*. 2017, 48:1. https://www.tandfonline.com/doi/full/10.1080/15575330.2016.1249491

Centre d'études sur les médias. *https://www.cem.ulaval.ca*

Chianello, Joanne. "Financial journalist makes Ottawa his home." *Ottawa Citizen*. March 25, 1996.

Chouinard, Tommy. "Saint-Charles-Borromée: des patients maltraités bientôt dédommagés." *La Presse*. April 18, 2013. https://www.lapresse.ca/actualites/sante/201304/18/01-4642073-saint-charles-borromee-des-patients-maltraites-bientot-dedommages.php

Cobb, Chris. *Ego and Ink: The Inside Story of Canada's National Newspaper War.* Toronto: McClelland & Stewart, 2004.

Collings, Anthony. *Capturing the News: Three Decades of Reporting Crisis and Conflict.* Columbia, MO: University of Missouri Press, 2010.

Conestoga-Rovers & Associates, Waterloo, Ontario. "Uniroyal Groundwater Clean-up and Treatment, Elmira." *Canadian Consulting Engineer*. October 1, 1999. https://www.canadianconsultingengineer.com/features/uniroyal-groundwater-clean-up-and-treatment-elmira/

Corra, Lisa. "News to Make a Difference: The Environment and the 4th Estate 1969-77." Master's thesis, Saint Mary's University, 2008. ISBN 978-0494-46156-3. ProQuest. https://library2.smu.ca/bitstream/handle/01/22435/corra_lisa_masters.PDF?sequence=1&isAllowed=y

Coyle, Emily, and Jackie Olmstead. "The use of solitary confinement continues in Canada." *Policy Options Politiques*. January 18, 2022. https://www.policyoptions.irpp.org/magazines/january-2022/the-use-of-solitary-confinement-continues-in-canada/

Cribb, Rob. "Cash for marks gets kids into university." *The Toronto Star*. September 16, 2011. https://www.thestar.com/news/canada/2011/09/16/star_investigation_cash_for_marks_gets_kids_into_university.html

Cribb, Robert, Patti Sonntag, P.W. Elliott and Elizabeth McSheffrey. "That rotten stench in the air? It's the smell of deadly gas and secrecy." *The Toronto Star*, October 1, 2017. https://www.thestar.com/news/world/2017/10/01/that-rotten-stench-in-the-air-its-the-smell-of-deadly-gas-and-secrecy.html

Crozier, Cullen, Kenneth Jackson and Margo Goodhand. *The 2020 Michener Awards Ceremony.* The Michener Awards Foundation. Aired June 16, 2021 on Vimeo. https://vimeo.com/566610045

"Daily News wins national award." *Halifax Daily News,* April 28, 1998, A3. Author's collection.

Davey, Keith. "How the Media Withheld the Message in Kitchener: For Good Journalists, Boosterism is Fatal." *Maclean's.* June 1972.

Deachman, Bruce. "Clark Davey, 1928-2019: 'The true journalist of journalists'." *Ottawa Citizen.* February 26, 2019. https://ottawacitizen.com/news/local-news/clark-davey-1928-2019-the-true-journalist-of-journalists

Debarats, Peter. *Guide to Canadian News Media.* Don Mills, ON: Harcourt Brace Jovanovich, 1990.

Delacourt, Susan. "Private lives, public scrutiny: Julie Payette and the media." *Ipolitics.* June 18, 2017. https://www.ipolitics.ca/news/private-lives-public-scrutiny-julie-payette-and-the-Media

Diamantopoulos, Mitch. *-30- Thirty Years of Journalism and Democracy in Canada: The Minifie Lectures, 1981-2010.* Regina, SK: Canadian Plains Research Center Press, 2009.

Donovan, Kevin. "Incoming governor general Julie Payette drops fight to keep divorce records sealed." *Toronto Star.* August 21, 2017. https://www.thestar.com/news/canada/2017/08/21/incoming-governor-general-julie-payette-drops-fight-to-keep-divorce-records-sealed.html

Doolittle, Robyn. "The Story behind The Globe's Unfounded series." *Globe and Mail.* February 3, 2017. https://www.theglobeandmail.com/news/investigations/unfounded-backstory-sexual-assault-claims/article33891825/

Doolittle, Robyn. "Police dismissals of sexual-assault claims as 'unfounded' dropped by more than half since 2017." *Globe and Mail.* December 26, 2022. https://www.theglobeandmail.com/canada/article-unfounded-sexual-assault-2022/

Doyle, Richard J. *Hurly-Burly: A Time at the Globe.* Toronto: Macmillan, 1990.

Drew, Karl. "Inter-Provincial Homes for Young Women, Inc." https://www.riverviewhistoryproject.ca/clubs-lodges-societies/inter-provincial-homes-for-young-women-inc

"Enhancing Royal Canadian Mounted Police Accountability Act." S.C. 2013, c. 18. Assented to 2013-06-19, Justice Laws. https://laws-lois.justice.gc.ca/eng/annualstatutes/2013_18/FullText.html

Fetherling, George. *A Little Bit of Thunder.* Toronto: Stoddart, 1993.

Files, Gemma. "Dr. Jackman Wants you to Feel Good about Yourselves." *Ryerson Review of Journalism.* June 9, 1991.

Fillmore, Frank. "Farewell to the People." *The 4th Estate.* April 17, 1969. https://archives.novascotia.ca/newspapers/archives/?ID=378&Page=200909211

Fillmore, Frank, and Debbie Sprague. "The Coverdale Report." *Scotian Journalist.* August 3,1972. Author's collection.

Fotheringham, Alan. "Rideau Rebellion." *Toronto Sun.* November 10, 1980.

Francis, Annette. "Grassy Narrows members demand compensation because of mercury poisoning." *APTN.* July 22, 2022. https://www.aptnnews.ca/national-news/grassy-narrows-members-demand-compensation-because-of-mercury-poisoning/

Free, Clinton, and Vaughan Radcliffe. "Accountability in Crisis: The Sponsorship Scandal and the Office of the Comptroller General in Canada." *Journal of Business Ethics.* Vol. 84, No. 2. 189-208. January 2009. https://www.jstor.org/stable/40294737

Gerber, Leah. "Why you still can't drink the local water in Elmira." *The Observer.* November 2, 2020. https://www.observerxtra.com/2020/11/02/why-you-still-cant-drink-the-local-water-in-elmira/

Globe and Mail. "Protected B, Final Review Report, Privy Council Office, Ottawa, Ontario." Quintet Consulting Corporation. January 12, 2021. https://www.theglobeandmail.com/files/editorial/News/GG/Report-into-workplace-conditions-at-Rideau-Hall.pdf

Globe and Mail. "About Us." https://www.theglobeandmail.com/about/the-trust-project/

Globe and Mail. "Halifax weekly wins Michener Journalism Award." April 28, 1998.

Greenspon, Edward. "Reporting and friendship at its best." *Globe and Mail.* April 8, 2006. https://www.theglobeandmail.com/news/national/reporting-and-friendship-at-its-best/article794398/

Harkness, Ross. *J.E. Atkinson of the Star.* Toronto: University of Toronto Press, 1963.

Hayden, Al. "Mercury in Lake St. Clair Walleye." *State of the Strait.* University of Windsor. http://web2.uwindsor.ca/softs/keyindicators/old/hg-walleye.htm

Hayes, David. *Power and Influence: The Globe and Mail and the News Revolution.* Toronto: Key Porter, 1992.

Honderich, John. *Above the Fold: A Personal History of the Toronto Star.* Toronto: Penguin, Random House Canada, 2022.

Howard, Ross. "Leading B.C. radio station lands in warm water." *Globe and Mail.* April 3. 1997.

Howlett, Karen, and Colin Freeze. "Black abandons his Post, sells out to Aspers." *Globe and Mail.* August 24, 2001. https://www.theglobeandmail.com/news/national/black-abandons-his-post-sells-out-to-aspers/article4152189/

Hutchinson, George. "Poisonous post-mortem on a northern native tragedy." *Toronto Star.* April 9, 2010. https://www.thestar.com/opinion/2010/04/09/poisonous_postmortem_on_a_northern_native_tragedy.html

Hutchinson, George, and Dick Wallace. *Grassy Narrows.* Scarborough, ON: Van Nostrand Reinhold, 1977.

Inflation Calculator. "1983 CPI and inflation rate for Canada." https://www.inflationcalculator.ca/1983-cpi-inflation-canada/

"Investigating police misconduct: Ricochet wins 2021 Michener-Deacon Fellowship." April 14, 2021. https://ricochet.media/en/3600/investigating-police-misconduct-ricochet-wins-2021-michener-deacon-fellowship

Investigative Journalism Bureau. "Generation Distress." November 23, 2020, https://ijb.utoronto.ca/projects/generation-distress/

Jackson, Joseph. "Newspaper Ownership in Canada: An overview of the Davey Committee and Kent Commission Studies." Government of Canada: Political and Social Affairs Division, December 17, 1999. https://publications.gc.ca/Pilot/LoPBdP/BP/prb9935-e.htm

Jobb, Dean. *Media Law for Canadian Journalists*. 3rd ed. Toronto: Emond, 2018.

Jones, Frank. "Khristine's downhill run to tragedy." *Sunday Star*. April 29, 1979. Retrieved from https://ezproxy.torontopubliclibrary.ca/login?url=https://www.proquest.com/historical-newspapers/page-a3/docview/1395087518/se-2

Jones, Frank. "Indian's 'murder' verdict wiped out." November 21, 1980. Retrieved from https://ezproxy.torontopubliclibrary.ca/login?url=https://www.proquest.com/historical-newspapers/page-a1/docview/1398214954/se-2

Keener, Kayla. "Alternative Facts and Fake News: Digital Mediation and The Affective Spread of Hate in the Era of Trump." *Journal of Hate Studies* 14, no. 1 (2019): 137–51.

Kershaw, Anne. *Rock A Bye Baby: A Death Behind Bars*. Toronto: McClelland & Stewart, 1991.

Kierans, Kim. "Media Concentration in Atlantic Canada: Media by Monopoly." Center for Journalism Ethics. University of Wisconsin at Madison. August 18, 2016. https://ethics.journalism.wisc.edu/2006/08/18/media-concentration-in-atlantic-canada-media-by-monopoly/

Kosh, Eric. *Inside Seven Days, The Show That Shook the Nation*. Scarborough, ON: Prentice Hall, 1986.

Kosh, Eric. "CBC Management Versus CBC Delinquents: The Case of 'This Hour Has Seven Days'." May 8, 2015. https://erickoch.wordpress.com/2015/05/08/cbc-management-versus-cbc-delinquents-the-case-of-this-hour-has-seven-days/

Krook, Lennart, and George A. Maylin. "Industrial fluoride pollution. Chronic fluoride poisoning in Cornwall Island cattle." *Cornell Veterinarian*, 69 (Suppl. 8): 1-69, 1979, PMID: 467082. https://pubmed.ncbi.nlm.nih.gov/467082/

Lagerquist, Jeff. "Julie Payette: Things to know about the woman chosen as the new governor general." CTVNews.ca. July 12, 2017. https://www.ctvnews.ca/politics/julie-payette-things-to-know-about-the-woman-chosen-as-the-new-governor-general-1.3500650

"Laurent Commission report on Quebec youth protection to be released Monday." *The Canadian Press*. May 2, 2021. https://montreal.ctvnews.ca/laurent-commission-report-on-quebec-youth-protection-to-be-released-monday-1.5410989

Library and Archives Canada. Media Club of Canada fonds. MG 28 I 232-21, 1971-72 21-45.

Library and Archives Canada. Registry files from the Office of Governor General Roland Michener. Office of the Governor General fonds. 1984-85/054 GAD, RG7 G28 Vol 67 ID 133543.

Library and Archives Canada. Michener Awards for Journalism - General fonds. RG71990-1991/016 Box 55 620-2-70 (1970).

Library and Archives Canada. Roland Michener fonds. General Correspondence. R3331-0-X-E, MG32-A4 Vol. 73.

Library and Archives Canada. Michener Awards for Journalism - General fonds. RG7 1990-1991/016 Box 55 620-2-78 (1978).

Library and Archives Canada. Awards Ceremonies - Governor General's Awards Michener Award for Journalism (1984-1989) fonds. SAUV RG7, G29 802-09 Vol 24/43.

Library and Archives Canada. Award Ceremonies - Governor General's Awards Michener Award for Journalism.1996/10/01-1997/10/30. R178, RG7. Vol: 12801. File: LEBL-813-2, File part: 3.

Library and Archives Canada. Office of the Governor General fonds. Michener Award for Journalism (1990-1994). 5/02/1990 – 10/04/1991, RG7 G 30 Vol 49, File No: HNAT 802-9 File Part: 1. ID:3786268.

Library and Archives Canada. Office of the Governor General fonds. Michener Awards for Journalism. HNAT 802-9 Vol 49, Part 3, 22-04-1992 3-05-1993. ID3786207.

Library and Archives Canada. Office of the Right Honourable Adrienne Clarkson fonds. RG7/R178 13399 File CLAR 813-2 Vol 1.

Library and Archives Canada. Roland Michener fonds. R3331-10-2-E, MG32-A4 Vol 74.

Ljunggren, David. "Canada brushes off allegations of Afghan torture." *Reuters*, October 29, 2007. https://www.reuters.com/article/us-afghan-canada-idUSN2949198720071029

Lowman, Ron. "Fraser MacDougall steps down after 15 years at press council." *Toronto Star*. June 18, 1987.

Mackie, Victor. "Bugging reaches the Hill." *Winnipeg Free Press*. October 18, 1973, Final edition.

Mair, Rafe. *Rafe: A Memoir*. Madeira Park, BC: Harbour Publishing, 2004.

Malarek, Victor. *Instinct: The Making of an Investigative Journalist*. Toronto: Macmillan, 1996.

Marotta, Stefanie. "The Globe and Mail's False Promises investigation wins Michener Award." *Globe and Mail*. December 10, 2020. https://www.theglobeandmail.com/canada/article-the-globe-and-mails-false-promises-investigation-wins-michener-award/

Maru Public Opinion. "Canada's Most Respected Occupations, 2022." May 18, 2023. https://www.marugroup.net/public-opinion-polls/canada/canadas-most-respected-occupations-2022

Max Bell School of Public Policy. "Max Bell School of Public Policy." https://www.mcgill. ca/maxbellschool/about

McKay, John. "Systemic Racism in Policing in Canada: Report of the Standing Committee on Public Safety and National Security." June 2021. https://www.ourcommons.ca/ Content/Committee/432/SECU/Reports/RP11434998/securp06/securp06-e.pdf

McSheffrey, Elizabeth, Mike De Souza, Robert Cribb, Patti Sonntag and Patricia W. Elliott. "Screams from the Yard." *National Observer.* October 1, 2017, https://www. nationalobserver.com/2017/10/01/inside-saskatchewans-failure-stop-silent-killer

Michener Awards Foundation. Electronic and paper files. Includes official documents such as the Letters Patent and Certificate of Incorporation, as well as minutes of annual general meetings and special general meetings, board of directors meetings, executive committee meetings, internal and external correspondence, memoranda, financial documents, newspaper clippings, photographs and so on.

Michener Awards Foundation. *Positive Change for a Public Good: Michener Award Laureates Live.* Aired November 16, 2021 on YouTube. https://www.youtube.com/ watch?v=XraiJRJW9YI&ab_channel=UniversityofKing%27sCollege

Michener Awards Foundation. "*The 2019 Michener Awards Ceremony.*" Broadcast December 7, 2020 on Vimeo. https://www.vimeo.com/489538006

"Michener Award goes to the Telegraph-Journal." *Cision.* June 14, 2019. https:// www.newswire.ca/news-releases/michener-award-goes-to-the-telegraph- journal-883276411.html

Michener-Rohr, Joan. *Memories of a Governor General's Daughter.* London: Bedford House Press, 1990.

Miller John. *Yesterday's News: Why Canada's Daily Newspapers are Failing Us.* Halifax: Fernwood, 1998.

Monsees, Linda. "A war against truth' - understanding the fake news controversy." *Critical Studies on Security,* 8 no.2 116-129. May, 2020. https://typeset.io/papers/a-war- against-truth-understanding-the-fake-news-controversy-44b3ampe69

Moon, Peter. "Law amendment gags media, MPs." *The Globe and Mail.* February 14, 1986. ProQuest Historical Newspapers. https://ezproxy.library.dal.ca/login?url=https:// www.proquest.com/historical-newspapers/law-amendment-gags-media-mps-say/ docview/1151428281/se-2

Moscovitz, Jason. "Jeanne Sauvé: Governor General ceremony delayed." *CBC Archives,* January 28, 1984. https://www.cbc.ca/player/play/1775385927.

National NewsMedia Council. "Fraser MacDougall Prize." https://www.mediacouncil.ca/ fraser-macdougall-award/

"New York Department of Health expands advisory against eating fish caught around Cornwall Island." *Nation Valley News.* April 13, 2019. https://www. nationvalleynews.com/2019/04/13/new-york-department-of-health-expands- advisory-against-eating-fish-caught-around-cornwall-island/

Neiman Foundation at Harvard. About - History. https://nieman.harvard.edu/about/history/.

Oda, Bev. "Response to the Report of the Standing Senate Committee on Transport and Communications: Final Report on the Canadian News Media." Canadian Heritage. November 23, 2006. https://publications.gc.ca/collections/collection_2007/ch-pc/CH44-80-2006E.pdf

O'Callaghan, J. Patrick. *Maverick Publisher: J. Patrick O'Callaghan*. Toronto: Carrick, 2015.

Oliver, Craig. *Oliver's Twist: The Life and Times of an Unapologetic Newshound*. Toronto: Penguin, 2011.

Outhit, Jeff. "Clean up launched after Elmira chemical factory taints farm next door." *The Waterloo Region Record*. January 3, 2019. https://www.therecord.com/news/waterloo-region/cleanup-launched-after-elmira-chemical-factory-taints-farm-next-door/article_d6fcf89a-20fc-5902-81d3-aa10dcc1d7e8.html

Picard, André. "Tenacious activist lobbied for the victims of Canada's tainted blood tragedy." *Globe and Mail*. August 26, 2022. https://www.theglobeandmail.com/canada/article-tenacious-activist-lobbied-for-the-victims-of-canadas-tainted-blood/

Picard, André. *The Gift of Death: Confronting Canada's Tainted Blood Tragedy*. Toronto: HarperCollins, 1995 and 1998.

Pitts, Gordon. *Kings of Convergence: The Fight for Control of Canada's Media*. Toronto: Doubleday, 2002.

Platiel, Rudy. "Tragic honour: Editor risked exploitation charge to sound suicide alarm." *The Globe and Mail*. March 26, 1984. Retrieved from https://ezproxy.torontopubliclibrary.ca/login?url=https://www.proquest.com/historical-newspapers/tragic-honor/docview/1313823198/se-2?accountid=14369

Porter, Jody. "Ontario announces $85M to clean up mercury near Grassy Narrows, Wabaseemoong First Nations." *CBC Online*. June 27, 2017. https://www.cbc.ca/news/canada/thunder-bay/ontario-mercury-cleanup-1.4180631

"Protection of Privacy Act." *Canada's Human Rights History*. https://historyofrights.ca/wp-content/uploads/statutes/CN_Privacy.pdf

Public Policy Forum. "The Shattered Mirror: News, Democracy and Trust in the Digital Age." January 26, 2017. https://shatteredmirror.ca/

Public Policy Forum. "The Shattered Mirror: 5 Years On. March 3, 2022. https://ppforum.ca/publications/shattered-mirror-5-years-on/

Québec gouvernement. *Rapport du Comité d'étude sur la réadaptation des enfants et adolescents placés en centre[s] d'accueil: guide des centres d'accueil de transition et de réadaptation du Québec gouvernement*. Ministère des affaires sociales. Direction des communications, 1976.

Québec gouvernement. *Instaurer une société bienveillante pour nos enfants et nos jeunes*. April 2021. https://numerique.banq.qc.ca/patrimoine/details/52327/4289583

Quebéc Superior Court. No: 500-06-001022-199, Eleanor Lindsay vs. Attorney General of Quebec et al., January 17, 2020. https://cbaapps.org/ClassAction/PDF. aspx?id=12545

Rankin, Jim, Jennifer Quinn, Michelle Shepherd, John Duncanson and Scott Simmie. "Singled Out." *Toronto Star.* October 19, 2002, A1.

Rankin, Jim, Jennifer Quinn, Michelle Shepherd, John Duncanson and Scott Simme. "Police target black drivers." *Sunday Star.* October 20, 2002. A1.

Ressa, Maria. *How to Stand Up to a Dictator: The Fight for Our Future.* New York: HarperCollins, 2022.

Richmond, Randy. "Indiscernible." *London Free Press.* October 11, 2016. https:// medium.com/@London.Free.Press/by-randy-richmond-the-london-free-press-507bd5a1d462

Rideau Hall Library: His Excellency David Johnston uncatalogued papers. Her Excellency Michaëlle Jean uncatalogued papers.

Robb, Amanda Robb. "Anatomy of a fake news scandal." November 16, 2017. https://www. rollingstone.com/feature/anatomy-of-a-fake-news-scandal-125877/.

"Roland Michener." *Toronto Star.* August 8, 1991.

Rosner, Cecil. *Behind the Headlines: A History of Investigative Journalism in Canada.* Toronto: Oxford University Press, 2018.

Ross, Selena. "Kids at risk of abuse need earlier intervention, with more help for their parents: Youth protection commission." CTV News Montreal. May 3,2021. https:// montreal.ctvnews.ca/kids-at-risk-of-abuse-need-earlier-intervention-with-more-help-for-their-parents-youth-protection-commission-1.5411886

Roston, Margo. "Margo's People." *Ottawa Citizen.* November 15, 1984.

Rusnell, Charles, and Jennie Russel. "Private Health, Public Risk: How the Alberta government allowed a private foundation to offer an unproven 'experimental' health program to its citizens." *CBC News,* July 14, 2017, https://www.cbc.ca/news/canada/edmonton/topic/Tag/Private%20Health%20Public%20Risk

Rusnell, Charles, and Jennie Russel. "Private Health, Public Risk?" *CBC News,* May 25, 2022, https://www.cbc.ca/news2/interactives/unproven/.

Saskatchewan. Court of Queen's Bench. Prince Albert (City) v. Zatlyn, 1995. CanLII 5965 (SK QB). https://canlii.ca/t/1nrsf Accessed April 7, 2022.

Seamans, Robert and Feng Zhu. "Responses to Entry in Multi-Sided Markets: The Impact of Craigslist on Local Newspapers." *Management Science* 60(2) (2013) 476-93. https://doi.org/10.1287/mnsc.2013.1785

Segal, Hugh. "The media through a looking glass: Building the brand by getting it right." *Policy Options Politiques.* February 2010. https://policyoptions.irpp.org/fr/magazines/after-copenhagen/the-media-through-a-looking-glass-building-the-brand-by-getting-it-right/

Siekierski, B.J. "PMO has no comment on Julie Payette's expunged 2011 assault charge." *IPolitics*. https://www.ipolitics.ca/news/pmo-has-no-comment-on-julie-payettes-expunged-2011-assault-charge

Smith, Graeme. "From Canadian custody to cruel hands." *Globe and Mail*. April 23, 2007. https://www.theglobeandmail.com/news/world/from-canadian-custody-into-cruel-hands/article585956/

Staff. "The Shawinigate affair: a timeline." *National Post*. May 2010. https://nationalpost.com/news/canada/the-shawinigate-affair-a-timeline

Star Editorial Board. "Julie Payette as GG sends a powerful message: Editorial." *Toronto Star*. July 13, 2017. https://www.thestar.com/opinion/editorials/2017/07/13/julie-payette-as-gg-sends-a-powerful-message-editorial.html

Statistics Canada. "Fifty years of family in Canada: 1961-2011." July 23, 2018. https://www12.statcan.gc.ca/census-recensement/2011/as-sa/98-312-x/98-312-x2011003_1-eng.cfm

Statistics Canada. "Literary and Journalistic Awards in Canada / Le prix de littérature et de journalisme au Canada: 1923-1973. " Ottawa: Information Canada, 1976. https://www.publications.gc.ca/collections/collection_2016/statcan/81-407/CS81-407-1973.pdf

Statistics Canada. "Table 7.1 - Interest rates and exchange rates." Last modified December 19, 2012. https://www150.statcan.gc.ca/n1/pub/11-210-x/2010000/t098-eng.htm

Statistics Canada. "Chart 3 - Unemployment rates in Canada and the United States, 1976-2016." Last modified July 7, 2017. https://www150.statcan.gc.ca/n1/daily-quotidien/170707/cg-a003-eng.htm

Statistics Canada. "150 years of immigration in Canada." June 29, 2016. https://www150.statcan.gc.ca/n1/pub/11-630-x/11-630-x2016006-eng.htm

Statistics Canada. "The Daily - Household Internet Use." May 19, 2000. https://www150.statcan.gc.ca/n1/daily-quotidien/000519/dq000519b-eng.htm.

Stursberg, Peter. *Roland Michener: The Last Viceroy*. Toronto: McGraw-Hill Ryerson, 1989.

Stursberg, Peter. *Lester Pearson and the Dream of Unity*. Toronto: Doubleday, 1978.

Supreme Court of British Columbia. "950204 between Thomas Siddon (Plaintiff) and Rafe Mair Westcom Radio Group Ltd. (Defendants), Statement of Claim," January 13, 1985.

Supreme Court of Canada. "Case in Brief - Resolute FP Canada Inc. v. Ontario (Attorney General)." https://www.scc-csc.ca/case-dossier/cb/2019/37985-eng.aspx

Supreme Court of Canada. "Coroner's Inquest Touching the Death of Ashley Smith." Corrections Service Canada. December 19, 2013. https://www.canada.ca/en/correctional-service/corporate/library/coroners-inquest-touching-death-ashley-smith.html

Supreme Court of Canada. "Backgrounder: 'A Preventable Death'." Office of Correctional Investigator. April 28, 2014. https://www.canada.ca/en/correctional-service/corporate/transparency/audits-evaluations/review-practices-place-prevent-respond-death-custody.html

Thompson, Glenn R. "The Coverdale Report: A Consultation Committee Appraisal of Correctional Services for Women in New Brunswick, Nova Scotia and Prince Edward Island." December, 1972. https://www.publicsafety.gc.ca/lbrr/archives/hv%209506%20c39.1-eng.pdf

Thorsell, William. "The rights of the innocent can be easily trampled." *Globe and Mail*, March 27, 2006.

Toronto Star. "The Toronto Star." https://www.thestar.com/

Tower, Taylor. "Concordia's Institute for Investigative Journalism facilitates the largest collaborative investigation in Canadian history." November 4, 2019. https://www.concordia.ca/news/stories/2019/11/04/concordias-institute-for-investigative-journalism-facilitates-largest-collaborative-investigation-in-canadian-history.html

"Troubling Issues in Saskatchewan Oil Boom." Global News. October 1, 2017. https://globalnews.ca/video/3779475/troubling-issues-in-saskatchewan-oil-boom

The Trust Project. https://thetrustproject.org/

Tuters, Marc, Emilija Jokubauskaitė and Daniel Bach. "Post-Truth Protest: How 4chan Cooked Up the Pizzagate Bullshit." *M/C journal* 21, no. 3 (2018). https://www.journal.media-culture.org.au/index.php/mcjournal/article/view/1422

Uncatalogued. Michener Awards Foundation Papers, Carleton School of Journalism and Communication, Ottawa. Includes minutes of annual general meetings and special general meetings, board of directors meetings, executive committee meetings, internal and external correspondence, memoranda, financial documents, newspaper clippings, photographs and so on.

Vipond, Mary. *Mass Media in Canada*. 3rd Ed. Toronto: Lorimer, 2000.

Watkins, Lyndon. "Press award is painful to rival." *Globe and Mail*. April 7, 1973.

"Wendy Roland Michener." *Ottawa Journal*. January 3, 1969. https://www.newspapers.com/clip/24869668/wendy-roland-mitchener-obit/

Westell, Anthony. "Journalism Foundation in the Works." *Content*. May-June 1989.

"When 'a flood of free newspapers' washed over Toronto." CBC Archives. June 27, 2019. https://www.cbc.ca/archives/when-a-flood-of-free-newspapers-washed-over-toronto-1.5180505

White, Patrick. "Despite new laws, inmates still face time in solitary confinement." *Globe and Mail*. October 31, 2022. https://www.theglobeandmail.com/canada/article-despite-new-laws-too-many-inmates-in-isolation-are-indigenous-panel/ Accessed November 2, 2022.

Wilson-Smith, Anthony, John Demont and Luke Fisher. "Somalia Inquiry's Damning Report." *The Canadian Encyclopedia*, March 13, 2014. https://www.thecanadianencyclopedia.ca/en/article/somalia-inquirys-damning-report

Winseck, Dwayne. "Figure 2: Major Communications and Media Ownership Changes in Canada 1994-2020, Media and Internet Concentration in Canada, 1984-2020." Global Media and Internet Concentration Project, Carleton University, 2021. https://www.doi.org/10.22215/gmicp/2021.2

Wood, Shirley. *Her Excellency Jeanne Sauvé*. Halifax: Goodread Biographies, 1982.

Young, Christopher. "Farewell to a Champion of Public Interest." *Ottawa Citizen*. June 23, 1995.

Index

Romahn, Jim, 59, 60, 101, 242n46
Roseberry, René, 150, 157
Rosner, Cecil, 14, 15, 20, 44, 45, 46, 140, 168
Ross, Sam, 29, 109, 230n2, 231n23
Roston, Margo, 83
Royal Canadian Air Force, 25
Royal Commission on Media 1981, 66
Royal Commission on Newspapers, 69
rubrics, judging, 111
Ruby, Clayton, 77, 86
Ruperthouse, Sindy, 245n39
Rusnell, Charles, 126, 127
Russell, Jennie, 126, 127–128
Russia, 183
Ryerson Polytechnical Institute, 17, 134
Ryerson Review of Journalism, 129
Ryerson University, 104, 115

Saint-Charles-Borromée Hospital, 151
Sampson, Constance, 141
Samson, Constable Robert, 45
Sarnia, Ontario, 48
Saskatchewan, 70, 83, 119, 121, 141
Sault Star, The, 72
Sault Ste. Marie, Ontario, 72
Sauvé, Jeanne, 82, 83, 85, 100
Sauvé, Maurice, 83
Sawatsky, John, 45–46
Schreiber, Karlheinz, 170, 171
Schreyer, Ed, 32–33, 58, 63, 69, 85
Schreyer, Lily, 58
Scotian Journalist, 37, 39, 40, 62
Scott, Gail, 133, 134–135, 141, 147, 154
Securities Act, 62
segregation, practice of, 138
sexual abuse, 140, 151
sexual assault, 119–120, 129, 140, 151, 178–179, 180, 195–196, 197
sexual harassment, 179
"Shattered Mirror, The" (Public Policy Forum), 169
Shawinigate, 161
Shelburne, Nova Scotia, 128–130
Sherbrooke Record, 149
Sherman, Paddy, 244n14
Siddon, Tom, 122, 124
Sikh community, 82
Silver Donald, 17
Simon, Mary, 212
slander chargers, 121. *See also* libel charges
small media outlets, 110, 133–134, 153–158
Smith, Ashley, 136–137
Smith, Graeme, 172
social media, 183, 184
societal change, 13–14, 36, 175, 183, 201–202

Société Radio-Canada, 119, 152, 173
solitary confinement, 52, 54
Somalia, 178
Sonntag, Patti, 104
"Sounding the Alarm" (*Telegraph Journal*), 198–199
Southam Fellowships, 100
Southam newspaper chain, 69, 70, 71, 99, 113, 145
Special Award, 89–90, 91, 92–93, 206
Special Committee on Mass Media report, 163–164
Special Senate Committee on Mass Media, 14, 18, 19–21
sponsorship scandal, 168, 169
spousal abuse, 77–78
Sprague, Debbie, 39
Standing Committee on Citizenship and Immigration, 82
Standing Senate Committee on Transport and Communication, 164
Stanfield, Robert, 36
Stanley Cup, 22
Stapon, Grant, 126, 127
Star Metro, 163
Starnes, John, 46
Starowicz, Mark, 17
Star Phoenix, 119
Star Weekly Magazine, 26
Statistics Canada, 97, 197
St. Catharines Standard, 198
Stevens, Geoffrey, 43, 86, 87
St. Lawrence River, 67, 236n9
Stocker, Shirley, 124
Strashin, Jamie, 10
strategic plans, 205
structured intervention units (SIU), 138
St. Thomas, Ontario, 140–141
Stuart, Penny, 67
students, journalism, 94, 102, 104, 105, 160, 210, 211
Studler, David, 119
Stursberg, Peter, 13, 25
submissions for Michener Award, 47, 56, 57, 59, 65, 66, 150–152
suicide, 55, 74, 75, 76, 80, 136
Sunday Express, 135–136
Sun group, 70
Supreme Court of Canada, 122, 179, 180, 181
Supreme Court of Ontario, 86, 87
Sutherland, Darryl, 167
"System of Abuse" (Rodenhiser), 128

"Tainted Water" (Sonntag and Cribb), 105
Taser stun guns, 32, 171–172

MIX
Paper
FSC® C100212
FSC www.fsc.org

Printed by Imprimerie Gauvin
Gatineau, Québec